Advances in Game-Based Learning

Series Editors
Dirk Ifenthaler
Scott Joseph Warren
Deniz Eseryel

More information about this series at http://www.springer.com/series/13094

Elena Dell'Aquila • Davide Marocco
Michela Ponticorvo • Andrea di Ferdinando
Massimiliano Schembri • Orazio Miglino

Educational Games for Soft-Skills Training in Digital Environments

New Perspectives

 Springer

Elena Dell'Aquila
Plymouth University
Plymouth, Devon, UK

Davide Marocco
University of Naples Federico II
Naples, Italy

Michela Ponticorvo
University of Naples Federico II
Naples, Italy

Andrea di Ferdinando
Aidvanced S.r.l.
Rome, Italy

Massimiliano Schembri
Aidvanced S.r.l.
Rome, Italy

Orazio Miglino
University of Naples Federico II
Naples, Italy

Advances in Game-Based Learning
ISBN 978-3-319-06310-2   ISBN 978-3-319-06311-9   (eBook)
DOI 10.1007/978-3-319-06311-9

Library of Congress Control Number: 2016957711

Printed on acid-free paper

This Springer imprint is published by Springer Nature
The registered company is Springer International Publishing AG Switzerland

Introduction

The book explores methodological and technological aspects underpinning the training of soft skills through the migration and adaptation of psycho-pedagogical methodology, such as role playing and psychodrama, to digital and online environments, the so-called EduTechRPG (Technologically Enhanced Educational Role Playing Game for soft skills training). Intelligent tutorship, psychological modelling and feedback mechanisms for ensuring the success of the learning process represent the fundamental characteristics of the proposed methodological approach to soft skills training. Soft skills can be defined as personal attributes that contribute to better express how people know and manage themselves, as well as their relationships with others. Their importance has been greatly recognised by the European Union in the past few years. The advent of new and powerful enhanced learning technologies, which is currently challenging traditional professional practice in many areas, is now also challenging this new domain, and the range of approaches and applications is growing fast.

The proposed exploration is conducted by the authors with the discussion of several concrete experiences of educational games and training tools applied to a variety of soft skills, such as negotiation, decision-making, leadership and problem solving. The experiences reported in the book are the synthesis of several European projects, coordinated by the authors, aiming at applying well known psycho-pedagogical training models to online, technology-enhanced learning contexts in a broad range of applications and target groups. The specificity of such a psycho-pedagogical methodology, applied throughout all the discussed EU projects, is mainly represented by the importance of feedback and debriefing processes that can be conveyed to learners through different means, such as online group or individual chats with tutors, automatic reports and a psychologically informed scoring system. Tutors that can be either real or artificial are seen as the key factor facilitating the training process.

More specifically, the book discusses the approach used by the authors to design EduTechRPG along with different EU-funded projects, such as the conception and use of the Eutopia platform in Eutopia MT, Proactive and S-Cube projects (Chap. 4), ENACT (Chap. 5), DREAD-ED (Chap. 6) and Learn to Lead (Chap. 7). This approach reflects two main dimensions: psycho-pedagogical and technological.

These should not be considered as mutually exclusive dimensions but rather as complementary. Indeed, the ability of integrating such dimensions in a single game implementation contributes to the design of an educational tool to create meaningful learning.

The first dimension specifies the psycho-pedagogical foundations of the learning approach adopted and identifies two main categories of EduTechRPG: drama-based and rule-based. Drama-based EduTechRPG allows users to experience direct involvement with the learning objectives through a personal dramatisation by acting out roles and competences. Rule-based EduTechRPG points instead more on the logical and reasoning aspects involved by the user for achieving a specific learning objective. A set of formal rules and interactions embedded in the game needs to be followed in order for learners to achieve the relevant learning objectives.

Conversely, drama-based EduTechRPGs are based on informal rules and open dynamics; therefore, there is not a unique way to achieve the desired learning objectives. This will depend on the specific situation in terms of aims and peculiarities of dynamics occurring among people involved in the specific game scenario.

With regard to the second dimension, EduRPGs are substantiated by the use of two main technological systems. One allows a virtual extension of traditional face-to-face psychodramatic mechanism and experience that is transposed to a digital setting (see Chap. 1). A second technological approach permits the production of "artificial" micro-worlds based on computer-simulated, formal models about social and psychological phenomena. We will refer to the former dimension and to the EduRPGs that predominantly exploit it as Communication Technology (ComTech) and Simulation Technology (SimTech) based. Characteristics, limitations and strengths of the above-mentioned four categories will be analysed in detail in the dedicated chapters.

Both drama-based and rule-based, as well as ComTech and SimTech, educational role-play games (EduRPG) can be characterised by the presence of a real or virtual trainer, also referred to as a backstage agent, as she does not intervene and directly affect the dynamics of the game, although she supports its interpretation and wielding.

Conversely, the actors of the game, whether real or artificial, represent the on-stage agents because it is only through their choices and actions that the game comes to life.

The virtual tutor is an expression of a computational model that embeds and describes a set of rules according to certain soft skills theories that drives the player to a stable training outcome. Indeed, the advantage of this method lies in the fact that it is very low cost, as after an initial phase to familiarise users with the system, it can be used without the guidance of a real trainer, as the system is self-regulated. Participants are offered an opportunity to experience an intense and effective learning experience and at the same time rapidly acquire competences directly applicable to real-life context. Learn to Lead and ENACT are both examples of Simulation Technology-based EduRPGs and, respectively, rule- and drama-based, using an artificial backstage agent, that is, an intelligent tutor system that guides and supports players in the learning process.

Conversely, drama-based EduTechRPGs that involve the use of the Eutopia platform require real agents both on the stage and backstage, where principles of the traditional face-to-face role are maintained and boosted by enhanced ICT systems. Learners' experiences are fundamentally based on open dynamics; therefore there may not be a unique way to achieve the desired learning objectives. This will depend on the specific situation in terms of time and peculiarity of interactions among people involved in a specific scenario, as will be described in detail for Eutopia MT, Proactive and S-Cube projects. On the other hand, disadvantages of this method are represented by high cost and time consumption in organising and managing the complexity of the virtual learning scenarios, as well as interactions among real participants. In addition, there is the need to involve experienced trainers also skilled in mastering the use of the technological tools and therefore of online role plays.

We believe that the book could be of interest to a wide community, which includes computer scientists and software developers, as well as e-learning specialists, trainers, psychologists and pedagogists, who should work closely to draw a system of essential educational/psychological principles and its effective and meaningful application. The book will serve as a useful guide, based on practical examples, of how training methodologies can be adopted by a wide range of professionals and for a wide range of purposes, such as to enhance traditional training practice, boost participants' learning experience, heighten participants' self-awareness and self-confidence, facilitate knowledge and promote skills, and competencies and personal, as well as group, development. The book will offer a factual support for choosing the most appropriate methodology in the specific domain of practice and will suggest effective means for the design of tailored role-playing games for different training purposes and contexts of application. The ultimate objective of this book is to offer a theoretical framework where real examples, direct experiences and possible indications on how rule-based and drama-based EduTechRPGs supported by Communication and Simulation Technology models can boost traditional practice for enhancing soft skills to a wide community of trainers, coaches, HR advisors, consultants and psychologists.

Specifically for such reason and for supporting the wider audience we intend to reach, we have devised a book that presents relevant theoretical and methodological aspects, together with a large number of examples and experiences, without the burden of several technical details, which are available in the publications referenced in every chapter.

Chapters 1 and 2 present the background and motivation for editing this book and set the frame within which the project experiences should be considered.

In particular, Chapter 1 is focused on the definition of what is meant for soft skills in current educational and psychological literature, and the relevance of soft skills in modern society that complements any sphere of human life, whatever is related to personal, social or professional environments.

Chapter 2 describes traditional settings and new technologies for role-play implementation. Psycho-pedagogical techniques widely used in psychological, sociological, educational and organisational settings for developing soft skills which will form the ground for the rest of the book will be described. The chapter will conjointly present the current state of the art regarding enhanced learning technology for soft skills training

Chapter 3 draws a definition of a possible taxonomy of EduRPG from both a technological and educational viewpoint resulting in "rule-based" and "drama-based" and "Communication Technology"- and "Simulation Technology"-based EduRPGs. Their characteristics, strengths and limits, and potential preferable context of applications, will be also explored. This chapter will also introduce the proposed taxonomy, based on the results and experiences from several European projects, described in the dedicated following chapters. The core elements of such a methodology are the gaming experience, the presence of feedbacks from the system (either from real or virtual tutors), the modelling of relevant psychological and pedagogical theories and the creation of an adaptive profile of learners.

Chapter 4 will be dedicated to the description of Eutopia, an example of drama-ComTech-based EduRPG that embeds role-play methodology as a psycho-pedagogical approach and takes inspiration from the MMORPG technology, that is, the massively multiplayer online games. The multiplayer authoring platform has been employed for the design of role-play games for the training and the development of soft skills employed in different EU projects, such as Eutopia MT, Proactive and S-Cube. Project-related experiences of the use of the platform will be also presented and discussed.

Chapter 5 will describe ENACT, a drama-SimTech-based EduRPG, based on a single-player 3D role-play game intelligence-based tool to train and assess the user's negotiation and communication skills in realistic scenarios during the interaction with artificial agents, for schools, enterprises, professional training and sport contexts.

Chapter 6 will be dedicated to the description of the DREAD-ED project that resulted in the development of a multiplayer ComTech-rule-based EduRPG for training communication, problem-solving and group decision-making skills of a team that works for crisis management in order to promote effective management situations in the context of disaster.

Chapter 7 will describe experiences derived by the EU project Learn to Lead that represents an example of Simulation Technology- and rule-based EduRPG for use in SMEs and small government offices for the development of effective leadership and management applied to team leadership.

Lastly, some tentative conclusions are drawn to examine strengths, limitations, similarities and differences between the EduTechRPG tool and experiences for training and developing soft skills that have been outlined throughout the chapters of the book.

The games and many of the project outcomes presented in the book, as well as supporting materials, are available at "http://softskillsgames.net/".

Contents

1 Soft Skills 1
    1.1 Soft Skills, Beyond the Concept of Intelligence 3
        1.1.1 Multiple Intelligence 5
        1.1.2 Other Concepts to Define Soft Intelligences 7
    1.2 Nature of Soft Skills 9

2 Traditional Settings and New Technologies for Role-Play
Implementation 19
    2.1 Role Play in Traditional Settings 22
        2.1.1 Role Play in Digital Environments 26
    2.2 Digital Role-Playing Games 27

3 Methodology and Design of Technologically Enhanced
Educational Role-Playing Games for Soft Skills Training 39
    3.1 Gaming Experience and Education 40
    3.2 Fundamental Concepts and Structure of EduTechRPGs 42
        3.2.1 Narrative Structure and "Mise en Scène" 43
        3.2.2 Assessment and Tutoring of Learners 44
    3.3 Analysis and Design Principle of EduTechRPGs 47
        3.3.1 Teaching and Learning Should Be Intrinsic to the Game 48
        3.3.2 Educational Games Should Follow the Same
              Game Design Principles as Entertainment Games 49
    3.4 Technological and Psycho-pedagogical Dimensions
        in EduTechRPG Design 50
        3.4.1 Modelling of Relevant Psychological
              and Pedagogical Theories 51
        3.4.2 Assessment Design and Techniques 57
    3.5 Conclusions 61

4   Eutopia: Transferring Psycho-pedagogical Role Play
to the Multiplayer Digital Stage 63
  4.1   Multiplayer RPG Games 63
  4.2   The Eutopia Platform: Communication-Technology Dimension 65
        4.2.1   Trainers 65
        4.2.2   Learners 69
  4.3   Methodological Aspects 71
        4.3.1   Gaming Experience 71
        4.3.2   Modelling of Relevant Psychological
                and Pedagogical Theories 74
        4.3.3   Feedback, Debriefing and Back-Stage Agents 75
        4.3.4   Blended Methodology 76
  4.4   Results and Experiences 77
        4.4.1   Negotiation and Soft Skills in SISINE and SINAPSI 77
        4.4.2   Conflict Management in Eutopia-MT 80
        4.4.3   Proactive 82
        4.4.4   Entrepreneurship Training in S-Cube 84
  4.5   General Remarks 86

5   ENACT: Virtual Experiences of Negotiation 89
  5.1   Theoretical Background and Psycho-pedagogical Modelling 90
        5.1.1   Negotiation Concept Adopted Within ENACT 91
        5.1.2   Psychological Modelling 91
  5.2   Design of the ENACT Platform 93
        5.2.1   Psychological Model Implementation
                and Behavioural Indicators 93
        5.2.2   User Representation and Avatars 94
        5.2.3   The Visual Interface and Game Dynamics 95
  5.3   Assessment in ENACT 97
        5.3.1   Tutoring System 99
  5.4   Results 99
        5.4.1   Training Need Analysis 99
        5.4.2   Pre-validation Testing Data 100
  5.5   User-Centred Approach and Flexibility 102

6   DREAD-ED: Improving Communication Skills
in Critical Situations 105
  6.1   A Game Designed to Teach Disaster Communication 106
  6.2   DREAD-ED Game Description 109
        6.2.1   Game Parameters 110
        6.2.2   Game Loops 111
        6.2.3   Avatars and Chat System 112
        6.2.4   Resources 112
        6.2.5   Actions 113
        6.2.6   Roles 114

6.3   DREAD-ED Game Mechanics 114
      6.3.1   Metaphor and Narrative 114
      6.3.2   Triggering Communication.. 115
6.4   DREAD-ED Evaluation Layer: Role of the Tutor 116
6.5   DREAD-ED as an Example of ICT and Rule-Based RPG............... 117
6.6   Testing DREAD-ED as a Training Tool.. 119
      6.6.1   The First Testing of DREAD-ED.. 119
      6.6.2   DREAD-ED Potential as a Training Tool
              for Decision-Making.. 121

7   **Learn to Lead: An Educational Game for Leaders to Be** 123
7.1   The Soft Skill to Be Transferred: Leadership 123
      7.1.1   Theories About Leadership 124
7.2   Learn to Lead Game Description.. 126
7.3   Learn to Lead Game Mechanics 130
7.4   Learn to Lead Evaluation Layer... 133
7.5   Learn to Lead as an Example of Computational
      and Rule-Based RPG 137

Conclusions.. 141

References... 145

Index.. 159

Chapter 1
Soft Skills

This chapter addresses the question of what is meant by the term soft skills, draws on various sources in literature to define the concept and explores how soft skills are important to everyone in every context, as it entails the involvement of personal aspects within any relationship. Soft skills are important to students, as they are linked to job performances and career development; they are crucial for employees who need to manage their interactions and emotions in order to interact effectively with customers and get engaged with the workplace missions; for management and leadership skills, as they help lead teams towards common and shared goals, accomplish organisational missions and support organisations in their future directions and visions.

There has been a growing recognition by researchers; managers; representatives of industry, commerce and organisation; and educational policymakers that "soft skills" are crucial for promoting personal and collective growth for creating new practices in professional, vocational and educational contexts. Today soft skills are recognised as transversal competencies existing in a reciprocal relationship with hard skills (technical, task-job related, specific knowledge) complementing any spheres of human life, whatever is related to personal, social or professional environments.

Soft skills, also commonly referred as "people skills", are recognised as personal attributes or a cluster of personal traits that optimise and enable positivity and enhance people's interactions and relationships with each other. They are in everyday use by most people, at different levels of existence, and are commonly regarded as a combination of competencies that are an expression of how people know and manage themselves, as well as their relationships with others.

However, people skills, social skills, social competence, interpersonal skills, social self-efficacy, managerial competence and social and emotional intelligence are just a few terms often used to describe soft skills, as we will see in the following paragraphs.

© Springer International Publishing Switzerland 2017
E. Dell'Aquila et al., *Educational Games for Soft-Skills Training in Digital Environments*, Advances in Game-Based Learning, DOI 10.1007/978-3-319-06311-9_1

In literature, it is difficult to find a universal definition of soft skills or an all-encompassing definition that provides a succinct insight. It is a broad concept that subsumes many dimensions of the personal sphere development that involves a combination of emotional, behavioural and cognitive components. Soft skills are related to interpersonal and intrapersonal areas; therefore, there is a relational dimension involved.

Due to the intrinsic complexity of the relational dimension, it is arduous to define and what to include or exclude in the definition of soft skills. However, it is useful to explore different approaches to defining soft skills in relation to their use and related concepts such as competence, emotional and social intelligence, multiple intelligences and communication.

Conversely, the concept of hard skills relates to technical, professional knowledge and abilities, usually referring to a skill that has been learnt through training and educational programmes, and to the ability or capability of an individual to perform a specific task within a specific area or domain. Hard skills and soft skills are never meant to compete with each other, but should ideally be complementary.

Soft skills are very often viewed as behavioural competencies (Boyatzis 1982), referring to personal attributes or characteristics that contribute to "how" a job is done or the process of the job or task, as opposed to the end product of the completed job. Boyatzis (1973) describes a competency thus: "… an underlying characteristic of an individual, which is causally related to effective or superior performance in a job which could be a motive, trait, skill, one's self-image or social role, or a body of knowledge which she uses". McClelland (1973) first referred to competency as "a critical differentiator of performance" and portrayed by the same author as a significant predictor of employee performance and success.

Soft skills include interpersonal capabilities such as proficiencies in the area of communication, conflict resolution and negotiation, leadership, personal effectiveness, active listening, creative problem solving, strategic thinking, decision-making, team building, influencing skills and selling skills, just to name a few. An additional source of confusion and complication is given by the association of the concept of soft skills to the notions of competence and/or competency, concepts that have dominated the literature concerning management strategy in the 1990. The terms competency and competence are often used interchangeably for defining the same concepts, causing confusion and misunderstanding. Considering all the different ways the two concepts are used (Sultana 2009; Pate et al. 2003; Snyder and Ebeling 1992; McClelland 1973; Boyatzis 1973; Woodruffe 1993; Dubois 1998) is almost impossible to identify a clear, univocal distinction.

Woodruffe (1993) offers one of the clearest distinctions between the two terms, relating soft skills to the concept of competency while further relating hard skills to the concept of competence. Competency is a person-based concept which refers to the dimensions of behaviour lying behind competent performances. Dubois (1998) concurs with these delineations while defining competency as a set of skills, knowledge, attributes and desirable behaviours thought to be required for successful performance. He describes competence as being a work-related concept which refers to areas of work for which the person is required to have hard skills to perform: "what" people have to be able to do and expected to know in order to effectively perform in their work.

The following paragraphs will be exploring first of all the approaches to defining soft skills in relation to their use and related concepts such as emotional and social intelligence, multiple intelligences, communication and competence and afterwards more detail of the controversy surrounding various definitions of soft skills, as identified from a search and review of soft skills literature.

1.1   Soft Skills, Beyond the Concept of Intelligence

As mentioned earlier, there is no formal and unique definition of soft skills in literature, as they are also referred to a wide variety of terms and associated concepts such as emotional intelligence (Sjöberg 2001; Goleman 1995; Bar-On 1997; Salovey and Mayer 1989), social intelligence (Marlowe 1986; Sternberg 1985), life skills (Gardner 1993a), social competence (Oppenheimer 1989; Zigler 1972), managerial competencies (McClelland 1998) and interpersonal skills (Klein et al. 2006; Skulmoski and Hartman 2010) with regard to different areas of use such as psychology, healthcare, accounting, sale and entrepreneurship, business and management (Thorndike 1920; Goleman 1998; Klein et al. 2006; Sadler-Smith and Shefy 2010; McClelland 1998; Salovey and Mayer 1989; Sternberg 1985; Joseph et al. 2010). All these different terms are often used interchangeably. In fact, as discussed below, many of the basic concepts associated with soft skills overlap with issues of communicating and interacting effectively with others and appropriately interpreting different social situations.

The growing interest and research around emotional intelligence (Goleman 1995) and social intelligence (Spearman 1904; Marlowe 1986; Salovey and Mayer 1989) have progressively increased the appreciation of soft skills as crucial for learning and personal development.

The ability of emotional intelligence represents the basis for the construction of human relationships, communication skills and sensitivity to errors which are described as social intelligence (Murata 2008). In other words the concept of social intelligence is multidimensional and defined as the ability of being aware of others and to adapt responses to others and social situations.

Since Daniel Goleman published his work on emotional intelligence (EI) in 1995, placing the family of soft skills at the heart of learning and personal development, appreciation of these skills has progressively increased. They are considered crucial both to life and business, because they affect how people learn and develop. As they involve intrapersonal as well interpersonal dimensions, soft skills help to manage ourselves, create and maintain effective relationships and understand others.

According to the definition given by the psychologist Goleman (1995), soft skills are a combination of competencies that contribute to how people know and manage themselves, as well as their relationships with others. Goleman considers soft skills to be twice as important as intelligence quotient (IQ) or technical skills in the context of success. Gardner (1983) describes the IQ movement as being blindly empirical, basing their outcomes on the ability to reach the correct answer while not addressing the process of thinking but merely its products.

Interestingly from our perspective, Boyatzis and Goleman (2001, 2002, 2007), who have been working in a strong partnership together, stated that emotional and social competencies can be assessed and can be developed in adults through training, education and development programmes.

Emotional intelligence is a phrase used to focus attention on a particular aspect of human talent. Although emotional intelligence is simple as a phrase, it incorporates the complexity of a person's capabilities. Earlier psychologists who explored this area of social intelligence offered the notion as being a single concept (Thorndike in the 1920s and 1930s and Goleman 1995), while more recent psychologists have appreciated the complexity of this concept and described social intelligence in terms of multiple capabilities (Bar-On 1992, 1997; Goleman 1998; Saarni 1990). Gardner (1983) theorised within a broader spectrum of the individual possessing multiple intelligences while including the areas of intrapersonal and interpersonal intelligences as part of a suite of intelligences (Boyatzis et al. 2000). The area of multiple intelligence will be explored in the following paragraph. Salovey and Mayer (1989), Mayer and Salovey (1993), who first used the expression "emotional intelligence", described it in terms of four domains incorporating knowing and handling one's own and others' emotions. In this regard they asserted that social intelligence is a broader construct that subsumes emotional intelligence (Salovey and Meyer 1990).

Other concepts and theories have used labels such as "practical intelligence", "intuitive intelligence" and "successful intelligence" (Sternberg 1985), concepts that will also be explored in the following paragraphs, that recognise the integration of emotions and intellect in our personal lives and organisations, because not all problem-solving situations are cognitive as they involve interpreting and reacting to personal and others' emotions. These often blend the capabilities described by the other psychologists with cognitive abilities and anchor the concepts around the consequence of the person's behaviour, notably success or effectiveness (Boyatzis et al. 2000).

The construction of EI incorporates the complexity of a person's capability. The model introduced by Daniel Goleman focuses on EI as a wide array of competencies and skills that drive leadership performance. In fact, Goleman defines "emotional intelligence" as a trait not measured by IQ tests (Goleman 1995) and specifies that outstanding performers are not defined by their IQs or even their job skills, but by their emotional intelligence, as a set of competencies that distinguishes how people manage feelings, interact and communicate (Goleman 1998). The construction of emotional intelligence introduced by Goleman focuses on emotional intelligence as a wide array of competencies and skills that drive leadership performance, where the capability of managing oneself and the ability to relate to others count twice as much as hard technical skills in job success. Goleman (1998), basing further claims on extensive research on more than five hundred organisations, proves that factors such as self-confidence, self-awareness, self-control, commitment and integrity not only create more successful employees but also more successful business and companies. In particular he affirms that a high level of individual success at work is characterised by emotional intelligence, or skills of social awareness and communication. Typically, these include the ability to motivate and influence others, to give effective feedback, to develop relationships, to monitor one's own behaviour, to manage emotions both of self and others and to read interpersonal situations.

Also Marlowe (1986) starting from the works of earlier social intelligence pioneers like Thorndike (1920), suggests that social intelligence comprises five components: prosocial attitude (interest and concern for others), social performance skills (appropriate interaction with others), empathetic ability (one's ability to identify with others), emotional expressiveness (way to express emotions towards others) and confidence. His definition of social intelligence refers to soft skills as the ability to act appropriately in any given social situation upon an understanding of the feelings, thoughts and behaviours of individuals (including oneself) which allows people to experience meaningful affective experiences (Marlowe 1986).

An additional definition of emotional intelligence offered by the integration of the work of Goleman (1995 and 1998) and Boyatzis (1982) is provided as follows: "emotional intelligence is observed when a person demonstrates the competencies that constitute self-awareness, self-management, social awareness, and social skills at appropriate times and ways in sufficient frequency to be effective in the situation". This definition offers more than a framework for describing human dispositions by offering a competency approach that can predict outcomes of effectiveness and job performance. The process of describing, evaluating and understanding competencies and/or capabilities that can be related to effectiveness and the possibility of clustering the way those competencies are organised can help to implement transformative learning and in so doing, enhance key skills.

In fact, Goleman and collaborators' studies reveal not only that emotional intelligence is important but also demonstrates that the skills that contribute to emotional intelligence can be taught and developed over time.

1.1.1 Multiple Intelligence

The work of Goleman (1995) and Mayer et al. (2004) on the theory of emotional intelligence has striking similarities to Gardner's work. In 1983, Howard Gardner, a professor of Education at Harvard, by introducing the concept of multiple intelligence challenged the hegemony of the IQ concept that considers intelligence as being a single measurable entity predicting mental capabilities and as a genetically inherited characteristic not increasing through adulthood.

Interestingly, around the same period of time, at the beginning of the 1980s, management consultants began challenging the notion IQ as associated to business and career success. McKinsey and colleagues (Watson, 1983) found that the most successful companies tend to put more emphasis on what they called the four soft Ss—style (leadership and management), skills (core organisational competencies), staff and shared values—than on the three hard Ss: strategy, systems and structure. Organisations able to use and cultivate the concepts represented by the 4 S promote organisational cultures and encourage individual and group initiative, development and responsibilities. This underpins efficacy, efficiency and effectiveness of organisations.

Gardner suggested that intelligence is constituted; however, a wide range of talents are not taken into account within the traditional IQ tests. The idea of multiple intelligences is a broad flexible concept constituting by several separate intelligences.

Gardner and colleagues agreed on the definition of the first seven intelligences after having examined a vast amount of literature regarding the "development of cognitive capacities in normal individuals, the breakdown of cognitive capacities under various kinds of organic pathology and the existence of abilities in special populations, such as prodigies, autistic individuals, idiots savants, and learning disabled children"… "forms of intellect that exist in different species, forms of intellect valued in different cultures, the evolution of cognition across the millennia, as well as two forms of psychological evidence, the results of factor-analytic studies of human cognitive capacities and the outcome of studies of transfer and generalization" (Gardner and Hatch 1989).

Intelligence is defined as a set of abilities and skills that all individuals possess. They differ only in the level of their skills and how these intelligences combine. No type of intelligence is more important than the other, as people can be intelligent in many different ways.

In his first work (*Frames of the Mind: The Theory of Multiple Intelligences*, 1983), Gardner proposes that there are seven possible intelligences—linguistic intelligence, logical-mathematical intelligence, musical intelligence, bodily-kinaesthetic intelligence, visual-spatial intelligence, interpersonal intelligence and intrapersonal intelligence. In a later book in 1999, *Intelligence Reframed: Multiple Intelligence for the 21st Century*, he discussed the possibility of adding three more intelligences to the list of the original seven: naturalist, spiritual and existential intelligences. At the end, Gardner concluded that these merit addition to the list of the original seven intelligences.

Two of the areas of intelligence identified by Gardner are closely related to soft skills. These are the two inextricably interconnected personal intelligences: interpersonal (external) and intrapersonal (internal) intelligence. Intrapersonal intelligence, (Gardner 1993a, b, 2006), involves aspects of personal development such as the ability to identify, recognise and, at a more advanced level, symbolise differentiated sets of feelings. This is prerequisite guiding how we interact with others appropriately. Interpersonal intelligence is the ability to understand people's intentions, motivations and desires that builds on a core capacity to notice distinctions among others, i.e. temperament, contrasts in moods, motivation and intentions. It is through sensitivity to ourselves (intrapersonal intelligence) that it is possible to relate to and understand deeply other people; likewise it is through sensitivity to other people (the interpersonal intelligence) that we can get in contact and know ourselves.

In more advanced forms of interpersonal intelligences, human beings can excel in areas involving communication (verbal and non-verbal), the ability to see situations from other perspectives, the creation of positive relationships with others and being competent in positively resolving conflicts with others. Intrapersonal intelligence is based on the capacity to understand oneself, to be aware of and recognise personal feelings, fears and motivations. This intelligence has to do with introspective and self-reflective capacities. Individuals that practise self-reflection are able to explore themselves in relation with others and assess with a certain level of accuracy, personal strengths and areas that need to be further developed and predict and manage their own reactions and emotions. According to Gardner a high quotient of intrapersonal intelligence indicates a high degree of self-awareness. This intelligence entails possessing an effective model of oneself and being able to use such information to regulate interactions and relationships in lives. The two personal intelligences are indissolubly related with the symbolic systems supplied by people's culture (rituals, religious codes, mythic and totemic systems) which provides a way and a map to make sense of the experience of self and others.

Despite the criticism towards the idea of MI considered as an ambiguous and subjective concept that cannot be validly and objectively measured, it offers valuable insights about new alternative ways of thinking about learning and education. This approach highlights how learners are intrinsically different and thus the importance of providing flexible programmes and active methods within professional practice in order to address individual needs. In this respect, the educational implications of the model proposed by Gardner stand in a direct line with and from the work of Dewey (1966) and Kolb (1984). He is joined by Goleman (1995) in holding the view that while all intelligences are present, individual or all can be nurtured and strengthened by different interventions, one example of which is training and education.

1.1.2 Other Concepts to Define Soft Intelligences

Although Gardner's concepts have also business relevance, the concept of multiple intelligence was mainly developed thinking about educational contexts. Other concepts of intelligence such as intuitive and practice intelligences were instead developed with business applications in mind.

In the same decade, Wagner and Sternberg (1985) defined practical intelligence as "purposive or successful adaptation in real-world context". Purposive means that intelligence is directed towards goals and is showed by our attempts to adapt to the environment we interact with. According to Sternberg, by this definition intelligence includes whatever characteristics lead to such adaptation, and the latter includes changing the environment or selecting a new one if necessary. In this perspective, the way to progress our knowledge of intelligent functioning consists of comparing individuals who have had varying degrees of success in adapting to a given set of demands and challenges of the real world, in order to understand the characteristics that differentiate people (Klemp and McClelland 1986).

This view is interesting as it focuses and points on experience within our environment, as a major source for acquiring knowledge and skills. One measure of the ability to learn from experience is the acquisition of "tacit knowledge". Tacit refers to the knowledge not explicitly taught or even verbalised that individuals need to know in order to get along in daily life. Sternberg considers the acquisition and utilisation of tacit knowledge, often characterised as "street smarts" or "common sense", to be an aspect of practical intelligence (Sternberg et al. 2000). Manifestations of practical intelligence are "professional intuition" or "business instinct". These two terms characterise the tacit quality of knowledge associated with individuals who are successful in their respective domains and reflect knowledge that was neither taught in school nor read in a textbook or manual.

Recently, in business and management contexts, a number of authors have proposed and used the term "intuitive intelligence" (Dreyfus and Dreyfus 1989; Sadler-Smith and Shefy 2004). They have suggested that intuitive intelligence has three main attributes (Sadler-Smith and Shefy 2004, 2010): expertise (in-depth knowledge of a certain domain), understanding and self-awareness, which are closely related to soft skills.

Being intuitively intelligent requires, in addition to knowledge, appreciation of one's own intuition and understanding of how it differs from instinct and insight, how it works and when it is likely to help or hinder (Hogarth 2001).

Self-awareness involves being aware of own intuitions recognising when they occur and being able to distinguish between intuitive feelings and emotional feelings, learning and understanding how personal biases and prejudices can affect and contaminate intuitions (Sadler-Smith and Shefy 2004). In addition to these, there are other intuitions having soft skills relevance, such as social intuition (related to the capability of quickly assessing what other people might feel or think, their intentions and motives), creative intuition (referring to an instinctive feel that occurs in advance of a creative idea or insight and that can suggest a favourable direction that might be followed; the creative outcome combines knowledge in novel ways not previously thought of) and moral intuition (a rapid and automatic feeling that comes in response to an ethical dilemma that offers an emotional signal as to whether or not a particular course of action is morally correct).

Pink (2005) also recently delineated soft aptitudes as "six senses" that everyone should build to set a new mind. He claimed that focusing on the development of soft aptitudes is the only way for individuals, firms and organisations to stand out in a crowded marketplace mostly driven by three main forces: lower labour costs (Asia), increasing demand for products or services that are pleasing and appealing (abundance) and machine and computers substituting what once only people were able to do (automation). Pink claims that we should shift our attention from skills such as linear thinking, analytic hard logic and step-by-step methods of problem solving to the development or refinement of our interpersonal soft aptitudes. They involve persuasion, communication, self-understanding, creativity and the ability to detect patterns and opportunities, combine apparently unrelated ideas into a novel invention, empathise, play, understand the subtleties of human interactions and stretch in pursuit of purpose and meaning.

Moreover, the area of soft skills has been biased by unhelpful theoretical models, often based on popular "neuromyths" and the assumptions that soft competencies reside in the "right brain", which will not be the objective of this chapter.

1.2   Nature of Soft Skills

The following paragraph addresses the difficult issue regarding a unique definition of soft skills and draws on various definitions in the literature to delineate what are the aspects advocated as distinctive for describing and defining the concept.

Soft skills have been a significant challenge for practitioners, policymakers, trainers and researchers because of a lack of unique definition and a specific conceptual framework for understanding soft skills domain. This has been the result of a series of diverse perceptions around the area of soft skills, mainly related to the difficulty of defining what they are exactly and sometimes to the idea that they are vague, indistinct and indiscernible.

The attempt of gaining greater clarity and a more precise conceptual weakness around this concept has produced a significant number of definitions of soft skills that will be examined below.

As previously highlighted, people skills, social skills, social competence, interpersonal skills, social self-efficacy, managerial competence and social and emotional intelligence are just a few terms often used to describe soft skills in different areas such as psychology, healthcare, accounting, sale and entrepreneurship, business and management and economy (Thorndike 1920; Goleman 1998; Klein et al. 2006; Sadler-Smith and Shefy 2004, 2010; McClelland 1998; Salovey and Mayer 1989; Sternberg 1985; Joseph et al. 2010; Bacolod et al. 2009).

Historically researchers have debated on whether soft skill is a stable trait personality-based characteristic (Robles 2012) or a situation specific aspect subject to the specific surrounding environment and situations (Bedwell et al. 2011). Research has highlighted that both components of learning from experience and traits are incorporated in those skills (Burgoon and Dunbar 2000; Hochwarter et al. 2006; Klein et al. 2006). Klein states that there is a consensus in literature to consider soft skills not only as simple trait-based orientations but instead as behaviourally based competencies, expressed independently of personality and capable of improvement through training. Therefore we aim to make training and learning as accessible and flexible resource for boosting soft skills awareness and development.

An additional complication to the already imprecise conceptual framework around the definition of soft skills is given by the study on the competence areas, where terms as "competency" and "competence" are often used interchangeably for defining sometimes the same concepts (such as soft skills) and other times different concepts (both soft and hard skills), causing confusion and misunderstanding (Sultana 2009; Pate et al. 2003; Snyder and Ebeling 1992; McClelland 1973; Boyatzis 1973; Woodruffe 1993; Dubois 1998).

Proctor and Dutta (1995) offer some common characteristics of the domains of "hard" and "soft" skills, in the following definition: "skill is goal-directed, well-organized behaviour that is acquired through practice and performed with economy of effort" (Proctor and Dutta 1995, p.18). As will be described in the following, soft and hard skills differ for many significant factors. More in general, in the literature it is possible to identify a variety of perspectives and distinction between knowledge, skills and competencies for defining skills (soft and hard). In this work we will refer more specifically to the distinction literatures between soft and hard skills (e.g. Klaus et al. 2007; Clark 1995; Wellington 2005; Rainsbury et al. 2002) as used in policy and practice literature.

However neither soft skills nor hard skills can be considered better than the other, as they are complementary to each other and good for being applied to a diversity and variety of things and situations (e.g. Ashton 1994; Caudron 1999; Jackson 2010; Mullen 1997; Strebler 1997; Wellington 2005). The distinction between soft and hard skills is interesting as it helps to identify the different frameworks wherein they have been conceptualised and applied. A more general concept of competence encompasses the ability of an individual to activate, use and connect the acquired knowledge, skills, motives, self-image and values as a whole in complex, diverse and unpredictable situations (Perrenoud 1997).

Hard (technical) skills can be codified and transmitted and are referred to as goal-directed behaviours that draw on the capability to perform a specific task within a specific area or domain. They refer to education, knowledge, training and experience. Soft skills, on the other hand, are subject independent and focus on individual and relational spheres, although as we will see the following are often employed in response to the demands of a task in order for this to be efficiently completed.

How can soft skills be classified? Based on the review of the nature of the different definitions existing in literatures, it is possible to summarise that soft skill has been explained by analysing a number of its component parts such as *personal and behavioural attributes* (explaining the different intra-/interpersonal dimensions supporting and defining soft skills), *domain attributes* (defining and distinguishing soft skills from hard skills) and *outcomes towards which soft skills are directed* (how soft skills are linked to other key skills to drive individual, team and organisational objectives and performance attributes, including their nature of being goal-directed behaviours, and act as predictors for potential development and job suitability).

However it is easier to find more material related to the last two categories, than the first. This is because soft skills as transversal competence indispensable also for everyday life have started being recognised only recently.

Anyhow, regardless of the different classifications, many definitions place soft skills in the context of learning and development practices which is one of the primary aspects on which this book focuses.

Accordingly with these distinctions, in the following we provide definitions identified from a search and review of the soft skills in literatures that put the accent more on one of the three dimensions than the others, although they often shade into each other areas of definitions. However, it is clear that all these aspects represent different facets of soft skills that include people interpersonal skills, personal qualities, career attributes, communication, teamwork, leadership and customer service. Therefore, soft skills are made up of the combination of interpersonal (people) skills and personal (career) attributes (Robles 2012). A summary of the definitions is provided in Table 1.1.

Table 1.1 Summary of soft skills definitions

Soft skills	
Intra-/interpersonal oriented	Intangible knowledge related to personal characteristics and acquired with experience and practice (Svetličič and Kajnč 2009)
	Inherently relational and process oriented, focused on the effect of communication on another person (Duffy et al. 2004)
	Educational skills not domain specific, including communication and interpersonal skills, problem solving skills, conceptual, analytical and critical skills, visual, oral skills and judgement and synthesis skills (Boyce et al. 2001)
Outcomes oriented (goal and performance directed)	Soft employability skills that increase individual's opportunities in the labour market (Martin et al. 2008)
	Help students and people stay employed (Pratt et al. 2010)
	Abilities and traits pertaining personality, attitude and behaviour rather than to formal technical knowledge that are required to each level of skilled service jobs (Moss and Tilly 1996)
	Skills related to critical thinking, oral communication, personal qualities and interpersonal and/or teamwork that workers in contemporary businesses require (Giloth 2000)
	Communication and interpersonal skills required to elicit the activities performed by different stakeholders to support business (Jeyaraj 2010)
	Describe a set of abilities or talents (work in teams, communication, leadership, customer service, problem solving) that characterise career attributes that individuals can bring to the workplace (James and James 2004)
	Acquired through experience concern with managing and working with people are essential for software project management (Sukhoo et al. 2005)
	Essential for engaging effective and productive interpersonal interactions (Bacolod et al. 2009)
	Goal-directed behaviours, including verbal and non-verbal communication and relationship-building competencies, characterised by complex perceptual and cognitive processes (Klein et al. 2006)
	Are integral to effective leadership and related high degree of emotional intelligence (Goleman 1998)
	Distinguishing factor between successful and unsuccessful manager and leaders (Hayes 2002)
	Requisites for success in performing the complexity of manager role (Gillard 2009)
	Support individuals and organisations accomplish goals (Conrad 1999)
	Are related to effective organisational outcomes, such as managerial success and leadership achievement (Bray et al. 1979; Connelly et al. 2000)

(continued)

Table 1.1 (continued)

Soft skills	
	They are context specific and regard practical intelligence comprising managing tasks, career, self and others (Joseph et al. 2010)
	Micro-social differentiating skills (team building, leadership, management, planning skills team building) that allow truly engaging with customers and stakeholders (Muzio et al. 2007)
	Allow to better understand personal ways to act, how to work better in teams and to be more productive and successful (Muzio and Fisher 2009)
	Combination of personal, interpersonal and group skills needed for enhancing the performance of individuals, teams in workplace and organisations (Whetten et al. 2000, Whetten and Cameron 2001)
	Competencies (intra-/interpersonal skills) related to work and interview success (Chia 2005)
	Behaviours that make employees effective in their roles and distinguish some as candidates for leadership positions (Ranade et al. 2010)
	Refer to personality traits, attributes and high levels of commitment to the job that would make the candidate stand out ahead of his peers (Deepa and Seth 2013)
	Those personal values and interpersonal skills that determine a person's ability to fit in a particular structure such as a project team or a company (Gonzalez et al. 2013)
	Personal qualities, attributes or the level of commitment of a person that set him or her apart from other individuals who may have similar skills (hard/technical) and experience (Perreault 2004)
Domain oriented	Interpersonal skills, while hard skills are domain and discipline specific (Skulmoski and Hartman 2010)
	Refer to trans-situational, non-technical skills performed in the intra- and interpersonal spheres that facilitate the application of technical skills and knowledge, including problem solving, personal qualities and work ethic, communication, and interpersonal and teamwork skills (Kantrowitz et al. 2002)
	While soft skills are expressions of emotional intelligence, hard skills are manifestations of cognitive intelligence (Newell 2002)
	Interpersonal qualities encompassing character traits, attitudes and behaviours rather than technical aptitude or knowledge needed to find a job (Robles 2012)
	Non-technical skills involving interpersonal and intrapersonal capabilities to handle performance in different contexts (Hurrell et al. 2012)
	Soft skills are the personal and social skill that a person possesses, while hard skills are job objectives, work experience and academic background (Hutchinson and Brefka 1997)
	Soft skills concern with people or behavioural skills and are essential to apply technical knowledge in the workplace, whereas hard skills are cognitive in nature and associated with the technical aspects of performing a job (Weber et al. 2009)
	While soft skills are non-technical traits and behaviours needed for successful career navigation that allow more effectively use of technical abilities and knowledge, hard skills refer to the technical ability and the factual knowledge needed to do a certain job (Klaus et al. 2007)

Some definitions point more on personal and relational attributes as key components of representing soft skills.

For example, Svetličič and Kajnč (2009) in international relationship studies refer to soft skills as soft knowledge depending on the environment and situation … "soft knowledge is intangible knowledge, which is difficult to quantify, codify, store and transmit, because it relates to more personal characteristics and includes judgment and experience… It is hidden within the answers to questions like "*how*"… To know "*how*" relates to the ability to implement certain tasks, to know "*who*", on the other hand, relates to who possesses the knowledge of what and why (hard knowledge)". Soft knowledge is tacit–internalized skills acquired with experience and practice.

Duffy et al. (2004) in the areas of healthcare state that interpersonal skills are inherently relational and process oriented and focus on the effect of communication on another person, such as relieving anxiety or establishing a trusting relationship; they build on basic communication skills, which alone are insufficient to create and sustain a therapeutic relationship.

Boyce et al. (2001) argue that a key component of educational reform in accounting is the development and enhancement of soft skills in students, which are defined as the range of educational skills that are not domain or practice specific, including communication and interpersonal skills; problem-solving skills; conceptual, analytical and critical skills; visual skills; oral skills; and judgement and synthesis skills.

Other definitions point more on the character of soft skills of being goal-directed behaviours, enabling goals of individual, teams and organisations to be pursued (and more in general to have a significant impact on the economic growth) and their value of predicting how people will perform new or different job roles.

Paraphrasing Martin and colleagues (2008), "In the 21st Century, our natural resource is our people – and their potential is both untapped and vast". The importance of developing "soft" employability skills impacts both at molecular and macro levels. On one hand soft skills increase an individual's opportunities in the labour market; they are considered as "deal-breakers" for many employees when they need to get and progress in a job. On the other hand, soft skills development contributes to increase productivity of teams and organisations and impact on economic growth.

Pratt et al. (2010) with regard to successful training initiatives for workplace state that the most valuable employees to organisations are able to forge partnerships, build relationships, communicate effectively with the business and find creative ways to manage costs, as these soft skills help Information Systems students and people stay employed.

Service and information industries rely on employees that are rich in human capital, creativity and soft skills. According to Moss and Tilly (1996), soft skills refer to skills, abilities and traits pertaining to personality, attitude and behaviour rather than to formal technical knowledge that are required to each level of skilled service jobs.

Giloth (2000) claims that a more robust understanding of soft skills is needed, as all workers in contemporary businesses require skills related to critical thinking, oral communication, personal qualities and interpersonal and/or teamwork, but many of these skills are newly shaped by structural changes in the economy, technology and new forms of work organisation.

For Jeyaraj (2010) soft skills may be viewed as the communication and interpersonal skills required to elicit the activities performed by different stakeholders to support the business process, verify the process models and determine any problems with the process experienced, all of which need to be accomplished through dialogue with stakeholders.

James and James (2004) agree that soft skills are a new way to describe a set of abilities or talents that individuals can bring to the workplace. They characterise certain career attributes that individuals may possess such as work in teams, communication, leadership, customer service and problem-solving skills.

Sukhoo et al. (2005) consider soft skills essential for software project management. Acquired through experience, "they are concerned with managing and working with people, ensuring customer satisfaction and creating a conducive environment for the team to deliver high quality products within budget and on time, and exceeding stakeholder expectations".

For Bacolod et al. (2009), soft skills are the skills that any worker needs for engaging effective and productive interpersonal interactions.

Klein et al. (2006) define soft skills as "goal-directed behaviours, including communication and relationship-building competencies, employed in interpersonal interaction episodes characterized by complex perceptual and cognitive processes, dynamic verbal and non-verbal interaction exchanges, diverse roles, motivations, and expectancies". Interestingly also this definition of soft skills as skills displayed in goal-directed behaviours, which are based on specific competencies that are expression of both attitudinal and cognitive processes, offers a precise route for exploring the competencies underpinning those specific behaviours. Thus, this perspective opens opportunities for creating space for training and development initiatives, as well as performance and potential appraisal systems.

For Jackson (2010) soft skills are deemed essential for enhanced productivity and innovation in the workplace. He has provided a competence profiling by assessing the most relevant soft skills for employability (i.e. problem solving, communication, teamworking and work ethic, adaptability and change management) that may inform training employability programmes.

The definitions of soft skills highlighting their value as predictors for potential development and job suitability are provided in the following.

According to Chia (2005), soft skills competencies [such as those relating to the emotional intelligence soft skills variable] include interpersonal skills, intrapersonal skills, stress management and thinking skills and communication skills; these are factors related to work and interview success (that provide indications of the potential suitability of candidates to work in the firms). In his study Chia (2005) examined interviewing activities and the number of final job offers given by the multinational public accounting firms to college graduates and found that soft skills of candidates were taken into high consideration during the recruitment process. In short, the level of soft skills as portrayed by the candidates during the different interviewing stages of the recruitment process influenced the decision to make the final job offer. The study identifies the relevance of soft skills competencies in enhancing a graduate's performance at a job interview and suggests that the enhancement of these competencies, not always adequately emphasised in a formal accounting education programme, can be attained through participation in related training and development courses.

Similarly, Ranade et al. (2010) warns on the new urgency of developing a clear competence mapping in today's professional world requiring a complex level of competencies. These include soft skills or behaviours that make employees effective in their roles and distinguish some as candidates for leadership positions. In this perspective soft skills development can assist the goals of individuals, teams as well as organisations.

Perreault (2004) defines soft skills as personal qualities, attributes or the level of commitment of a person that set him or her apart from other individuals who may have similar skills (hard/technical) and experience. The mastery of soft skills is instrumental to success for individuals entering the twenty-first century workforce.

Very recently, also Deepa and Seth (2013) stated that soft skills refer to personality traits, attributes and high levels of commitment to the job that would make the candidate stand out ahead of his peers.

Also Gonzalez et al. (2013) define soft or social skills as those personal values and interpersonal skills that determine a person's ability to fit in a particular structure such as a project team or a company.

The definitions pointing more specifically on domain attributes are helpful in distinguishing soft skills from hard skills, as non-technical competencies needed for effective job performance.

For example, Skulmoski and Hartman (2010) define soft skills as interpersonal skills while hard skills as domain and discipline specific.

According to Kantrowitz (2005) soft skills refer to trans-situational, non-technical skills performed in the intra- and interpersonal spheres that facilitate the application of technical skills and knowledge, including problem solving, communication skills, personal qualities and work ethic, interpersonal skills and teamwork skills.

For Newell (2002), while soft skills (self-awareness, self-regulation, motivation, empathy and social skill) are expressions of emotional intelligence, hard skills (e.g. logic, analytical thinking rigour and strategic, long-term vision) are manifestations of cognitive intelligence.

Weber et al. (2009) pointed out that hard skills are associated with the technical aspects of performing a job. They require the acquisition of knowledge and are primarily cognitive in nature. Whereas soft skills concern with interpersonal, human, people or behavioural skills, they are essential to apply technical knowledge and skills in the workplace.

Robles (2012) describes soft skills as interpersonal qualities encompassing character traits, attitudes and behaviours rather than technical aptitude or knowledge needed to find a job.

According to Hurrell et al. (2012), a soft skill is a non-technical skill that involves interpersonal and intrapersonal capabilities to handle performance in different contexts.

Hutchinson and Brefka (1997) define soft skills as the personal and social skill that a person possesses while hard skills as job objectives, work experience and academic background.

Klaus et al. (2007) define soft skills as non-technical traits and behaviours needed for successful career navigation that allow a more effective use of technical abilities and knowledge, while hard skills refer to the technical ability and the factual knowledge needed to do a certain job. Moreover, soft skills compliment the hard one: "You can have all the technical expertise there is, but if you can't sell your ideas, get along with others, or turn your work in on time, you'll be going nowhere fast".

The other definitions of soft skills focus instead more on managerial factors enhancing performance and effectiveness of workplace, as they facilitate and support in ascertaining one's strengths in leadership, facilitating, mediating and negotiating.

Goleman (1998) stated that interpersonal skills are integral to effective leadership, and the most effective leaders have a high degree of emotional intelligence. Individuals with high emotional intelligence and therefore with personal and social competencies are oriented towards a transformational leadership style with emphasis on motivating and influencing others impacting on cooperation, motivation and productivity (Palmer et al. 2001; Bass and Avolio 1990; Gardner and Stough 2002).

Hayes (2002) has identified interpersonal skills as a key distinguishing factor between successful and unsuccessful manager and leaders (Hayes 2002): "the successful enactment of interpersonal skills enables individuals to manage successfully the challenges and opportunities of their job role".

Similarly, Sharma (2009) defines soft skills as "the extra edge that set apart the leader from the followers" and includes communication skills, interpersonal skills, negotiation skills, emotional intelligence, teamwork and cooperation.

Within the field of project management research, Gillard (2009) recognises interpersonal or soft skills, necessary requisites for success in performing the complexity of manager roles. These are skills that can be taught and learnt rather than skills that are innate or genetic.

Leadership skills are important to the domain of soft skills because they support individuals and organisations accomplish goals: (a) they assist the way information or services are delivered to customers and co-workers and inspire confidence of supervisors and management (Conrad 1999) and (b) they are related to effective organisational outcomes, such as managerial success (Bray et al. 1979) and leadership achievement (Connelly et al. 2000).

With regard to the IT professional roles, recently Joseph et al. (2010) defines soft skills as practical intelligence comprising of four management dimensions: managing tasks (knowing where and how to obtain non-IT domain knowledge); managing career (understanding career goals and how to structure an existing assignment in order to progress along a successful career path); managing self (related to the intrapersonal competencies of self-motivation and self-management, both essential for achieving performance excellence); and managing others (superiors, subordinates, peers, users, clients, vendors). Their nature is tacit and context specific and this helps to distinguish experts from novices.

Muzio et al. (2007) refer to soft skills as micro-social skills, such as team building, leadership, management and planning skills. They are differentiating factors that allow truly understanding the needs of customers and engaging effectively with key stakeholders. Moreover, soft skills are the skills that allow a person to better understand his or her own actions, how to work better in teams and how to be more productive and successful. Moreover, hard skills (innate and cognitive intelligence) and soft skills (emotional intelligence) are discussed in light of Maslow's hierarchy of needs model (1970), linking the first group to lower-order skills (physiological needs) and soft skills to higher-order skills (e.g. self-actualisation).

Interestingly Whetten et al. (2000) identifies ten core management skills organised around the three main groups of soft skills: personal, interpersonal and group skills. Overlap occurs among the three groups of skills; this means that as people progress from personal to interpersonal to group skills, the core competencies developed in the previous skill area help support successful performance of the new skill area. Management skills are the skills needed to manage one's own life as well as relationships with others, and thus represent a ceaseless endeavour. They are responsible of enhancing the performance of individuals or teams in workplace as well as organisations.

More specifically, Whetten and Cameron (2001) define several characteristics of management skills that differentiate them from other kinds of managerial characteristics. Managerial skills are:

1. Behavioural and not personality attributes or stylistic tendencies, consist of identifiable sets of actions that lead to certain outcomes, can be observed by others and are common across a range of individual differences.
2. Controllable: The performance of these behaviours is under the control of the individual; this means that they can be consciously demonstrated, practised, improved or restrained by individuals themselves.
3. Developable: Unlike IQ, certain personality or temperament, individuals can improve their competency in skill performance through practice and feedback, progressing from less competence to more competence in management skills. That outcome is one of the primary aspects on which this book focuses.
4. Interrelated and overlapping: Skills are not simplistic, repetitive behaviours, but they are integrated sets of complex responses; therefore, it is difficult to demonstrate just one skill in isolation from others.
5. Contradictory or paradoxical in their complexity: Meaning that they are neither all soft and humanistic in orientation nor all and hard and directive in driving people. They are neither exclusively oriented towards teamwork and interpersonal relations nor towards individualism and technical entrepreneurship.

Whereas these skills are called "management skills", meaning the core competencies that a managerial role should encompass, they are relevant not only in organisation or work setting; they are applicable in different spheres of personal life with families, friends, volunteer organisations and your community.

Moreover, as we have seen in the previous paragraph, we can summarise that social skills involve the following key components: self-awareness, ability to express oneself in social interactions and ability to read and understand different social situations, emotional expressiveness, empathy, sensing non-verbal emotional signal, understanding other's thoughts, feelings and intentions and act accordingly.

In examining all these definitions, it is possible to detect the complexity of the different factors that have been used to define the concept of soft skills and way to apply them to social, working or organisational contexts. However, despite of the different views and terminologies employed for defining soft skill, whether its components are considered more as behavioural, relational, emotional or cognitive, the different definitions proposed converge on the idea that soft skills is multidimensional, involving a complex blend of psychological components (Bedwell et al. 2011).

A possible attempt of a comprehensive definition encompassing what is intended and described as soft skills in literature could be the following: "Soft skills are not domain or practice specific (Boyce et al. 2001); experientially based (Sukhoo et al. 2005), both self (Gardner 1993b; Moss and Tilly 1996) and people orientated (Duffy et al. 2004); goal-related behaviours (Duffy et al. 2004; Hayes 2002); inextricably complementary to hard technical knowledge and skills enabling completion of activities and accomplishment of results (Kantrowitz 2005; Wellington 2005); and crucial for effective leadership performance".

In summary as they are task related means that can be employed in response to the demands of a task, to support the application of a harder skill in order to obtain the completion of a specific task.

In relation to hard skills, they are detected as more based on experience than on specific rules of procedures as per hard skills. They are less specialised and more transferrable than hard skills, and their outcomes are less predictable and measurable than technical skills. They are oriented more on people and significant interactions than specific domain oriented.

However soft and hard skills exist as part of a skill continuum. If we refer to the task-related soft skills, these can be considered harder than people-related and self-related soft skills and seen as a bridge between soft and hard skill domains; moreover they exist in reciprocal relationship, as one without the other does not make possible people to fully express themselves and their capabilities.

As soft skills are fundamentally behavioural, they can be learnt through training and development, unlike intelligence and personality (McClelland 1998). Because of their intrinsic nature of being real-world oriented and developed within real-word situations, soft skills training programmes, mainly conducted in face-to-face settings, employ a series of active methods including group discussions, interactive exercises, role-play simulations and case studies. In fact soft skills are displayed, then possible to observe, through behaviours and more specifically through goal-directed behaviours. These behaviours are based on specific competencies both expression of attitudinal and cognitive processes. This definition offers a precise route for exploring those competencies underpinning specific behaviours, thus opening space for training and development initiatives, as well as performance and potential appraisal systems.

We strongly share the vision that soft skills can be learnt and developed through personal experience, interaction, disclosure, feedback and reflection. Soft skills can be exercised within "learning-by-doing" environments that enable opportunities for practice and on-going and constructive feedback (Svetličič and Kajnč 2009). Through a guided process of learning, personal experiences can be transformed and internalised, become meaningful and people learn how to learn.

Chapter 2
Traditional Settings and New Technologies for Role-Play Implementation

It is widely recognised that role play is particularly suited to experiential leaning. It is a powerful tool that enables participants to draw into an experience and move the learning experience from an impersonal, theoretical and notional form into interactive and participative dimensions.

Regardless of the field and discipline of application, we believe that role-play technique does not simply enhance experiential learning. Role play uses the art form of dramatisation onto an educational stage, enabling learners to increase awareness of self and others, enhance mental flexibility and imagination, enlarge personal perspectives and create multiple perspectives and extend thoughts and feelings beyond the horizon of personal interpretation. Role enactment nurtures both cognitive and emotional skills and capabilities that can open up new solutions and opportunities for actions, and helps to identify and face a new level of reality and interpretation of the surrounding environment, both in relation to ourselves and in the interaction with others (Boggs et al. 2007).

Since its origins, role-play technique has been variously adapted and applied to different settings and contexts, for different purposes and to many disciplines, such as psychology, organisational change, sociology and pedagogy.

Psychodrama, sociodrama and simulation settings can be seen as different implementations of role play, which according to different purposes have been exploited in psychotherapy, education, counselling, personal development, business and organisational and training contexts. Role play has extensively been recognised as a powerful technique for enhancing the traditional training practice, boosting participants' learning experience, facilitating knowledge and promoting skills, competencies and group, as well as personal development, in face-to-face activities (e.g. McGill and Beaty 2001; Shaw et al. 1980; Turner 1992; Van Ments 1999). Thus, the term role play describes a range of activities where two or more people act out the part of individuals in a hypothetical situation (Black 1978) who are involved in "as-if" or simulated actions and circumstances (Yardley-Matwiejczuk 1997) that project participants into an imaginative-creative process established through the

© Springer International Publishing Switzerland 2017
E. Dell'Aquila et al., *Educational Games for Soft-Skills Training in Digital Environments*, Advances in Game-Based Learning,
DOI 10.1007/978-3-319-06311-9_2

interpretation of a real or fictional role in a specific given situation (Aronson and Carlsmith 1968).

The term role play was originally introduced by J.L. Moreno in 1934 after his experience and findings with the "theatre of spontaneity" in 1921. Moreno discovered the therapeutic potential of dramatic improvisation activity, as the enactments had positive effects on the personal lives of actors involved in the representations, and he called role-playing techniques the application of the principles of the "theatre of spontaneity" to educational purposes, in order to avoid any confusion with therapeutic psychodrama. Acting spontaneously does not mean being driven by uncontrolled emotions or impulsive activities. Instead, it is the psychological state to respond with new and adequate actions to external circumstances without being influenced by prescriptive social roles. This, according to Moreno, means to act creatively. Role play as a derivative of an art form invites the expression of novel or original ideas (Blatner 1995). Moreno developed and formalised these ideas into the methods of psychodrama and sociodrama, addressed briefly below.

Moreno (1946a, b) defines role as the functioning form that individuals assume in the specific moment they respond to specific situations in which other persons or objects are involved and highlights that roles do not emerge from the self, rather the self emerges from the roles.

The dynamic relationships between the individual and others are expressed through roles and can be explored through sociometry (Moreno 1953), a method that identifies the socio-emotional networks of relationships between group members. In terms of role theory, each individual can be imagined as constituted by multiple roles reciprocally interacting. Individual ways of being and behaving are an expression of this interaction of roles in combination with a series of personal attributes (abilities, interests, life story, cultural and social components, genetics aspects, etc.). Role play allows exploration of how personal individual and social roles interact with others' individual and social roles.

Although the different purposes of role play depend on the specific setting in which they are applied, they share similar principles and dynamics. Role plays can be adopted to deal with personal (psychodrama) or collective (sociodrama) issues and used to exercise a variety of specific skills (learning simulations). However, overall role-play technique is recognised as an effective vehicle for accelerating learning and stimulating interpersonal and intrapersonal communication.

Role play encourages new ways of thinking and interacting with things and people of our personal environment. This technique uses a variety of dramatic instruments derived from sociodrama and psychodrama, such as replaying a scene or a part of a scene, role reversal, making asides, mirror and double. These enactment tools facilitate learners to explore their emotions, concepts and thoughts from a detached perspective and the development of metacognition capacity (Weinert and Kluwe 1987). Thus, it is an effective method for fostering the skill of empathy and self-awareness. In the double, a group member (auxiliary) takes the role of the inner voice of the protagonist, helping to express and clarify feelings, thoughts or experiences unspoken and unaccepted by the individual. In role-reversal participants are invited to temporarily exchange their roles in the drama with others' roles.

In using the mirror technique, the protagonist steps out of the scene, while another member (auxiliary ego) is asked to replay the role and behaviours portrayed by the individual. The protagonist of a role play can be involved into the scene contemporarily either as outside the situation being represented by auxiliary egos or as active participant in role-reversal or mirroring positions.

A crucial role is played by the role-play director, who guides, coordinates and monitors the process. The director facilitates the role-play enactment and more specifically suggests possible actions to be undertaken, according to the needs expressed by protagonists and/or the group. He can review the performance and intervene during the enactment, invite protagonists to play different roles, exchange parts and introduce, support and instruct the auxiliary players.

Once the performance is concluded, the director invites all participants, including audience and auxiliaries, to self-reflection and discloser process of what the enactment meant in personal terms and group experiences.

One of the key aspects supporting self-awareness enhancement is represented by the personal dialogue that participants can entertain with the director during the pauses allowed in the action. From this pausing and the feedback offered by the director, the learner can experience the so-called phenomenon of role distance. Through this process, the player can meta-communicate with the role she represents, as she is encouraged and supported to look at himself in the performance "from the outside", considering the different point of views of other players and audience. This process helps to develop the competency of building mental flexibility and creative adaptation. Role-play technique develops a type of knowledge that transcends procedural knowledge. Indeed, role players are involved in experiences concerning a level of "conditional knowledge" that refers to being aware of the "why" and "when" to use and apply what has been learnt. Role plays should train and develop a general aptitude in individuals, although focusing on specific behaviours and aspects. The aim is to promote transferral of the learning to both similar and different situations from those experienced, therefore generalise and apply behaviours different from those that have been the object of attention (Perkins and Salomon 1992).

Two fundamental characteristics of role play emerged from this discussion: one is related to the role of the director who can be referred to as the therapist, educator, trainer, coach, consultant or psychologist (within a specific setting, she defines scenarios to be performed, harmonising roles to be explored, feedback and debriefing processes with layers, as well as group needs); and the other is that role play implies a level of personal growth through experiences that is possible, thanks to the presence of a group. Indeed, the peculiarity of role-play activities and its learning potential is represented by the interactions between members of the group involved in the enactment. Regardless of the nature of problems or dynamics represented either at individual and social level, the group itself represents the metaphoric stage allowing roles and dynamics to be revealed and disclosed.

It is interesting that, in recent years, role-play technique and its principles have been also implemented in digital environments and thus used in relevant context of applications by different professionals according to specific needs and purposes.

In literature, it is possible to find various and diverse examples of how role play transferred to virtual environments has been used and applied. Some of them can complement face-to-face activities, or provide stand-alone solutions, and envisage single-player or multiplayer interactions. Both multiplayers and single-player applications can be based on approaches characterised by conversational and emotional interaction, in other words open dynamic, or interaction mediated by objects and action exchange. In this case, the training methodology relies on defined steps. For a more detailed discussion of differences and peculiarities of the two approaches, the reader is referred to Chap. 3 of this book.

The following paragraph explores principles and applications of role-play technique in traditional settings. Subsequently, a review of online role-play examples and their main features, proprieties and applications to different contexts is described.

2.1 Role Play in Traditional Settings

As mentioned earlier, because of its intrinsic nature of being a vehicle for learning, role-play technique has been widely used in therapeutic, psychological, sociological, educational and organisational settings, thus with different implementations according to given specific needs.

A particularly interesting aspect of the current research findings in this area is that interactive training methods proved especially effective at enhancing cognitive, affective and skill-based outcomes of interpersonal skills; therefore, it is crucial to realise the link between training of soft skills and enhancement of individuals' relationships with others, their personal (or self) evaluations and job performance (Klein 2009).

Role play is used to create simulated scenarios where individuals are assigned specific roles to enact specific defined situations within a system of rules or guidelines (Betts et al. 2009). More specifically, role play exploits its learning potential through the interactions between group members enabling both individual and group learning and change. However, although its origins lie within group dynamics, role-play technique is also applied to situations involving only two people interactions (Bell 2001), with the advantage of focusing on specific aspects of interest without the need of managing the complexity of group dynamic as well.

As previously discussed, role play derives from psychodrama and sociodrama, methods introduced by J. Moreno for investigating, respectively, individual and social problems and dynamics, or more specifically, as a way to heal both individuals and groups (Sternberg and Garcia 2000).

As Moreno clarifies, while psychodrama deals with problems and dilemmas of an individual in psychotherapy, sociodrama works in mainly nonclinical contexts to clarify the issues involved in intergroup conflicts (Moreno 1946b). They are both grounded on Moreno's role theory and utilise group dynamics, enactment and principal psychodramatic methodologies. It is possible to state that the main differences between the two methods reside in the types of role that are explored. Psychodrama deals with individual problems and involves the role playing of personal aspect of individuals' life, as result of the concourse and concurrence of many different roles. Diversely, sociodrama focuses on the exploration of conflicting interactions at the level of social-common roles. In other words, if the action aims to explore parents' roles, we refer to a social role; conversely, if the focus is on how a specific parent is experienced, conceptualised and performed by a single individual, we refer to a psychodramatic role. Therefore, while in psychodrama, the enactment process is focused on individuals taking on the role of protagonists, in sociodrama, the protagonist of the session becomes the group itself.

Psychodrama and sociodrama are similar in that they employ common psychodramatic tools considered as invaluable experiential resources for cultivating empathy, effective feedback culture, self-disclosure, self-awareness and mental flexibility, such as "double", "role reversal", "mirror" and their combinations.

Over the years, the so-called classical Moreno psychodrama has been adapted and integrated with a variety of therapeutic approaches such as Gestalt, behaviour, family and psychoanalytic group therapies.

Although psychodrama is most often known in its form of group psychotherapy, Moreno believed that this method should also have been made available to a more general public in order to benefit people who were not psychotherapy clients. Moreno always tried to show that his method was meant as much more than a psychotherapeutic method, as his idea empathised as creativity and spontaneity affect our involvements in every sphere of our lives.

For example, people might wish to experience the psychodramatic method for educational purposes or for personal growth or for increasing emotional fulfilment. From the same perspective, role play for psychodramatic as well as sociodramatic methods may be effectively integrated in many fields aside from psychotherapy, which require some exploration of the psychological dimension of a problem or situation such as education, training programmes, organisational development and change, consulting to business, self-help groups' sense, industrial relations, mental health and primary and secondary education. Therefore, psychodramatic techniques can be employed to address socio-economic issues, social conflicts in communities, professional subgroupings, group and organisational climate changes, workplace and public relationships and peer and parental relationships (Blatner 2000; Betts et al. 2009; Zanardo 2011).

In literature, the term role play for learning purposes is often used interchangeably and inconsistently with the term simulation. Indeed, we believe that they can be considered as different points along a continuum; as the difference, it is a matter of learning purposes and objectives rather than typology (Sutcliffe 2002; Ladousse 1987). According to this view, role play engages participants in acting in a given role in a specific situation and can leave space for individual initiative, improvisation and imagination. Simulations could instead include role play involving participants to act a role which is bounded by the rules and the degree of structuration of the simulation itself. In general, they tend to mimic more familiar or realistic situations than role play. On the other hand, it is true that role play is based on a simulation process, since participants are invited to act in "as-if" actions and circumstances. Other authors identify the term role play as techniques used in therapeutic situations (Ruben 1999).

In this work, we use the term simulation to refer to role-play activities for training and educational purposes.

Role plays applied in educational and training settings create a stimulating opportunity for simulating particular events or situations that can help, for example, to master key aspects of a specific theory or deepen the understanding of a certain topic of study.

This is evidenced by the work of Hollander (1978) and Hollander and Hollander (1978) demonstrating that role-playing and sociodramatic enactments can help children in subject matter learning. They placed great emphasis on role reversal as being crucial in the learning process.

Applications of role playing in primary and secondary education settings—in their form of psychodrama and sociodrama for training purposes—have involved a variety of settings (Blatner 1996; Hollander and Hollander 1978; Altschuler and Picon 1980; Schlanger and Birkmann 1978; Lee 1991) such as:

1. Discussion of class material
2. Family life education programmes for exploring dating, marriage relationships and conflict resolution
3. Creative drama, more based on improvisation than prescribed scripts
4. Special situations involving issues concerning, for example, parent-student conflicts, ethnic strife and alcohol abuse programmes
5. Special education, which refers to special classes for people with learning disabilities that are helped with problems related to defeatism, poor self-esteem, behaviour problems, crippling disabilities, diabetes, deafness and blindness. Special classes can also include children with severe emotional disturbances, psychosis or problems with hyperactive, impulsive behaviours and autism
6. Learning about feelings, which refers to what is also known as emotional intelligence (EI), education regarding emotions and feelings experienced, teaching children to recognise personal emotions and learn how to manage those feelings along with the development of coping skills in interpersonal relationships (soft skills). These applications can be possible only if pupils are highly supported by professionals in personal exploration and self-discovery. Other researches in educational settings have emphasised the influential effect of role play for the development of social values (Shaftel and Shaftel 1967), interpersonal abilities (Schonke 1975) and creativity in the classroom (Torrance and Myers 1973) and therefore the potential of introduction of role playing as a teaching method in the curriculum (Shaftel and Shaftel 1982).

A recent and important area for the application of psychodramatic role-play methods regards professional training and industry. The major application of role play in both contexts is to develop interpersonal and intrapersonal skills (soft skills) of professionals, employees, managers, personnel and staff. Special attention has been given to the enhancement of sensitivity for students in training for care professions, such as nurses, teachers, policemen, doctors and so on.

Blatner (2006), for example, with regard to the use of the sociodramatic technique in education, argues that role play is the best way to develop soft skills such as initiative, communication, problem solving, self-awareness and working cooperatively in teams. Also Bollens and Marshall (1973) have highlighted the fact that role play finds particular application in relational contexts, typically in such areas as counselling and soft skills training.

The use of sociodrama, psychodrama and simulations recognises the fact that people better learn "by doing" and by experiencing situations in practice. In these contexts, people can practice and exercise skills explicitly and rehear individual and group effective behaviours in not treating and non-judgemental environments through the interaction of different roles. In role play, there is always a chance to learn from one own mistakes as they are source of self-reflection.

For example, the benefits to using role play in psychodrama for training purposes can help to focus on the representation of professional roles associated with real working contexts in order to investigate personal emotions, fears and expectations associated with that role. This process can help participants to disentangle roles from unpleasant perceptions and to regain a more effective vision and potential of possible personal evolution of the role and within the role.

Yet, sociodramatic role playing can focus on political, organisational and collective issues (e.g. economic crisis, abortion, organisational culture change, immigration streams and so on) played out by groups of people. The mechanisms of role reversal, mirroring and doubling foster deep and true understanding of people and problems, contribute to identify values, convictions and perspectives and expand people's mental maps with new perceptions and experiences.

Simulations can focus on a specific theoretical area (leadership, negotiation, decision-making) that is transferred into experiential role-play activities, where the aim is to complement the mere theoretical acquisition of knowledge by supporting learners in mastering practical aspects and relational dimensions that can be related to a specific theory, to be applied to real-life contexts and situations.

During the simulation, for example, a player can be invited to exchange her role with another one so to understand situations experienced by other people, while observers can be asked to play the role of the double with the aim of helping players to become more aware of feelings and thoughts not completely expressed. Once the simulation is concluded, a debriefing process takes place. The postgame session allows players, observers and trainers to share the experienced feelings, to examine behaviours acted and to elaborate on individual and group experiences (Kozma et al. 1978). As Thatcher (1990), Petranek and colleagues (Petranek et al. 1992) have also pointed out, the value of the debriefing process is crucial because throughout the discussion between trainers and trainees, learners clarify their objectives and reflect on their own learning process. Towards more conventional methods, the benefits of using simulations have shown to enhance learners' motivation and interest and promote a positive impact on attitude change (Pierfy 1977; Bredemeier and Greenblat 1981; Van Sickel 1986) and may provide better behavioural, cognitive and affective learning and personal understanding of social issues and events (Bredemeier and Greenblat 1981; Foster et al. 1980; Hankinson 1987).

In organisational contexts, role playing and simulating real-life situations are extensively used for selection and development under the method of assessment centre in combination with a variety of other criteria (interview, paper-pencil questionnaires and business cases). When applied for selection purposes, role play can support understanding of how a person would act when placed in a given organisational role or react to a problematic situation, as, for example, dealing with a passive-aggressive boss or a passive co-worker or yet with stress and anxiety in the workplace. The use of role play within potential and performance appraisal processes helps to identify and evaluate an employee's job performances both individually and collectively, as well as their potential to assume higher positions and responsibilities. Role play can simulate situations eliciting behaviours and outcomes that bear evidence about key competencies associated with a strategic role or position in the organisation, such as decision-making and leadership power, resistance to stress, organisation and planning abilities, analytical thinking and capacity of vision.

2.1.1 Role Play in Digital Environments

As highlighted earlier, because of their experiential and behavioural nature, soft skills cannot be effectively imparted and accomplished with traditional pedagogical approaches. For meaningful transfer of relevant skills and behaviours to real-life and working contexts, a pedagogical shift to participating-active methods is needed.

Several studies have confirmed that training methods involving only symbolic modelling, such as lectures and presentations, rank lower in cognitive and behavioural involvement than methods that involve participative modelling processes, as role plays (Klein 2009; Bandura 1977).

Multimedia and simulation-based training systems and digital role playing have become increasingly adopted for soft skills development. For the purpose of this book, we will specifically focus on digital role playing.

The advent of personal computers and the Internet has dramatically changed the domain of applicability of role-play techniques, by allowing the exploration of novel settings, based on artificial and digital environments. Indeed, the use and the growth of online games have been swift and widespread in the last decade, and the intrinsic power of this form of games for engaging large groups of people for significant periods of time and for creating community culture and sharing common interests and objectives is consistently more and more evident.

Literature has already highlighted the increased interest around online games as a medium for learning and demonstrates how these could be adopted within education and training contexts (Squire 2003; Egenfeldt-Nielsen 2005; Michael and Chen 2005a, b; de Freitas and Oliver 2006). Within this context, particular attention has been given to games that encompass both the engaging and immersive principles of games and the effectiveness of simulations as a meaningful learning space (Martens et al. 2008). From this perspective, the key challenge for effective learning games is about creating experiences that are engaging, motivating and interesting for learners that need to be supported through a system of feedback, reflection and transference to real-life situations. Therefore, consideration of using games for learning purposes has been changing in recent years, especially the perceptions about the suitability of commercial-off-the-shelf role-play simulations and games to support learning (Egenfeldt-Nielsen 2007) as well as skill assessment (Gee and Shaffer 2010). The key to success for e-educational role-playing games resides in being different from commercial online video games that pursue different objectives from education and workplace skill acquisition. Everquest and World of Warcraft, the two most subscribed fantasy-themed, massively multiplayer online games (MMORPG) based on role-play technology, are examples of leisure games used for educational purposes although not explicitly designed for learning objectives. Moreover, the development of e-educational role-playing games cannot compete with multinational millionaire budgets.

More and more, researchers, psychologists, tutors, educators and game developers have recognised the importance of working together to draw a system of principles that could help in the design and use of games as effective learning tools. In this domain, role-play simulation games can be conceived as tools that can boost effective learning when appropriately integrated in a training program designed on clear and predefined learning objectives and desired outcomes, as we will see in the next chapter.

In literature, there is no unique definition of game for learning purposes, such as serious games, simulations and virtual worlds, and this is not the objective of this work either. However, they can be considered as points along a continuum, according to the rigorous structure of the game and the specificity of learning goals (Aldrich 2009; Carr et al. 2010). Nevertheless, those are all forms of experiential learning activities or active methods (Dewey 1938, 1966) used for developing different skills, at different levels (procedural knowledge technical and vocational skills, social and soft competencies), with distinct purposes and in multiple environments, such as health, military, education, training and vocational areas.

2.2 Digital Role-Playing Games

As this work aims to focus mainly on role-play simulations for boosting effective learning processes, in the rest of this section, we will focus on the implementation of digital role-play setting and some platforms which have been specifically designed for role-play simulations.

It has been already said that role-play methodology derives from psychodrama and sociodrama (Moreno 1934) and that they have been adapted and applied to various domains, such as psychotherapy, education, business and organisational and training settings to intensify and accelerate learning. Recently, a variety of factors such as the introduction of the Internet, the progressive development of new technologies, the newest communication social systems and the innovative applications of artificial

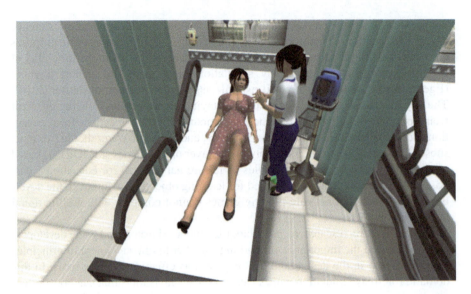

Fig. 2.1 Secondhealth: Virtual hospital in the 3D virtual world of Second Life-Scilands (Screenshot by Dave Taylor, Copyright Imperial College London, reproduced with permission)

intelligence have allowed role play to be performed on a computer screen and on a number of other platforms including consoles and portable devices.

Role plays in e-learning environments provide a learning experience where both interactive (Wills et al. 2010) and reflective (Laurillard 2001) dimensions take place.

Among the possible implementations of role-play games for learning purposes, multiplayer online role-play games (MORPGs) are considered one of the most powerful forms of modern gaming avatar-based role plays, and they seem to embed the methodology and the psycho-pedagogical principles originally expired by J. Moreno more closely than other types of role playing. There are limitations, however. As we will see below, there are circumstances in which multiplayer role playing is not always the best scenario for learning.

One of the most successful examples of this kind of virtual world is Second Life. The potential of using Second Life and other immersive virtual worlds initially created with social and entertainment purposes for supporting educational purposes has been presented in the work of Kirriemuir (2008), de Freitas (2008), and more recently by Gregory and Masters (2012) and in a review on the use of Second Life in primary, secondary and higher education (TOJDE 2011). For example, SciLands is a virtual environment within Second Life dedicated to science and technology. Secondhealth[1] represents a virtual operating theatre within the 3D virtual world of Second Life-Scilands, used for testing standardised training modules for surgical students through a series of hands-on lectures (Fig. 2.1).

---

[1] http://secondhealth.wordpress.com

Another example is represented by the VirtualPREX[2] project that uses classroom environments from Second Life for creating role play for pre-service teachers in order to enhance teaching skills before teaching in real professional contexts.

There are few examples of open-source platforms that deploy learning-oriented 3D virtual environments. Among them, some worth mentioning are Croquet (2006), Open Wonderland (2011) and OpenSim (2010). However, it seems that none of these platforms are currently actively used in educational and training contexts. OpenSim is the alternative open-source multiplatform of Second Life used to create persistent shared multi-user 3D virtual environment (metaverse). It may be accessed using a variety of clients on multiple protocols and has been applied to support learning across a range of computer science topics, such as human-computer interaction, data communications and computer networks (Miller et al. 2010).

Croquet has been conceived as a complete development and delivery platform for context-based collaboration to support communication, resource sharing and synchronous computation among large numbers of users. Diversely from the commercial virtual world Second Life or the related OpenSim, the platform offers much more flexibility to end users. Implemented in squeak language (based on Smalltalk-80), its flexible peer-based architecture enables the creation and deployment of collaborative multi-user online applications across multiple operating systems and devices. Any user has the ability to create and modify a personal information world and create links to any other Croquet world and network-deliverable information networks (as the World Wide Web). User or groups of users can visit and work inside any other world on the net, via spatial portals (Smith et al. 2003). After 2007, when Croquet SDK was released; the development of the technology continued under the Open Cobalt[3] project up to 2010.

Croquet has implemented interactive solutions for the teaching of language, ancient history and architecture, collaborations and resources sharing for scholars' communities. *Croquelandia* is one of the first spaces developed within Croquet as an immersive language instruction tool, designed to support Spanish pragmatics teaching. The tool uses narrative-based activities that guide the learner on a quest.

Players, immersed into a 3D space reproducing various geographical locations of real Spanish-speaking areas (e.g. Otavalo, Ecuador, Merida, Mexico), are engaged in a variety of gamelike goal-directed activities. The users are provided with corrective feedback through the interaction with nonplayer character speakers.

Qwaq forum is a licensed-oriented version of Croquet software. It is a quick tool for creating virtual meeting places to support a range of academic groups, such as astrophysics (Hut 2008) where students have opportunities to intervene in real time and have live chats and ask questions to the scientists. For example, within Qwaq forums, astrophysicians can meet up, exchange documents, share knowledge and set up large-scale simulations.

---

[2] http://www.virtualprex.com
[3] http://www.opencobalt.org/

Another application using Croquet is Igrishe, developed to support arts-related topics. It allows artists to build and run real-time visual performances and installations in theatres, art galleries and learning labs.

A further interesting application is Ancient Spaces, a 3D modelling program for the study of antiquity, art history and archaeology that engages students in virtual reconstructions of Athens. The software gives students access to a repertoire of 3D primitive shapes and elements that can be assembled to model and populate the Athenian agora. Students can "learn by reconstructing" key architectural and artistic environments of the ancient world (Lombardi 2006).

Similarly, *Open Wonderland* is an open-source toolkit cross-platform that provides a client-server architecture and set of technologies for creating personal and specialised virtual and mixed-reality worlds. Open Wonderland provides a rich set of tools for creating environments supported by several technologies (e.g. jVoice-Bridge for creating realistic immersive audio models, Collada loader for importing 3D objects in the scenes), as well as supports shared software applications, such as word processors, web browsers and document-presentation tools. For example, users can draw on a virtual whiteboard and view documents and presentations. Users interact through avatars, digital representations of themselves in the virtual environments. Users communicate in the virtual world by means of headsets and speakers or dedicated chat windows for text messages. For the development of professional skills in a business context, Wonderland has been used to improve remote collaboration. Users are able to build reproductions of different settings, such as offices or lecture rooms where people can use their digital alter ego to attend meetings, give presentations and interact. Within the project SIMiLLE developed by Sun Microsystems, Wonderland has been used to design learning activity scenarios to boost foreign language learning competences and skills and help students to learn about UK cultural aspects. The platform tools allow teachers to develop realistic learning scenarios, observe student interactions and making records of the activities performed. Similarly, students acting in the virtual world will carry out tasks and assume roles, according to the defined learning objectives, and make recordings or producing reports of their experiences to foster further reflections (Gardner et al. 2011).

In spite of the applications described above, there are very few research studies regarding role-play methodology implemented in virtual environments (Gao et al. 2009) and very few e-leaning role-play environments explicitly designed for soft skills training and development. However, it is possible to find suitable examples in this direction represented by e-learning platforms such as *E-drama* and *Unigame*, where online learning scenarios and contents are designed and assessed by tutors, trainers and psychologists. These are integrated systems of learning tools to be used by trainers, teachers and learners to support the training experience. We will specifically refer to this technology with the term of EMORPG. *Educational* denotes both characteristics and purpose of the play; *multiplayer* refers to the fact that learners play simultaneously in the same online world; *online* specifies that the game to be played requires an Internet connection; *role-playing games* indicates that when players join the virtual environment, they interact with each other through controlling a digital alter ego (an avatar) with physical appearance and personality aspects that can be more or less related to the real player interpreting it.

Thus, our definition of EMORPG encompasses various aspects: it is an experiential and imaginative activity inspired by the role-play principles, taking place in a virtual world where interpersonal dynamics occur because of people interacting at the same time with each other through the presence of an avatar and under the supervision and guidance of a role-play director. The director (who according to the context of role-play setting applications can be a psychologist, teacher, trainer, educator, consultant or therapist) can play different roles. They can write a storyboard as a playwright, assign roles to players as a casting director, guide the action in the performances, as a movie director, and, finally, give personalised feedback to the group by recording and analysing significant parts of the scene of the enacted performance (feedback and debriefing phase). EMORPG provides a structure, a design of the narrative experience, processes of feedback, reflection and self-awareness, ensuring occurrence and transference of learning, as the simulation scenario is designed and implemented in line with identified pedagogical objectives and taking into account group training needs.

Moreover, among the e-learning technologies designed for training purposes, there are few examples of platforms based on user-avatar interactions presenting different characteristics. They may differ depending on various rules to be followed in order to achieve learning objectives, possibility of improvisation, time available to perform the tasks, type of interactions between players (with real users or with computer bots), number of players involved in the virtual environment (multiplayers or single player) and so on.

Interestingly, as will be seen in Chap. 3, some of the limits identified with EMORG (such as the complexity for facilitators to take into account too many variables during the role playing going from the observation of group dynamics to the feedback processes) have induced professionals to consider the advantages of introducing game technology less dependent on the supervision of real facilitators.

Some examples identified in literature are based on single players interacting with BOT controlled by a computer programme, such as At-risk (Kognito Interactive 2009) E-Adventure, and Not-Fear within the EU E-circus project-Education Through Characters with Interactive Role-playing Capabilities that Understand Social Interaction (Aylett et al. 2006).

At-risk is an avatar-based gatekeeper training simulation designed to allow university students (At-risk for students) and high school educators and staff (At-risk for educators) to build interpersonal skills and learn how to manage effective conversations in the area of behavioural health. The games are designed to support and prepare university and college students and staff to recognise, approach and refer students exhibiting signs of psychological distress including depression, anxiety and thoughts of suicide, in order to identify students that can be potentially at risk. Role play engages staff and students, respectively, in 45-min and 1-h conversations with an "expert student" computer-controlled avatar, with its own story and personality

Fig. 2.2 E-adventure: Learn about Galician traditions and culture

that guide the learner through the steps to follow in order to achieve the identified learning outcome.

Through these conversations, they practice and learn to use active and reflective listening techniques in order to effectively encourage disclosure of psychological distress, motivate students to seek help and avoid common pitfalls such as attempting to diagnose the problem and giving unprofessional advice. At-Risk for High School Educators is part of a suite of gatekeeper training simulations tailored to the needs of different groups of learners, such as university faculty, college students and families of returning veterans, multicultural teams, health providers and emergency department personnel.

E-adventure (http://e-adventure.e-ucm.es) is a single-player interaction-based educational authoring platform, created with the aim of facilitating both the development of 2D point-and-click games and learning simulations for various purposes (a well-known example of point-and-click adventure game is MonkeyIsland[4]). An interesting feature of it is the direct involvement of educators in its development. The platform is the result of a project developed by the e-UCM e-learning research group at Universidad Complutense de Madrid, with the aim to promote the integration of simulations and games in traditional education processes and more specifically in Virtual Learning Environments (VLE). E-adventures provide educators with a user-friendly game editor that allows them to define characters, rules, contents, items and scenarios of the game to be played both in first and third person. The E-adventure game learning scenarios can vary and regard different subject matters and contexts such as teaching history (Fig. 2.2) and English language, evacuation protocol principles, assembly of hardware components, etc.

---

[4] https://www.facebook.com/pages/Monkey-Island-Adventures/78883723363

Another example, based on the E-circus project, offers both a 3D single (*Fear-Not*) and multiplayer (*ORIENT*) virtual environments aiming at enhancing social and emotional learning through the interaction of users with virtual characters and establishing effective and empathic relations with learners. Similarly to the previous example, learners are presented with a series of options to be selected directing the learning path. Fear-Not and ORIENT are two types of software created for the use of children and young adolescents in schools to support students in dealing with bullying and foster intercultural empathy, in combination with traditional educational methods. Not-Fear is a single-player videogame consisting of a series of interactive, bullying stories where students aged between 9 and 12 years interact with virtual characters in the role of bullies, helpers or victims who are endowed with their own emotions and memories and behave according to the roles assigned (victim, bully, victim's friend, etc.). Users, after having observed a bullying episode, advise the victim about how to act, by choosing from a list of coping strategies, as, for instance, inviting the character to ask for support from a teacher. The user observes how this suggestion is enacted by the victim of the bully and which consequences occur. At the end of the scenario, a universal message regarding the most appropriate coping strategy is displayed to the user. ORIENT (Overcoming Refugee Integration with Empathic Novel Technology) is a multi-user game designed to be played by a group of 2–3 teenagers aged between 13 and 14 years aiming at the integration of refugee and immigrant children in schools, as well as boosting team building competence. The group plays the role of a spaceship crew that land on the planet ORIENT populated by aliens represented by virtual characters. Their mission is to understand the local culture and find and learn the most effective way of interacting and cooperating with the aliens inhabitants in order to save ORIENT form an imminent catastrophes (Lim, Dias et al. 2008, Lim, Aylett et al. 2009).

Continuing with the previous, other examples are represented by multiplayer platforms allowing real-time interaction between real participants, such as *Unigame, Infiniteams* and *E-drama*.

Unigame Social Skills and Knowledge Training web platform was developed within the Unigame project funded by the EU Socrates/Minerva program in 2003–2004. Unigame can be defined as an online group chat-based role-play game to be used by tutors within university and lifelong learning framework in order to support various domains, as part of face-to-face learning activities (Dziabenko et al. 2003). The final aim is to acquire knowledge within a specified topic area by interacting with other players and different team groups and by using different means of communication such as private or discussion forums. The interactions between participants are based on open dynamics; thus, there is no unique or prescriptive way to achieve the identified learning objective. This means that specific ways of interacting between specific people and within a specific context will always determine peculiar training dynamics. The nature of the interactive experience itself can boost soft skills such as problem solving, effective communication and teamwork as the overall aim of the game, regardless if the specific topic is to reach mutual agreement within team members as well as the other teams involved.

Unigame has often been used as part of a blended learning approach comprising of a number of sessions where players are introduced to topics to play and team to be part of and involved in discussions around topics for reaching consensus or reflecting on the specific part played in the game.

An example of team-based multiplayer online game is *Infiniteams*[5], developed by TPLD. It can be defined as an example of online multiplayer task-based activity game rather than a role-play experience (e.g. the team has to cooperatively build up a bridge over a river), which integrates education with gameplay (Seeney and Routledge 2011). It makes use of avatars to represent the players, and the game scenario is based on deserted island survival elements. This software has been designed to be used for team building, management training and recruitment in order to encourage teamwork, communication, leadership, trust, problem solving and negotiation. The training activity is organised around modules that are time based scored, depending on time taken to complete the game and strategy chosen by the team.

Each module (mini-game) is based upon 1-hour activities comprising of debriefing to set up and discuss about the scenario to play, two rounds of games spaced out by discussions and analysis of the team performance in the first game phase and conclusion and reflections facilitated by trainers. In education, TPLD has also developed *Eduteams* multiplayer software for providing experiential learning to pupils aged between 10 and 14 year old. It is used to support the development of a variety of skills such as communication, teamwork and problem solving, as well as IT skills.

From the perspective of the EMORPG, E-drama is probably one of the most renewed platforms; however, it was never actually meant to be used for education and training but as opposed to being a research prototype that could point towards development of a practical system. It was only briefly used in various schools in Birmingham for a couple of days in an evaluation study[6]. Initially developed in 1999 by Hi8us, E-drama is a web-based role-play multi-user environment that incorporates a variety of tools for creating and customising role-play sessions.

With E-drama, a group of five people can interact online under the guidance of a real or computerised director that initiates the simulation, changes the background of the scenarios, intervenes in the role play and communicates with players using text chat. Users, represented by avatars, can customise the physical appearance of their virtual alter ego according to the scenario that they are invited to enact by trainers (see Fig. 2.3).

The E-drama software comprises of two user interfaces, "Actor" and "Director" client applications, used, respectively, by learners and trainers. The first version of the software (E-drama) provides a 2D environment as interactive ground for both learners (actors) and trainers (directors), while the enhanced version introduces a 3D flash interface for scenario backgrounds and animated characters replacing the previous 2D static avatars. The new 3D version is referred as E-drama software and was the result of the collaboration between Hi8us, Maverick TV, Birmingham University and BT Innovate with the support of the PACCIT programme. The 2D

---

[5] http://www.infiniteams.com
[6] Prof. John A Barnden and Dr. Li Zhan, personal communication, October 9, 2014

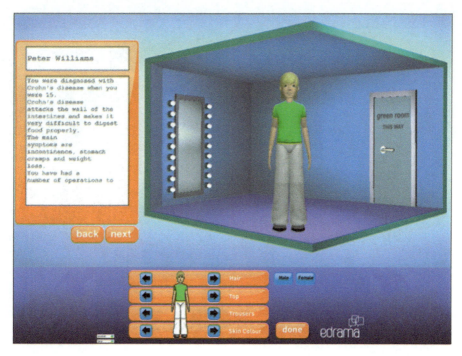

Fig. 2.3 E-drama, customisation of avatars (Screenshot by Dr. Li Zhang, reproduced with permission)

E-drama was used in formal education for teaching aspect of drama and supporting a different range of subject areas such as creative writing and career advice with a version of the software called Dream Factory, commissioned by the UK University for Industry (Dhaliwal et al. 2007). The enhanced version E-drama also introduces computerised AI-guided agents in order to offer new elements to the scenario for developing participants' dynamics and especially to reduce burdens and responsibilities of real directors in the role-play process (Zhang et al. 2009). The AI actor is driven by a system called EMMA (emotion, metaphor and affect).

The impact played by EMMA and the 3D animated characters on users' experiences was assessed in various trials in secondary schools that involved participants in dealing with scenarios regarding homophobic and school bullying and Crohn's disease (Zhang et al. 2009).

Within E-drama, trainers and trainees can communicate to each other by typing in messages that are shown in speech bubbles above avatars' heads (see Fig. 2.4). A variety of non-verbal signals, such as facial expressions, gestures and a range of body movements, can animate the 3D avatars, with the aim of making the interactions between players more engaging emotionally.

In recent years, the interest towards the implementation of role-playing approach into technological artefacts is expanding, and a number of software have been developed, both from research institutions and the private sector. The latter case is

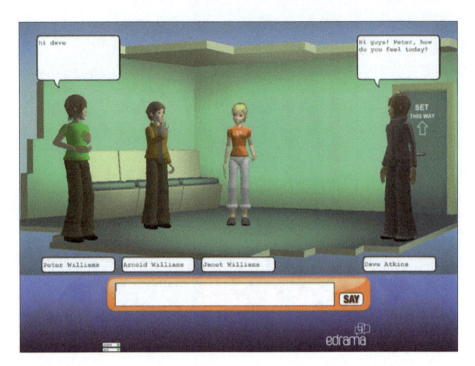

Fig. 2.4 E-drama improvisation interface with three human-controlled characters (on the stage) and one AI character, Dave (Screenshot by Dr. Li Zhang, reproduced with permission)

particularly interesting, as it demonstrates the real potential of the technologies we are discussing in this book. As we argue throughout the book, virtual role-playing games are mainly explored in the field of soft skills as a natural extensions of traditional training techniques. Indeed, the modern literature in this field presents some examples of virtual role-play application to communication and negotiation. The area of communication is currently the most promising and natural candidate. The US company Alelo has developed a suite of software for training cross-cultural communication skills in different critical environment which is currently used for training US military personnel deployed in conflict area, especially in the Middle East, and for colloquial English training (Johnson 2014).

Communication skill is also the target of a platform developed by the University of Utrecht in the Netherlands (Jeuring et al. 2015). The platform name is *Communicate!* and is a serious game for practicing communication skills. It supports practicing interpersonal communication skills between a healthcare professional such as a doctor or a pharmacist, or a (business) psychologist, and a patient or client. A player selects a scenario and holds a consultation with a virtual character. In the consultation, the player chooses between the various options offered in the scenario. The player scores on the learning goals addressed by the scenario and gets immediate feedback through the effect of the choice between the answer options on the utterance and emotion of the virtual character. *Communicate!* also offers an editor for developing role-playing scenarios.

In the field of negotiation, besides our platform ENACT, that will be described in a dedicated chapter, an increasing body of research is particularly focusing of training negotiation skills in virtual environments with role-playing approaches.

The platform *BiLAT* (Kim et al. 2009) and related instantiations described in, e.g., (Gratch et al. 2015) is a role-playing serious game for the training of bilateral negotiation through interactions with virtual agents in a simulated environment. The platform is enhanced by an intelligent tutoring systems that provide guidance and feedback on the user's performance. The system is particularly interesting as it is based on a long stream of research around the design of a virtual human, involving both advanced 3D graphic techniques and artificial intelligence (Core et al. 2006).

A different perspective in role-playing implementation is taken from a different group of game, in which a set of formal rules and interactions has to be followed in order for learners to achieve the relevant learning objectives. These set of steps are embedded in the software; they do not require the presence of any experienced external guidance and drive the player to a stable training outcome. Indeed, the advantage of this method lies in the fact that it is very low cost, as after an initial phase to familiarise users with the system, it can be used without the guidance of a tutor, as the system is self-regulated. Although this methodology enables players to rapidly learn and asses specific skills or behaviours (e.g. problem solving), on the other end the richness of the unpredictable dynamics occurring between trainees may be lost, especially when we refer those soft skills that require continual guidance and feedback. DECIDE-IT and Learn to Lead are examples of formal rule-based role-playing technology.

As discussed more in detail in Chap. 3, we will propose a possible taxonomy of games reflecting the approaches, namely, psycho-pedagogical and technological, used by the authors to designing Technologically Enhanced Educational Role-Playing Game (EduTechRPG) for soft skills training along different EU funded projects. The first dimension specifies the psycho-pedagogical foundations of the learning approach adopted and identifies two main categories of EduTechRPG: Drama-based and Rule-based depending whether the objective of the game focuses more on a direct involvement with the learning objectives through a personal dramatisation (Drama-based) or more on the logical and reasoning aspects involved by the user for achieving specific learning objectives (Rule-based).

Moreover, EduTechRPG are exploited by the use of two main technological systems that result in Communication Technology-based (ComTech) EduTechRPG and Simulation Technology-based (SimTech) EduTechRPG. The first system allows a virtual extension of traditional face-to-face psychodramatic mechanism and experiences that are transposed to a digital setting (see Chap. 1). The second technological approach permits the production of "artificial" micro-worlds based on computer simulated, formal models about social and psychological phenomena.

Eutopia (Chap. 4) and ENACT (Chap. 5) represent two different examples of drama-based training environments, respectively, a stand-alone SimTech and ComTech EduRPGs. DREAD-ED (Chap. 6) and Learn to Lead (Chap. 7) are instead examples of rule-based role-playing technology, respectively, ComTech based and SimTech based.

The peculiarity and the novelty of our psycho-pedagogical methodology, throughout all the above-mentioned EduTechRPG, are represented by the importance of feedback and debriefing processes that can be conveyed to learners through different means (online group or individual chats/meetings with tutors, a brief automatic report at the conclusion of a training session, etc.). Tutors, which can be either real or guided by an artificial agent, are a key factor facilitating the training process, the personal and group development through the interactions with learners, as we will see in the following chapters.

It is important to remark that the aforementioned dimensions used by the authors to develop those different EduTechRPG should not be considered as mutually exclusive but rather as complementary. Indeed, is the ability of integrating such dimensions in a single game implementation that contributes to the design of an educational tool to create meaningful learning.

Characteristics, limitations and strengths of the above-mentioned EduTechRPG will be analysed in detail in the following dedicated chapters.

Chapter 3
Methodology and Design of Technologically Enhanced Educational Role-Playing Games for Soft Skills Training

A wide range of information and communication technologies can be used to develop EduTechRPGs, and a number of pedagogical strategies can be applied, mainly developed for favouring different educational objectives and to meet specific technical requirements. Although formal categorisation of those approaches and models is a difficult exercise, in this chapter, we will attempt to present a rational view of the characteristics of EduTechRPGs from both technological and educational viewpoints. In particular, we will try to draw a general picture of the elements which, to different degrees, characterise the variety of models and implementations observed in modern EduTechRPGs. The categorisation that we will design in the following pages cannot be exhaustive, because such categories and denominations only aim to rationalise a complex and multifaceted panorama. Moreover, it should be noted that some of the categories might also be applied to more traditional implementations of EduRPGs and, to a certain extent, to analyse the characteristics of any type of game, especially for exploiting the educational potentiality of a given implementation and to identify the possible domain of applications. In particular, with the help of such reflections, we aim to introduce a unique methodology and the various elements to be taken into account in the process of designing and implementing an EduTechRPGs, both from technological and educational perspectives. The same categories will be used for embracing the experiences that will be discussed in the following chapters in a common framework. Such an exercise is particularly interesting when looking back to the technological and educational endeavours of the various implementations presented in Chap. 2 and looking at their characteristics from the perspective presented in the following pages.

This chapter will focus on the proposed methodology for soft skills training, based on the results and experiences from several European projects. The core elements of the methodology are the gaming experience, the modelling of relevant psychological and pedagogical theories, the tutoring and assessment of users, and the use of simulation and artificial intelligence techniques. Throughout the chapter,

© Springer International Publishing Switzerland 2017
E. Dell'Aquila et al., *Educational Games for Soft-Skills Training in Digital Environments*, Advances in Game-Based Learning,
DOI 10.1007/978-3-319-06311-9_3

there will be an attempt to draw general categories and the fundamental game structure that may help to better characterise the constituent parts of EduTechRPGs and their relationship with both technology and psycho-pedagogical concepts.

3.1 Gaming Experience and Education

There has recently been a great deal of interest in harnessing the motivational qualities of games in order to create powerful, engaging educational and training tools (Amory et al. 1999; Gee 2003; Garris et al. 2002; Brown 2014; Moreno-Ger et al. 2014; Riemer and Schrader 2015). This interest is unsurprising, given that games are carefully designed to engender user engagement (Dondlinger 2007; Mayo 2007) and that engagement is also a key predictor of success in any educational or training programme. Indeed, motivation is consistently found to be a key predictor of successful educational outcomes (Malone 1981; Filsecker and Hickey 2014). Specifically, the amount of time a student spends engaged in learning (or time-on-task; Admiraal et al. 1999; Fredrick and Walberg 1980) has a significant impact upon her learning. At the same time, games are a form of technology that specialises primarily in engaging and motivating users to spend time-on-task (Dondlinger 2007; Mayo 2007). The prospect of a form of teaching that inspires engagement on similar levels to those observed with computer games is very attractive to educators. Moreover, learning is also an essential part of successfully playing any game (Gee 2005; Koster 2013; Rosas et al. 2003). Indeed, all commercial games are educational to some extent, because they force players to learn the skills needed for gaining success within that game. When playing any game, it can be said that players demonstrate complex behaviours after a period of playing that they would have been incapable of performing before they started playing. Entertaining games require players to learn (Gee 2003), and those players engage in this learning willingly. It seems that game designers have hit on profoundly successful methods of getting people to learn and to enjoy learning (Warren et al. 2009; Warren and Dondlinger 2008).

For this reason, most of the successful game-based learning experiences have used mainstream games like Civilization, the Tycoon sagas or The Sims. Experiences specifically applied to role-playing games for soft skills training have been discussed in Chap. 2. However, despite their educational potential, most mainstream games lack integration with the current curriculum and appropriate assessment frameworks. As an example, in real-time strategy computer games like the RollerCoaster Tycoon saga, Virtual U or SimCity saga, players adopt the role of business managers and have to take the management decisions of an organisation. For example, in Roller Coaster Tycoon, the goal is to build and administrate a theme park that is profitable. The potential of these games is almost evident because they can help students in developing highly valuable skills like resources management or decision-making, but it is uncertain if this will result in a better performance in exams and, as a consequence, in a tangible academic improvement.

Nevertheless, the advantage of using mainstream games is clear: teachers or educational institutions only need to go to any retail store and purchase them, without the need of creating a new educational game. Indeed, creating a game is a time-consuming task, so in an already time-constrained curriculum where educators are usually struggling to achieve the goals defined by educational regulators and institutions, the question is "Is it worth taking the time?"

Notwithstanding, there are clear benefits that come from using custom games developed directly by educators instead of using mainstream games (Prensky 2005). Indeed, mainstream games are developed to be entertaining, not educative. They provide contents that are rich and valuable from an educational perspective but also include errors, misconceptions and inaccuracies to make the games more attractive. This is usually a concern that parents show when they are told that their kids will be using games in the classroom. In addition, mainstream games are not always easy to align with current curricula or do not meet educational standards.

However, starting from the obvious observation that entertainment games are hugely successful, especially because of the way in which they engender motivation, it is not a surprise that the creation of games which provide useful learning experiences for the player has been proposed. Indeed, educational games appear to offer the potential to improve learner motivation, time-on-task and, consequently, learning outcomes.

There are a number of reasons behind this view, which have been highlighted in many recent books and scientific articles (Aldrich 2005; Hussain and Coleman 2014; Giessen 2015; De Gloria et al. 2014). The main pedagogical element that stands out is that users experience the game in a direct, not mediated way. By simply playing the game, sometimes with the help of a light tutorial, the user can acquire the game dynamics, its foundation concepts and the entire body of knowledge necessary to progress deeply in the game and experience more advanced features. This is a fundamental psycho-pedagogical element of game-based learning, which in turn leverages on the concept of intrinsic motivation to achieve and win within the game (Csikszentmihalyi 2014; Malone and Lepper 1987; Dickey 2007) and seamlessly implements a wonderful example of learning-by-doing or experiential learning; that is, learning by actually doing and being active in the learning process, so to experience and reflect upon the characteristic of the experience. According to the main proposers of such pedagogical frameworks (Dewey 1938 and more recently Kolb, 1984), the process of experience and reflection is at the basis of knowledge acquisition in learners.

For these reasons, there have been a huge number of games developed in recent years with the intention of providing useful, engaging learning experiences. However, the application of such an approach to role-playing games explicitly dedicated to soft skills is still in its infancy.

3.2 Fundamental Concepts and Structure of EduTechRPGs

This section will present the fundamental concepts that form the theoretical and methodological background of any educational role-play game, with a special view on EduRPGs dedicated to soft-skill training. As we will see, the particular application domain requires specific features and a dedicated methodology.

Irrespective of their technical implementation and application domain, all EduTechRPGs share general features that can be found in every psycho-pedagogic role-playing game. Their fundamental structure can be viewed as the combination and interaction of three layers: (a) hidden layer; (b) visible, or external, layer; and (c) evaluation layer. It is worth noting here that, although in this present chapter and in the book as a whole we will focus our attention on the specific case of soft-skills training and EduRPGs, the first two layers present a general structure that can be found in any other game and similar concepts can also be applied to other domains, not restricted to games. The third layer, on the contrary, identifies a concept which is specifically related to the design and implementation of EduRPGs.

These layers are functional elements within the game that must be opportunely designed and implemented. Their relationships, including the target beneficiaries, are schematised in Fig. 3.1. In EduRPGs the fundamental element is the soft skill that the designer wants to teach, or evaluate, and whose training must be transferred to the game. Given the specific soft skill in mind, the structure that follows represents the fundamental content of the game, that is, its hidden structure and the visible layer. As suggested by the name, the visible layer is what the user will see and will act upon during the game. It represents the gamification aspect of the design and must be in perfect accordance with the hidden layer, so that the user is provided with the correct level of information and gaming operations to play with.

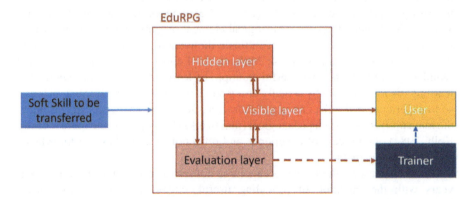

Fig. 3.1 Fundamental structure and functional elements of an EduRPG with their relationships. The starting point is the soft skill to be transferred through the game. EduRPG designers must work on three different levels: hidden layer, visible layer and evaluation layer. *Dashed lines* represent the information flow of the EduRPG when a trainer or tutor is present

In addition, given the specific educational purpose of the game, the accomplishment of the educational objectives is devoted to a specific element of the structure, which we call here the evaluation layer. The evaluation layer complements the hidden and visible layers. Its role is to analyse user's game performances in the light of the specified training objectives and to provide the user—and the trainer, if present (hence the dashed lines in the graph)—of meaningful information about the learning process and overall performances. Moreover, based on opportune learning analytics, the aim of this functional element of the EduRPG is to provide tutoring and guidance to the user throughout the game.

3.2.1 Narrative Structure and "Mise en Scène"

According to Barthes (1977), narrative is a pervasive feature of human cultural products and can be found in myth, legend, fairy tale, novel, epic, history, news, cinema, comics and, obviously, games. Speaking in terms of literary concepts, the relation between the visible layer and the hidden layer can be likened to the relationship that links the narrative of a novel, a theatrical representation or a movie, with the underlying narrative structure and moral of the story, that is, the development of the story itself and the message conveyed.

It is possible to make an association between the overall narrative structure and moral of the story with our concept of hidden layer. Indeed, this holds the constituent elements of the story and represents the hidden elements and the meanings upon which the training game is realised. Therefore, it is fundamental that the hidden layer embeds the psycho-pedagogical elements necessary for a successful transfer of the soft skills to be trained. As we will see later, the hidden layer in EduRPGs is usually based on certain psychological assumptions, similar to those assumed by the traditional role-playing games, often inspired by psychological theories pertaining to the training objectives and by pedagogical concepts. Of all concepts in pedagogy, the most important in this domain is learning through experience, a concept that we have previously encountered and forms the basis of any EduRPG game development. Those assumptions should be embedded in the narrative of the games, therefore in the hidden layer, or they can be modelled within the computer game by means of simulation techniques that permit reproduction of an artificial reality within which the user will be able to play a given role. In any case, the hidden layer is the element of the game that conveys the meaning of the training and the content, for the benefit of the user's learning process.

In the visible layer, the external layer, we find the game narrative proper. EduRPGs, as many other cultural products, are expressed through a narrative metaphor, so it is important to define those visible elements as instrumental for establishing the correct sets of experiences to be implemented for the benefit of the user. In particular, this means defining the plot, scenario, characters, roles and overall setting of the game. This layer is where the training context is defined: who are the characters, what actions they can perform and what kind of interactions is possible between characters. The characters can be the leader and the employees in a company or a group of students in a classroom. They can even be two armies on the chess board. The visible layer, therefore, together with the overall narrative of the game, also contains what in cinematography is called "mise en scène", which literally represents what and how the user will see the characters and the whole scene on the screen. This aspect is particularly important because it is the real front-end of the game and it offers a major contribution to the positive or negative perception of the user, which can in turn affect motivation and willingness to engage with the game.

What is important is that, in cooperation with the hidden layer, the narrative or visible layer can sustain the educational objectives of the game and permit the user to have a first-hand experience of the concepts to be learnt. In practical terms, if the game is about mathematics, the user must be able to experience mathematical problems for the accomplishment of the game.

In the case of soft skills, the realisation of such dynamics presents peculiar challenges. If we look at the ENACT project, for example, a case that will be thoroughly discussed in a different chapter, the central focus of the training and assessment is on negotiation skills and effective communication. It is therefore instrumental that the hidden layer takes into account the modalities in which the user can experience the dialogue with another person under controlled circumstances. In effective communication, besides the actual meaning of the sentences that can be expressed, the way in which they are expressed—the body language, the vocal tone, etc.—is also important. The narrative structure must be designed in such a way that the several components that usually play a role in communication acts can be experienced by the user through interaction with the computer. This poses several interesting problems. However, to produce a reliable EduRPG in such a domain, it is essential that the visible layer presents the user with the correct level of information (i.e. body language, eye contact, sentences) and the hidden layer implements a number of rules and dynamics that makes the user's experience interesting and full of educational content.

3.2.2   Assessment and Tutoring of Learners

The evaluation layer, as we have called it previously, holds all the assessment and tutoring elements of the game. An interesting organisation of such evaluation elements in educational games can be inferred from the combination of assessment methodology taken from entertainment games and traditional role-playing games. In particular, video games use well-known performance assessment techniques that allow for swift and challenging progressions of the player within the games, while psychological role-playing games for soft skills training present a peculiar assessment and tutoring techniques that should be present in EduTechRPGs. Therefore, the evaluation layer in EduTechRPGs is a blend of those two domains which must be carefully integrated and based on specific learning analytics and educational data mining (Bienkowski et al. 2012; Siemens and Baker 2012).

3.2.2.1 Performance Assessment

Even if not expressly designed as educational tools, mainstream video games have strong educational potential and rely, in part, on training mechanisms. This is evident if we consider the first phase in many games, when it is necessary for the player to learn how to play the game.

Gee (2003) observes that good video games are learnt well by the player, so that they are played long and hard by many people. Game designers could have easily solved their learning problems by making games easier, but most gamers do not want short and easy games; they want hard and challenging games in which they can perfect and progress. Game designers are able to get people to learn and master something that is long and challenging, and enjoy it, and evaluate players' learning outcome through pass or fail mechanisms even if the failure is not as important as in real life. When players fail, they can start again from the saved level, so it can be used as a strategy to better understand the game and perfect the gaming style.

Video games continuously assess the player's level, and educational games should use similar techniques (Michael and Chen 2005a, b online cit.). In traditional games, the main assessment techniques are the following:

- *Tutorials.* Tutorials introduce the player to the basic rules for interacting with the game and then test the player on them, proposing specific missions that introduce only a few game features and elements. Once the first tutorial missions have been successfully accomplished, the player can face greater challenges, until she has mastered the basic concepts.
- *Level completion.* This is the first indicator that the player has reached a specified standard performance within the game. Level completion allows us to say not only that player participated in a certain mission but also that she was able to manage it. On the other hand, the cons are that completing a level does not guarantee that the player has acquired the corresponding knowledge. Indeed, she could have just learned how to beat the game, for example, by cheating.
- *Scoring.* The scoring system teaches the player what is important within the game. After any action in the game, the player can observe its effects on the score. A positive effect indicates a good choice, a negative effect a bad choice, and no score indicates that the related action is probably not important. In this sense, scores correspond to grades in the classical educational context.

These techniques can all be included in educational games, but EduRPGs need even more specific and peculiar tools. In educational games, we need to know not only if the learners learned or not some material but also at which level they currently are, which problems they are encountering and which materials are instead managed well, and, more in general, we need to understand the strengths and weaknesses of learners.

The answer to this need come from the traditional exercise of role play in psychological settings, which roughly correspond to the teacher in more classical classroom settings; that is, the figure of the trainer or tutor.

3.2.2.2   The Role of Trainer/Tutor

As we have seen in the previous paragraph, assessing player's performances is not a unique prerogative of educational games, and every game does this to some extent. However, in educational games, the role of the trainer, or tutor, is particularly important, especially for preserving an effective methodological parallel with traditional role-playing games, where trainers play a fundamental role in facilitating the learning process, as in *face-to-face* training settings. Trainers manage the interactions among participants, analyse and interpret group dynamics, shape the learning experience to assist specific needs, provide feedback on areas to be further developed and finally indicate possible directions for personal development.

Indeed, the use of educational software per se does not ensure that learning actually takes place at all. The key to a successful training experience resides in the way the training is designed and helps to facilitate the learning process. This is particularly true for technology-enhanced role-play games, where the figure of the trainer can be somehow forgotten, while it has been argued that learning is particularly facilitated when trainers can participate in the learning process (Rogers 1983). Moreover, without facilitation, guide and support, an experiential learning activity can even lead to "miseducative experiences" (Dewey 1938). Indeed, experiential learning is about creating an experience where learning can be facilitated.

As it has been pointed out in the literature, the role of trainer is crucial through the entire process of role play: definition of the learning scenario-environment, monitoring of role play, its course and dynamics and the assistance offered with feedback and debriefing in order to maximise learning (Dawson 1990; Thatcher 1990; Perry and Euler 1988; Glandon 1978; Shirts 1976). Livingston (1970) highlighted how influential the role of a trainer can be, by describing a study in which significant differences in attitude change among groups of learners who played the same simulation under the guidance of different trainers were found.

The trainer is also present during the learning process, by providing feedback and by analysing the entire performance of the player in the light of the specific learning objectives. Feedback plays a very relevant role in behavioural psychology theory. Skinner (1938, 1953) devoted a great deal of work to reinforcement and punishment understanding and to reinforcement scheduling (Ferster and Skinner 1957), as well as later researchers, who focused on feedback timing on concurrent schedules (Catania 1998) and on methods for adapting schedules based on performance (e.g. matching law; Herrnstein 1961). All these studies aim at maximising attention and motivation in learners. Feedbacks, together with debriefing, are regarded as the most important elements for maximising the learning process (Coppard and Goodman 1979; Kollöffel and de Jong 2015), because they guide trainees through a reflective process about their learning (Thatcher, 1990), provide a space for giving personal meaning to the experience (Petranek et al. 1992) and help to relate the experience to real-life contexts.

The use of feedback and debriefing systems enables exploitation of the full potential of trainers' guiding, facilitation and support. Trainers guide the learning process and may intervene as facilitators at any time during the game and on completion of activities. Trainers can observe and analyse the evolution of the game, learner's actual performances, and monitor improvements, progresses and/or difficulties. They can also send comments and hints to players for soliciting an immediate reflection on the responsibility of the personal role played within the dynamics that have taken place.

The trainer therefore plays a prominent role in the successful experience of role playing, and this can be also be embedded in the game. As we will see, in EduTechRPGs the tutor can be a human being but also a virtual entity, thanks to artificial intelligence and learning analytic techniques. In both cases, the tutor should be able to "observe" the behaviour of learners during the game, similar to what happens in real, *face-to-face* contexts, and based on observations and statistical analysis should be able to create a "learner's profile". To create such a profile, educational games can rely on the huge amount of data available, even more than in real-life tasks, because within the game, it is possible to record every single action of the players, the time required for performing actions and the mistakes made.

Profiling the user is a fundamental achievement within EduRPGs, because it enables implementation of learner-centred strategies for the specific cognitive characteristics and learning style of every single user. It allows also the creation of specific training pathways specifically designed for the personal requirements of different users, in this way creating a profound divide between EduTechRPGs and more traditional and universal educational technologies.

3.3 Analysis and Design Principle of EduTechRPGs

Despite the fact that games appear to have a great potential for educational use, as discussed above, the specific features that make games so successfully engaging for users to play and learn with are not well understood (Linehan, Kirman, et al. 2011). This presents a serious problem for designers of educational games. Combining games design and educational goals in order to create a fun game that also helps people learn appears to be a very difficult task. This is particularly true when addressing the domain of soft skills, especially from a "learning-by-doing approach". In order to address this aspect of the creation of educational games for soft skills, with the specific focus on experiences and practice, the following pages will present the concept introduced above from a practical point of view, and new tools and concepts useful for the analysis and design of EduTechRPGs will be discussed. In particular, we will present two main concepts: (a) some principles that we think are necessary in order to make learning through role-playing games effective, engaging and fun and (b) a categorical structure based on the pedagogical and technological characteristics of EduTechRPGs.

Both elements will play a central role in understanding the type of game to be designed and the general design principles.

3.3.1   Teaching and Learning Should Be Intrinsic to the Game

In order to make the training provided by EduTechRPGs effective, it is essential that game mechanics, that is, the set of rules that define what the player actually can and cannot do when interacting with the game, must be integrated through an intrinsic link to learning contents. For instance, Habgood and Ainsworth (2011) have tested different versions of Zombie Division, a 3D adventure game that teaches mathematics to children through swordplay with skeletal opponents. In the "intrinsic" version, mathematical multiple-choice questions were integrated into the combat system, whereas in the "extrinsic" version, they were put between levels, without any link to the combats. The authors showed that children decide to spend more time playing the intrinsic version because of the perceived link between game mechanics and learning content.

This is an absolutely key point that has been missed in the majority of games designed for education. Indeed, educational software has traditionally used gaming elements as a separate reward for completing learning content, with no relation to the skill or knowledge being learned. Indeed, in the early phase of "edutainment" games, it has been often used a kind of "chocolate-covered broccoli" approach (Bruckman 1999). The idea was to make learning content more fun and attractive by tagging games to it. However, such methods have often proved ineffective (Kerawalla and Crook 2005; Trushell et al. 2001), failing to effectively harness the engagement power of digital games. The reason, as already noted, seems to reside in the extrinsically motivating design models of such systems (Lepper 1985; Parker and Lepper 1992).

On the other hand, teaching and learning are usually intrinsic to gameplay in successful games. When playing an entertainment game, everything the player learns during her play is necessary for the fulfilment of some specific goal within that game, not for some objective outside it. For this reason, the way a game should evaluate whether or not players have learned should be through simply monitoring their play, not with a different modality such as a questionnaire. More in general, teaching, learning and assessment should be carried out solely through the core mechanics of the game.

From a pedagogical perspective, it is worth noting that, although the process of learning can be frustrating, the good performance of a recently acquired skill is incredibly satisfying (Lindsley 1992; Gee 2003). Educational games, like entertaining ones, should provide this opportunity to learners, simply by letting them play.

In summary, when training soft skills by means of EduTechRPGs, we should link the learning outcome with the mechanics of the game we are building. As an example, if our goal is to teach leadership or negotiation, we should create a game that revolves around leadership or negotiation. And everything the player learns is learnt simply by playing, and rewards are given to the player inside the game.

3.3.2   Educational Games Should Follow the Same Game Design Principles as Entertainment Games

Given the success of entertainment games in making people learn and practise for many hours, often dedicated to enhancing skills that have no other scope than making the player satisfied, it is natural to look at those games as successful exemplary implementations. Therefore, the potential of games to work as valuable training tools can only be fulfilled through a deep understanding of how entertainment games motivate engagement and learning. To engender the same motivation observed with entertainment games, and obtain successful learning outcomes, we should design our educational programmes in a gamelike fashion, using the same principles and techniques adopted by commercial games.

The following is a short and an inexhaustive list of features shown by most engaging games:

- Games are complex, logical systems that allow interaction and trial-and-error learning (Randel et al. 1992).
- While playing, players are constantly presented with a series of short-, medium- and long-term goals (Swartout and Van Lent 2003).
- Games let players improve their abilities in an incremental manner, starting from basic skills to more complex ones. Usually, players are not allowed to advance to more difficult levels if they do not show excellent performance on the current one (Loftus and Loftus 1983).
- In order to reach their goals, players are typically required to take some actions or decisions during game play (Prensky 2001; Salen and Zimmerman 2003).
- During their play, players are not afraid to make errors. On the contrary, they usually accept repeated failures until they reach their goal.
- The level of autonomy of the players is high. Throughout the game, they take decisions and make actions in complete autonomy, although sometimes they can ask for help from other players (e.g. in dedicated forums).

Based on these principles, educational games should therefore:

- Clearly define not only the ultimate learning outcome of the programme but also intermediate steps that learners must reach on their way to the final goal. Once players have passed some level in the game, thus demonstrating mastery of some particular skill or knowledge, they should be allowed to advance to subsequent levels which build upon that newly acquired information. For each learning outcome, we should also define an acceptable mastery criterion.
- In every phase of the game, the difficulty level should be high enough to keep learners engaged, but at the same time, it should not surpass their abilities, in order to avoid frustration.
- Provide a personalised learning process according to the player's profile. It is important to first assess the player's level, her needs, learning speed and motivation, in order to create a learning path tailored to individual learners.

Finally, it is worth noting that games do not appear to be the ideal way for teaching everything. Given their structure and principles, they are most useful for teaching content that is organised in a way similar to gameplay. Thus, when deciding whether or not to build an educational game, we should first understand whether the topic is appropriate to be modelled as a game (Randel et al. 1992). If not, a different teaching method may be more appropriate.

3.4 Technological and Psycho-pedagogical Dimensions in EduTechRPG Design

From a general standpoint, it is possible to understand and categorise EduTechRPGs by looking at their technological and psycho-pedagogical characteristics. It is important to note that those views, as well as the categories that will be drawn in this chapter, should not be intended as mutually exclusive but as mutually complementary dimensions. Indeed, it is the careful choice and blend of such dimensions in a single, specific, implementation that will make the resulting product an effective and viable educational tool.

From a technological point of view, it is possible to identify two main dimensions which are distinct and complementary: (a) technologies that allow for a virtual extension of the action space (the scene) of traditional psycho-pedagogic role-playing games to technologically enhanced stages (see Chap. 1 for details) and (b) technologies that permit the production of "artificial" micro-worlds based on computer-simulated, formal models about social and psychological phenomena. We will refer to the former dimension and to the EduTechRPGs that predominantly exploit it, as *ComTech* and to the latter as *SimTech*.

From a psycho-pedagogical and user-centred perspective, that is, from the point of view of the type and characteristics of the soft skills training to be transferred and focusing on the experience that the user will have by playing the game, two more categories can be identified. One category can represent the extent to which, while playing the game, the user has to express herself through behavioural acts that involve her body or other forms of interactions that involve the personal sphere of expressions, such as an actor would do on stage. Those elements correspond to the traditional behavioural domain that plays a prominent role in psychodrama, and we will call the dimension that focuses on such behavioural aspects, and the EduTechRPGs that rely on it, *drama based*. Situations in which the user is asked to perform abstract and strategic forms of decision-making are different from yet complementary to the drama-based dimension. Here, user's logical and reasoning aspects are prominently highlighted, as may happen in simulation games such as SimCity or Civilisation or even in abstract games such as chess. We will call this game domain, and the EduTechRPGs that rely on it, *rule based*.

The four categories identified above are helpful both for the analysis of soft skill-based educational games and for identifying the correct level of design for one game, given the type and level of soft skills training to be transferred.

3.4.1 Modelling of Relevant Psychological and Pedagogical Theories

As described above, teaching and learning should be intrinsic to gameplay for the game to be fun and engaging. Teaching and learning should be carried out solely through the core mechanics of the game. Moreover, as a direct outcome of the previous categorisation, a fundamental element of EduTechRPGs design for soft skills training is that teaching and learning materials must seamlessly embedded within the gameplay in a way that is "invisible" to players. To this end, different technologies and approaches can be applied, and they will vary according to the type of gameplay to be created and the particular skills to be taught. That is, the design must always start form the soft skill to be taught and from the type of experiences that are relevant for training of the given skills. The technologies will then follow. For this reason, the above categorisation can be particularly helpful in moving from the beginning of the design process in the right direction.

In particular, in order to convey the right level of information correctly and to create an effective set of experiences within the educational game, it is fundamental that the target audience of the game and the relevant psychological and pedagogical theories are correctly identified because they will permit understanding of the typology of game to be designed that best embeds the training requirements. Such aspects will be discussed in more detail in following chapters, where specific cases will be presented. In the case of the ENACT game, for example, the theory at the basis of the RPG is the theory proposed by Rahim and Bonoma (1979) about conflict resolution. For the Learn to Lead game, the core theory is represented by the full-range theory of Bass and Avolio (1990) about leadership.

Identification of the relevant theory makes it possible to identify the game components, the interactions among characters and to design the game scenario, so that the basic components of the game, such as the hidden, the visible and the evaluation layers, can be outlined and implemented. At the same time, the psycho-pedagogical background of the game will help to identify the best training setting, according to audience needs. A multiplayer game will have different requirements than a single player, especially in terms of interactions modelling and hidden structure. Similarly, the live presence of a tutor/trainer, online or offline, will dictate different requirements with respect to implementation of an "artificial trainer" within the game.

Modelling interactions in EduTechRPGs is particularly important because soft skills are specifically defined as personal skills that have a great societal impact and are mainly effective in dealing with other people. However, the kind of interactions to be modelled strongly depends on the type of skills that must be trained and the overall educational requirements.

If the starting point is the soft skill that we want to teach and whose training must be transferred in EduRPG games, the type of interactions to be reproduced strongly depends on the number of participants allowed, the technology available and the pedagogy to be applied, that this, the educational focus of the game and the kind of training situations that the user should experience. In this case, a categorical distinction like the one outlined above is particularly helpful.

Role-playing games are fundamentally inspired by theatre metaphor and rely on features directly derived from this world. However, the gaming implementation of such features can vary drastically.

Drama-based games require at least a dyadic interaction in the plot, because in traditional role-playing games the player is assumed to perform a role in interaction with at least another role. Given that EduTechRPGs are expressed through a narrative metaphor, it is therefore important to define the characters, the scenario and all that lies in the visible layer. In this case, defining the plot also means designing the game core, because there is no clear boundary between the two layers. In fact, the game coincides with the kind of interactions among players, which are defined by the plot and the scenario. Inside the plot and in the corresponding hidden layer, every role is defined in relation to the simulated sensory features within the game, i.e. what the player can see, hear, smell or touch, and the actions she can perform must be all defined a priori, in order to provide the user with a rich environment which is functional to the educational purposes of the game.

The interactions within the game plot can be defined as competitive, synergistic, hierarchical, etc. In addition, we should also contemplate the possibility that, in digital EduRPGs, interactions can occur among human players, as in the case of Eutopia and DREAD-ED, or with one or more artificial agents serving as other players, as in ENACT. We thus have single-player or multiplayer EduRPGs, depending on the number of human players involved in the games. In the former case, in which humans interact with one another as if they were in the same classroom, Internet and various communication technologies will help to extend the stage to virtual environments (ComTech games). What must be defined here is what techniques can be employed to widen the classical EduRPG setting. In a digital EduRPG, one can choose to exploit 2D or 3D representation, action in first or third person, or even adopting novel interfaces such as holograms or virtual reality techniques. Such a choice will only affect what the game looks like but not the plot based on the narrative. In the latter case, additional technologies are needed to implement and model the artificial players that interact with the user, the human player, who is the target of the educational process. This is the domain of what we have called SimTech games.

Similarly, the live presence of a tutor, as in Eutopia, implies very different technological and pedagogical requirements than a game like Learn to Lead, in which the tutor is implemented as an artificial agent, requiring a totally different structure and implementation of the evaluation layer. In fact, in the case of Eutopia, the evaluation layer provides the tutor with useful statistics extracted by the gameplay of the user.

The tutor is even able to openly define the plot and the scenario and can also directly interact with the player during the game sessions and in ad hoc debriefing sessions (see Chap. 4). On the other hand, in Learn to Lead, the evaluation layer must be implemented in such a way that the statistics can be automatically analysed by some kind of expert system, as in artificial tutoring systems. The role played by the theory in this type of games is much more important, because the tutor must be implemented as an artificial agent interacting with the user at a game metalevel. That is, an autonomous system capable of analysing the game dynamics in lights of a psycho-pedagogical theory and providing feedback to the user according to her performance within the game must be implemented at the evaluation layer of the game.

Unlike Eutopia, Learn to Lead, for example, and ENACT are games that we can also define as SimTech EduTechRPGs, in the sense that beyond the technologies needed to connect the players within the game, a SimTech game tries to create virtual characters around the player, so that the player can interact with those characters rather than with other real players.

SimTech EduTechRPGs share both the narrative and the theatrical dimension with other traditional and technology-enhanced role-playing games. However, their specific feature, that is, the definition of what we have called hidden layer, makes them learning environments with peculiar functionalities, opportunities and limits. In particular, in order to create a dynamics within the game in which the player can experience realistic interactions, some fundamental modern technological approaches becomes fundamental, at least in our own experience: computer simulations, agent-based modelling and artificial intelligence.

3.4.1.1 Agent-Based Modelling in EduRPG

SimTech games, in particular, use computer modelling to create an *artificial reality* around the players that tries to reproduce the main dynamics of a specific social or psychological phenomenon, whose principles must be acquired and experienced by the user. In order to create such an artificial reality within the game, a computational approach using agent-based modelling (ABM) is often helpful.

ABM (Helbing 2012; Bonabeau 2002) is a class of computational models used to simulate phenomena belonging to various domains ranging from biology to psychology and sociology, starting from the action and interaction of simple agents. These agents are autonomous and can represent individual or collective entities such as groups.

In this book, we adopt a wide definition of ABM: in EduRPG, ABM is not used to understand collective behaviour starting from simple rules but aims to represent in detail agents' interactions and the agents themselves, in this multiagents systems approach (Van Der Hoek and Wooldridge 2008; Ferber 1999) where agents can be very complex, such as advanced cognitive agents often requiring a huge modelling commitment and a big computational burden.

Conceiving and designing an EduRPG according to the SimTech approach is much more similar to videogames design and realisation than to classical psycho-pedagogic role-playing games, and it is therefore conceptually appropriate to distinguish this kind of games from the ones produced under the ComTech frame.

ABM methodology is particularly important in this domain because all the interacting entities within the game can be conceptualised as agents, which are immersed in an environment and, by means of their interactions, can modify the state of the game. Both the players, real or artificial, and the professional figures that support the role-playing game, such psychologists, teachers or trainers, can be usefully conceptualised as agents. Within the game dynamics, they become special agents, or meta-agents, with the ability to observe the users' performance and to carry out a variety of functions, such as tutoring, advising or mentoring.

3.4.1.2   On-Stage and Backstage Agents

In this respect, it is possible to conceptualise different kinds of agents within the game. We define the agents interacting in the environment, or the game space, as on-stage agents (OSA), whereas the observer agents, that is to say the agents that can support play although not intervening directly, are defined as backstage agents (BSA), where each agent has its own sensory and behavioural apparatus, within an environment that has specific features in terms of dimensions, interaction possibilities among agents and other agents or objects, and game rules specifying legal and illegal game states.

An EduTechRPGs developed according to the agent-based modelling approach can therefore be described as a mise en scène of a plot by one or more agents interacting in a well- and formally defined game space: Actions performed by OSAs can directly modify the game state; BSAs support OSAs, but they cannot act in the game space and, therefore, cannot modify its state. In this way, we can identify a sharp separation between the visible layer and the hidden one, that is, the inner game mechanics. The visible dimension can be conceived trough traditional narrative techniques. The hidden layer can be expressed in terms of ABM and implies formal definition of the following components:

(a) Game space characteristics
(b) Sensory and behavioural components of agents, both OSA and BSA
(c) Rules presiding over OSA functions and interactions with other OSAs
(d) Rules presiding over OSA functions and interactions with the game space
(e) BSA functions and interactions with the player

Formal rules for controlling agents can be deterministic or probabilistic: in the former case, nothing in the game happens by chance, and there will be a well-defined outcome for every action. In the latter case, there will be a certain amount of stochasticity within the game, and actions will produce outcomes with a certain probability.

Adopting the ABM approach to develop SimTech EduRPGs opens the way to adopting automatic control systems and software based on artificial intelligence systems to model OSA and BSA behaviour. By this means, it is possible to delegate both on-stage and backstage functionalities to intelligent and autonomous artificial

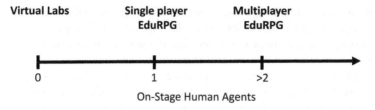

Fig. 3.2 According to how many human stages are on stage, we have virtual labs, a single-player EduRPG or a multiplayer EduRPG

agents, making it possible to run EduTechRPGs with mixed teams composed of human and artificial agents. In the case of artificial BSAs, artificial agents resemble collaborative or antagonist nonplayer characters in videogames.

By considering artificial OSAs operating in the same environment with humans, we can propose an additional taxonomy for SimTech games illustrated in Fig. 3.2 that distinguishes EduRPGs according to how many human agents are on stage.

The case in which no human agents are present on stage is called *virtual lab*. In a virtual lab, the learning environment becomes a place where it is possible to manipulate variables and observe what effects will be produced. It is not a role-playing game but an agent-based simulation that equally holds an educational potential (Sitzmann 2011), as will be discussed in the next paragraph.

When only one human player is on stage, we have a single-player EduRPG. In this case, the user interacts with artificial OSAs while involved in the micro-world and facing an individual character in a dialogic interaction (e.g. ENACT) or presiding a group of artificial agents (Learn to Lead).

When two or more players are on stage, we have multiplayer EduRPGs where players, in addition to what can be performed in single-player EduRPGs, can also interact with other on-stage human agents. In this characterisation, the extreme case in which there are only human players interacting in the virtual space is what we have defined as a ComTech game.

3.4.1.3 Computer Simulations, EduTechRPGs and Virtual Labs

SimTech EduRPGs exploit the specific kind of ABM methodology to quantitatively define the hidden content in terms of computational rules and/or mathematical functions. ABM methodology is widely used in social and psychological scientific research to translate what in human sciences is exposed verbally into quantitative and operational models. These verbally expressed theories are then simulated with computers. Therefore, theories can become computer programs.

Thanks to this method, neural, cognitive and social processes that occur in humans when interacting with the environment and with each other can be expressed in terms that are completely similar to the ones used in hard sciences (physics, chemistry, etc.). Therefore, in computer models in general and in ABM models in particular, a specific psychological or social phenomenon is expressed using two components: the verbal theory and the quantitative, operational model. The scientist developing a computer simulation model describes the study topic in narrative and verbal terms, then translates the underlying dynamics into quantitative terms and develops a computer simulation, and then finally manipulates the model to define the computational system that best reproduces the observations. In other words, the modeller exploits the possibility to simulate an artificial micro-world (Brehmer and Dörner 1993; Rieber 2005; Plass and Schwartz 2014) for micro-worlds in education in order to understand, study and explain some observations in the macro-worlds, the real world in which we are immersed.

In expressing psychological and pedagogical theories, as said above, a simulation-based model is an effective way to express a scientific theory (Shiflet and Shiflet 2014; Ostrom 1988). A simulation is a theory about mechanisms, processes and factors underlying a certain phenomenon that is translated into a computer program (Di Ferdinando 2002). In Parisi's (2001) words: "…to understand reality it is advisable to reproduce it" and, with the present technology, it is possible to reproduce reality with computers. Using simulations, reality can be reproduced, and given that the mechanisms governing reality are not known, reproducing realities means reproducing the reality as we think it is: that is, a theory about reality. Basically, a computer simulation, in this sense, is a model of reality that also embeds what is underlined behind the phenomena, their causes and mechanisms. After this translation process, using a computer monitor or other device, even a physical device such a robot, it is possible to observe and compare it with observations from the real world.

Simulations are therefore not simply models. They are rather models holding causes, and this makes them an extraordinary new way to express scientific theories (Casti 1997; Heermann 1990; Nahodil et al. 2003). With simulations, theory is the computer program underneath the simulation, and empirical phenomena are the program outcomes that the computer program generates. Theory and phenomena are then strictly linked, whereas in traditional science, they are completely separated: theory is in the scientist's mind, phenomena are in the real world. This powerful method can be applied to a huge amount of phenomena, ranging from oceans to society, from atomic movements to seasonal trends, and from the behaviour of simple organisms to human cognition and can be adopted from all disciplines in both natural and human sciences.

SimTech EduRPG yearns for transferring this particular learning strategy beyond research labs to formal and informal educational contexts, becoming a tool that can reach many people in many different contexts. Such operationalisation of the theory in the game design is also an interesting scientific exercise, other than a practical requirement, because it permits testing the psychological theory from a different perspective. Observing a simulation in the computer is like observing the phenomenon reproduced in a virtual laboratory. Computer simulations can therefore be seen as virtual labs in which phenomena can be reproduced, observed and studied. This perspective has a huge educational potential (Rieber 1996; Plass and Schwartz 2014), because it allows experimentation and direct observation of the creation and dynamics of a phenomenon starting from its basic principles.

In the context of social science and by looking at the relationships among computer simulations, education and EduRPGs, an interesting example of computer simulation as a virtual lab in social science is the TeamSim software (Miglino et al. 2008).

TeamSim is an educational micro-world that revolves around the exploration and understanding of team dynamics. With TeamSim, the user can interact with a group of agents in a 2D environment and can manipulate a number of variables, such as the structure of hierarchical relationships within the team, the structure of the communications network, and other environmental and group-dynamics parameters. In TeamSim, formally defined rules governing interactions between agents determine the efficiency of the team. The mechanisms on which the model is based are completely defined in the simulation code.

From an educational viewpoint, the simplicity of the model helps learners to grasp the underlying theoretical assumptions of group organisation. By interacting with the micro-world, the learner can design experiments (simulations), exploring and having first-hand experiences of notions in the dynamics of small groups.

It is interesting to note the difference between the user's experiences when interacting with virtual labs, such as TeamSim, compared with the experiences gained when involved in a SimTech EduRPG. In the former case, the user observes and manipulates from outside what happens in a micro-world, exactly as an experimenter would do in a lab experiment. In the latter case, the user is an agent who acts in the micro-world and operates and determines dynamics and evolution from inside the micro-world. The user is effectively immersed in the simulation. This concept of agency applied to the user involved in the gameplay of EduTechRPGs is the feature which is particularly relevant in applying EduRPGs to teach soft skills, as we will show in the following chapters.

It is worth noting that, from an implementation point of view, conceiving and designing a SimTech EduRPG requires two specific professional profiles which, in some cases, can be possessed by the same person and in others by different persons: the ability to develop a narrative for the game that consistently embeds the psycho-pedagogical theory on which the EduRPG is based and the expertise to transfer the narrative to a scientific agent-based simulation model in which the user's interactions must be consistently modelled and implemented according to the training to be delivered.

3.4.2 Assessment Design and Techniques

Together with the design and implementation of the core gameplay, which mainly focus on the visible and external layer of our scheme in Fig. 3.1, another compelling element in EduTechRPGs, as we have seen, is the design and implementation of the evaluation layer, because every educational game must assess the performances of the user. In this respect, a relevant role is played by the backstage agent (BSA), as we have called it, together with its functionalities and interactive modalities. Up to now, we have neglected BSAs, but their role is crucial in the educational process, as we will discuss in the next paragraph.

3.4.2.1   Feedback, Debriefing and Backstage Agents

Backstage agents have the role of supporting the learners involved in EduRPGs, not by intervening directly in the dramatic action but by providing what is required to enhance the learning process. In EduRPGs, these agents can cover specific roles, explicitly foreseen and functional to the target educational goals. This is the case of trainers, tutors, supervisors, facilitators, guides and all those figures responsible for assessment who implement and benefit from learning analytics. Indeed, a core element provided by BSA, as we have seen before, is feedback from real or artificial tutors.

Giving feedback is fundamental in every educational enterprise to allow learners to understand how close they are to their goals, and this is also true for teaching with games that aim at driving the learners toward excellent performances (see discussion above for details).

In our experience, we found that feedback should be given both during the game and through debriefing. An important feature of digital games that is remarkably aligned to good learning is that games provide short feedback cycles. This allows players to explore the game environment freely, trying out their hypotheses, learning by trial and error and getting immediate information that they can use to redefine wrong assumptions in a risk-free environment. This characteristic is well aligned with educational requirements, given that most educational approaches require the educator to provide students with feedback about their achievements. Nevertheless, in traditional educational approaches, where the instructor usually has to mark students' work using conventional means (i.e. manually), there is a significant delay until students can receive the appropriate feedback: computer games can help to reduce such delays almost to zero.

Therefore, as computer games set players in a world that they are free to explore without requiring the intervention of an instructor, they are an ideal medium to promote authentic learning and "learning-by-doing" processes, turning students into leaders of their own learning experience. In this sense, computer games can provide meaningful learning experiences by simulating highly interactive scenarios that professionals encounter in real-world settings, where they face open-ended, real-world problems.

As an example of such a feedback element, a player in Fig. 3.3 is receiving immediate feedback in an ENACT game session. In this case, the feedback is provided by the on-stage agent. The BOT which the user interacts with displays an angry facial expression and body posture (non-verbal communication) and gives a verbal feedback through the text.

Feedback should be provided through the entire game experience of the player. Moreover, a very important moment for delivering feedback is at the end of the crucial game phase, or at the end of the game, during the *debriefing* phase, when the player receives feedback about the overall performance.

Debriefing often provides a safe place to recognise and release emotions built up during the game. During the game, different kinds of emotions are commonly raised, but they cannot always be conveyed properly within the game. In this case, it appears fundamental to consider the right time and space to deal with them in

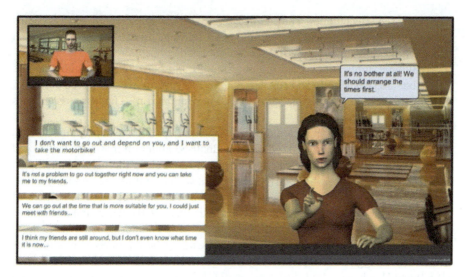

Fig. 3.3   Immediate feedback in the ENACT game

order to reach a better understanding of what happened emotionally. On the cognitive side, debriefing offers the opportunity of recognising mistakes as part of the learning process (Henneman and Cunningham, 2005). Even if the game provides online feedback during play, it is possible that the player understands that she has been wrong but cannot understand why or what action would have been appropriate in a certain situation. In this condition, debriefing allows the user to learn from her own mistakes.

Debriefing is also an activity that can benefit group work, either online or offline. Analysing what happened during the game, comparing their own performances and sharing the experiences with other people make it possible to compare different perspectives from other players or from other people involved in the learning process such as tutors. This shared task encourages collaboration and communication among all these people.

The last fundamental goal that debriefing helps to achieve is that of linking game events to the real world. That is, the debriefing phase should help the player to translate what happened during the game to everyday life situations and personal experiences.

In traditional EduRPGs, debriefing is usually provided by the trainer. The same can happen in ComTech games like Eutopia, where the players' actions are watched and analysed by a human tutor. Such a figure is what we have called a backstage agent. It can observe the game and interact with the player outside the game dynamics, but it cannot directly modify the game space. In SimTech games, the BSA is often, but not necessarily, demanded to a virtual agent. When a virtual tutor is used, artificial intelligence techniques can help to create a learner profile and ad hoc, personalised feedback, tuned with the specific performance of the player.

Artificial Intelligence in Education (AIED) is an interdisciplinary field that aims to produce educationally useful computer artefacts by incorporating artificial intelligence (AI) techniques. The premise of AIED is that implementing such systems involves the modelling and representation of relevant aspects of knowledge and hence requires the application of AI techniques and concepts.

Traditional applications used in education are not personalised to the learner's needs, but are rather static and rule based (e.g. if Question X is answered correctly, proceed to question Y, otherwise go to question Z, and so on). The learner's abilities are not taken into account.

While these kinds of applications may be somewhat effective in helping learners, they do not provide the same kind of individualised attention that a student would receive from a human tutor. This has prompted research in the field of intelligent tutoring systems (ITSs) which, in the framework we have outlined previously in this chapter, can either support BSAs or become BSAs themselves. The origins of intelligent tutor systems can be traced back to the late 1970s, when first attempts to create "intelligent" educational software called CAI (computer-assisted instruction) were based on a behaviourist perspective on learning based on Skinner's theories (Dede and Swigger 1988) whose limits were underlined by Sleeman and Brown (1982) and Hawkes et al. (1986). Carbonell (1970) suggested that computers could act as teachers rather than just tools. Carbonell's introduction of AI techniques into CAI marked the beginning of the era of ITSs.

ITSs are the results of collaborative work from different perspectives, such as cognitive psychology, computer science, and especially artificial intelligence (Larkin and Chabay 1992; Paviotti et al. 2012; Olsen et al. 2014). ITSs have some specific features that distinguish them from CAI programs, namely, ITSs are limited to a specific domain; they have a dynamic model of student performance used to guide education; they provide detailed diagnostics of errors rather than simply drill and practice; and they allow interaction with students.

In recent years, with the rapid expansion of Internet, new computer-aided instruction paradigms, such as e-learning and distributed learning, have provided an excellent platform for ITS ideas. Intelligent tutoring systems can now be found in online environments or in traditional classroom computer labs and are used in primary schools as well as in universities. ITS systems cover a wide range of domains, such as mathematics, health sciences, language acquisition and other areas of formalised learning.

ITSs may employ a range of different technologies and may vary greatly in design, implementation and educational focus. However, ITSs are usually based on four components (Nwana 1990; Freedman 2000; Nkambou et al. 2010): domain model, student model, pedagogical model and user interface components.

The *domain model* contains information the tutor is teaching and is the most important because without it, there would be nothing to teach the student. It contains the concepts, rules, and problem-solving strategies of the domain to be learned.

The *student model* can be thought of as an overlay on the domain model. It is considered as the core component of an ITS, paying special attention to the student's cognitive and affective states and their evolution as the learning process advances. As the student is involved in the learning process, the system engages in a process called model tracing, reporting any situation in which the student model deviates from the domain model.

The *pedagogical model* provides a model of the teaching process. It receives input from the domain and student models and makes choices about pedagogical strategies and actions: for example, information about when to review, when to present a new topic, and which topic to present. In addition, the system tracks the learner's progress from problem to problem in order to build a profile of the learner's strengths and weaknesses.

The *user interface component* contains the interactions with the learner, including dialogues and screen layouts. It manages how this information is presented to the learners in the most effective way.

ITS strategies can therefore be of great help in designing and implementing systems capable of following the learner during gameplay and creating a personalised and learner-centred environment in which focused experiences revolve around the real, measurable needs of the user. Also from the implementation point of view, a number of universities and EU projects (e.g. i-Tutor) are now focused on ITS applications and design and an open framework for the technical implementation of ITSs is freely available as an open-source project (GnuTutor).

3.5 Conclusions

In this chapter, we have introduced and described the pathway to be followed to conceive and design an EduTechRPG.

In the following part of the book, we will describe some examples of EduTechRPGs according to the proposed features we have introduced at both the technological and psycho-pedagogical levels. These examples derive from different experiences related to numerous projects we have been involved with in recent years. In the following chapters, the reader will find much information related to the EduTechRPGs design process, implementation and field experience connected to user experience with the specific games. In particular, we will present various games and related experiences according to the features we have introduced, namely, SimTech vs. ComTech and drama based vs. rule based.

The projects we are going to describe are in a different lifecycle. Some of them, for example, Eutopia, are quite old and have been proposed over the years in various contexts, generating various experiences and related outcomes; some others, such as DREAD-ED and Learn to Lead, have come to a conclusion and are currently used in vocational and training courses and for counselling about leadership; some others, like ENACT, are still ongoing.

For this reason, the reader will find varied descriptions about the platforms, related applications and collected data, but all of them will offer interesting hints and suggestions for designing and implementing her own EduTechRPG: while describing a specific project, each chapter will highlight different aspects that can be taken into account in this challenging process.

Chapter 4
Eutopia: Transferring Psycho-pedagogical Role Play to the Multiplayer Digital Stage

In this chapter, we will describe an EduTech-RPG platform called Eutopia, used to teach and develop a various range of soft skills by implementing ad hoc educational role-playing games. Results and experiences from a number of European projects that have applied the Eutopia platform will be presented and discussed, along with strengths and limitations of the tool.

According to the taxonomy presented in Chap. 3, Eutopia can be defined as a *Drama-Communication Technology-based Educational Role-Play Game* that embeds role-play methodology as a psycho-pedagogical approach and takes inspiration from technology used in multiplayer games. The learning approach is based on open dynamics; therefore, there is no unique way to achieve the desired learning objectives. The technological dimension enhances the potential of the training experience because it makes a virtual extension of traditional face-to-face role-playing activity possible, transposing it into a digital setting.

4.1 Multiplayer RPG Games

As previously discussed in Chap. 2, the role-play methodology has been adapted and applied to various domains and training settings for intensifying and accelerating learning and for developing new ways of understanding of concepts and knowledge. Moreover, role-play games can be considered as learning strategies that can be enhanced through technology, by extending learning through added dimensions that may be impossible to conduct in face-to-face situations (Garrison and Anderson 2003). Among them, the so-called massive multiplayer online role-playing games (MMORPGs) and multi-user virtual environments (MUVEs) such as Second Life (http://secondlife.com/education/) and Active Worlds (http://www.activeworlds.com/edu/).

© Springer International Publishing Switzerland 2017   63
E. Dell'Aquila et al., *Educational Games for Soft-Skills Training
in Digital Environments*, Advances in Game-Based Learning,
DOI 10.1007/978-3-319-06311-9_4

MMORPGs originate from role-playing video games, which in turn have origins in pen-and-paper role-playing games (such as Dungeons and Dragons) and use much of the same terminology, settings and game mechanics. Thanks to the explosion of Internet and the increasing power of modern computers and graphics cards, role-playing video games have evolved from simple text-based games into visually rich 3D experiences.

It is worth noting here the difference between role-playing methodology, which derives from psychodrama and sociodrama (Moreno 1934) with learning purposes, and role-playing videogames, which are created for recreational purposes and take inspiration from pen-and-paper role-playing games.

In both MMORPGs and MUVEs, a group of remote users interacts simultaneously through Internet by controlling a digital actor (an avatar), as it explores a wide and hugely varied artificial universe, rendered in 3D graphics. Via their avatars, players take on specific roles that represent their digital alter egos in their interactions with other players. Players communicate using the possibilities provided by the avatars. For instance, avatars can adopt a posture, make gestures or show specific facial expressions. They can also communicate via text or speech. In this way, the remote user becomes a kind of "virtual" puppeteer.

It has been suggested that players are less inhibited when playing electronic role-playing games than they would be in real life (Fleming Seay and Kraut 2007). Divested of their social, psychological and corporeal identity, players find it easier to identify themselves in other lives (other roles). The effects can be both negative and positive. Excessive use can create disassociation and dependency, while occasional, well-balanced use can stimulate players' skills, allowing them to freely explore multiple scenarios (Miglino et al. 2007).

In Chap. 3, we underlined the importance of games in improving user engagement and motivation. Virtual environments are good examples for creating effective, immersive and engaging learning experiences, using high-quality 3D game techniques and technologies.

As for immersion, we should differentiate between spatial immersion and psychological immersion. Spatial immersion occurs when the user feels that the simulated world is perceptually convincing, meaning that the simulated world looks and feels real. On the other hand, psychological immersion occurs when the user confuses virtual and real life, loses critical distance from the game and becomes emotionally fully involved (Bjork and Holopainen 2006). Of course, spatial immersion is often a prerequisite for psychological immersion, which explains the importance of 3D graphics in role-play games.

Although immersion is one of the most difficult patterns to instantiate in game design, common ways of achieving it have been proposed in game literature, such as using narrative structures, well-defined characters, good-looking graphics, the presence of goals to overcome and freedom of choice and allowing smooth learning curves. The focus of players can instead move away if the challenges are too easy or too hard, thereby making the game boring or frustrating, or if some technical problem occurs or a process takes too much time to complete, such as loading or saving game progress.

By applying the role-play methodology to MMORPGs and MUVEs, we aim to exploit the features of such virtual worlds for learning purposes, allowing the players to participate in virtual role play. Given that such worlds are already structured in a role-play setting, the adoption of role-play methodology appears well suited for transferring the psychodrama from the real world to the 3D digital world.

This chapter describes one such attempt.

4.2   The Eutopia Platform: Communication-Technology Dimension

Eutopia is an online platform which permits the development and deployment of educational role-playing games.

As already said, Eutopia is inspired by MMORPGs and MUVEs. However, in addition to the functions normally presented in such environments, Eutopia also provides additional features specifically designed to facilitate its use in distance learning. In particular, it has been used to develop a variety of role-playing games for the development of different soft skills.

In summary, the platform is based on a client/server architecture, which comprises three different software pieces for users:

- Editor—for trainers, allowing the design of personalised storyboards and role-play learning scenarios
- Client—for both trainees and trainers, allowing them to interact with the 3D environments and with each other through text chat messages and non-verbal modalities
- Viewer—for visualising recorded group interactions and sessions along with text-based exchanges.

In the following paragraph, we will describe the specific features of Eutopia for both learners and trainers.

4.2.1   Trainers

Eutopia provides a complete set of tools for trainers that enable them to wear different hats, designing and assessing the learning process around the identified learning objectives.

Eutopia allows trainers to write the scripts for online multiplayer games. The design of a multiplayer game requires accurate definition of learning goals, story and roles and of the physical and psychological features of avatars.

While the game is in progress, they act as a guide for using the learning platform features at their best, in order to explore the learning potential of available tools. They can observe what is happening among players and intervene at any time by writing messages to them or by activating special "events".

Finally, when the game is concluded, they can provide players with personalised feedback, encourage group discussion and analyse the strategies and behavioural styles adopted by players.

As specified in Chap. 3, we can refer to trainers as back-stage agents (BSAs), that is, observer agents, able to support and facilitate play without intervening directly in the game environment.

4.2.1.1   Editing Scripts

In an online training session, learners are less free to interact than they would be in a traditional chat session, because they have to follow a script, written by the trainer. In scripting the role play, the trainer designs prearranged roles in order to arouse and focus on specific dynamics. Players are given a set of precise instructions to follow with regard to the role they need to portray and the way their character needs to behave. This helps them to "learn about other characters", exploring emotions, concepts and thoughts about a role. That is especially true for the roles with which players do not feel strongly identified.

In order to script the role play, trainers use the Eutopia game editor (Fig. 4.1). This provides an authoring system that allows non-technical people such as trainers

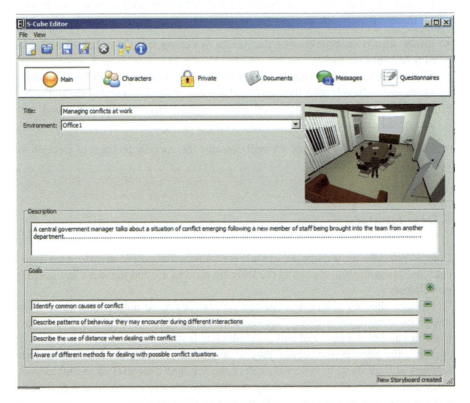

Fig. 4.1 Main screen of the editor during scripting. Trainers use the editor to define general aspects of the session, the characters involved, special events such as new documents and messages and questionnaires to be administered

to create learning simulation scenarios in a complex environment. In this way, Eutopia addresses one of the difficulties typically related to the use of computational simulations by non-technical users (Gaffney et al. 2009).

Scripts allow trainers to define various aspects of the session, such as:

- General aspects, including title, graphical environment in which the role-play game will take place, description of the story and its general goals which are shared by all characters.
- Characters involved, their names, their graphical avatars, their specific descriptions and individual goals. Such features are visible to all users.
- Private features of characters, such as hidden goals that are not publicly visible to other users. Moreover, it is possible to design a personality for each character by setting a number of "constraints" (i.e. behaviour and facial expressions that are not allowed). This is a key feature in helping players identify with their roles.
- Special events that can be activated by the tutor during the session, such as documents and special avatars that will appear in the scene to deliver a certain message.
- Surveys that can be administered, by supplying online questionnaires to players who have to fill them in before continuing playing. Trainers can thus have accurate and fast feedback about important aspects of the role play.

4.2.1.2   Starting a Session

Once a script has been created, it can be used to start role-playing sessions. The session can be launched by the same trainer that created the script or by another person. So, in principle, designers and online tutors can be represented by two different categories of professionals.

When starting a session, trainers can also decide the time available for its completion and can even spread a script over different sessions. That is, the same script can be used for different sessions, in each of which the trainer can add a specific sub-goal.

According to the script created, the trainer decides to associate to each participant the role of one of the characters, represented by a specific avatar. As soon as the session is started and learners log on, they take on the role of the character assigned by the trainer. It is only when a learner enters the session that she comes to know the story in which the personal avatar is involved, the common goals to be achieved, the specific goal assigned to her character and the other information included in the script.

When all players have logged in, play can start, guided by the tutor.

4.2.1.3   Participation in a Session

After scripting and starting the role-playing session, there are two ways in which trainers can intervene during interaction among learners. The first is by taking the role of a character in the role play. The second is to act as an invisible stage director.

Fig. 4.2 A screenshot of the tutor version of Eutopia Client: the trainer activates an event message included in the script

The first way moves the trainer from a perspective of back-stage agent to one of on-stage agent. In other words, she enters the session and plays the game like other players, taking one of the roles defined in the script.

On the other hand, the second way allows her to behave as a back-stage agent, providing a set of useful controls/features: observe interactions among players; access the private characteristics of players; listen to private messages ("whispers") among players; "broadcast" messages visible to all players; exchange private messages with a specific user; activate events, thus changing the course of the simulation; and so on. To access these features, trainers can use the *Tutor* version of *Eutopia Client* (see Fig. 4.2).

During the session, the trainer can introduce new elements in order to influence interactions among players, such as elements of difficulties that players need to overcome. All these additional events are in any case part of the game script, but it is the trainer who is responsible for activating them, when she judges the most appropriate moment. An event could be either a document which appears on the screen (e.g. letter, fax or email) or be represented by a new avatar who enters the scene and delivers a message, via text and with non- and para-verbal elements.

Trainers also have the possibility to bookmark relevant situations and dynamics that occur during the session. This provides the opportunity for rewinding the game session to that bookmark when needed. As an example, a trainer can create a "crossroad" situation: she can bookmark a starting point, let players interact and observe the results, eventually have a brief debriefing phase, then go back to the starting point and let players interact again but with a different perspective. Indeed, in this second case, players are aware of what happened previously and of tutor feedbacks.

Moreover, trainers can ask players to complete questionnaires about their learning process as a contribution to data collection and analysis of session outcomes. In fact, Eutopia also includes an *evaluation protocol* comprising of a set of questionnaires that can be used to assess the level of learners' skills before, during and after training has been taken.

4.2.1.4   Debriefing Tools

Eutopia allows trainers to record game sessions, which can be reviewed using the *Viewer* feature of the Eutopia Client. The recordings take the form of 3D interactive videos, in which it is possible to see the same scene from different points of view, shifting the virtual camera to the preferred position and thus "navigating" through the recording. It is also possible to insert notes and comments, change the playback speed, split the recording into chapters and modify it in various ways (e.g. cutting out irrelevant parts). Through these facilities, trainers can create a commented version of the recording to be used during debriefing.

During debriefing, it is very important that trainers assess whether group and individual goals have been achieved and to what extent. Trainers can examine the most significant aspects and dynamics of the role-play session and the way in which the participants have conducted themselves within the session. The trainer can then communicate to participants whether, and to what extent, they have achieved their individual and group goals. Feedback can be provided immediately after role play or in a later feedback session.

4.2.2   Learners

Learners who play out the scenarios reach the virtual stage set where they can interact with each other through controlling virtual alter egos, the avatars. These are also referred as on-stage agents (OSAs), which are the agents directly acting and interacting in the virtual environment.

Players cannot decide which avatar to use because it is the trainer that associates each user with a different character and a corresponding avatar, endowed with specific physical and emotional features.

Before and during the role-play session, learners can be asked to fill in a questionnaire or a set of questionnaires provided by the trainer, as part of the *evaluation protocol*. At the end of each session, learners can review the session and participate in a debriefing session with the trainer.

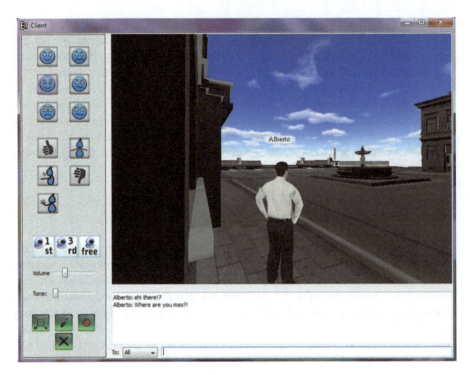

Fig. 4.3 Avatar control as a way to explore an online session

4.2.2.1   Participation in a Session

In order to access the system, learners participating in the online role-playing games use the *Learner* version of the *Eutopia Client* software. Once logged in, learners join a 3D graphical environment in which they are represented by avatars (Fig. 4.3). Learners can use their avatars to explore the environment and to communicate with other players. They can choose between playing in first person and third-person mode. The first person mode uses the player's perspective, with the scenario seen through her eyes. The third-person mode consists of a viewpoint from outside the player, with the scenario seen through someone else's eyes.

Players communicate via short text messages, which appear in bubble cartoons over their avatars' heads. They can also interact by using various forms of para- and non-verbal communication (expressed by emoticons and facial expressions that can be assumed by avatars). For example, players can decide loudness (shown by the font size of the text in the bubble) and emotional tone (shown by the shape and colour of the bubble) of a message. Players can control the gestures and body movements of avatars; for example, by making the avatar wave goodbye, point at someone or hug someone. They can "whisper" messages to each other, that is, send messages are that are visible only to players directly involved in the conversation and to the trainer. Finally, they can communicate with the trainer and raise any question to receive guidance or clarification.

4.2.2.2   Debriefing Tools

We have already seen how trainers can record and play back sessions using the Viewer feature of Eutopia Client. Players can also record the sessions in which they participate. The Viewer allows players to evaluate and review the way they acted and interacted from different viewpoints, providing useful insights for subsequent debriefing sessions.

Where useful, the trainer can provide them with a complete version of the recording, including information that was not accessible to them in the original session. For example, in the recording provided by the tutor, learners also have access to whispers among other players, which were not visible during the session; or learners can now know the hidden goals of other players.

As we have seen, trainers also have various ways of editing and commenting on the recordings, which allows them to provide useful feedback to learners. Trainers can also propose a special debriefing session with learners, in order to discuss a played session in greater depth.

4.3   Methodological Aspects

The methodology behind Eutopia platform is inspired by the methodology previously described in Chap. 3 and by the psycho-pedagogical principles of the role-play technique discussed in Chap. 2.

The technological dimension enhances the potential of the training experience, because it enables a virtual extension of traditional face-to-face role-playing activities, which are transposed to a digital setting.

4.3.1   Gaming Experience

In order to make the learning process more effective, the challenge of using Eutopia is to design role-play scenarios that are engaging, interesting and immersive for learners. These elements enable participants to experience an effective learning process through the enjoyment of playing and within a fun environment.

This increase in engagement can be addressed through the addition of game elements to the design of learning scenarios, such as an interesting plot/story, an appealing environment/virtual world, a contextualisation (space and time of the game), challenging goals for the player to overcome and a type of strategies for success (teamwork and cooperation).

Each Eutopia scenario presents clear goals and objectives that the player needs to accomplish in order to complete the game. Goals and objectives are specified in the storyboard and are distinguished between public (accessible to all) and private (accessible only to the player). The storyboard could also include intermediate/short-term goals in order to help the player reach the final objective.

The presence of the trainer helps learners to concentrate on their learning tasks and therefore avoid distractions from the main purpose of the game. Indeed, if needed, the trainer can intervene during discussion among players in order to keep them on track towards the desired learning outcomes.

The trainer also stimulates continuous learning by encouraging improved performance. As in a game, this can be achieved by increasing the level of difficulty of the task to be achieved. Of course, the level of challenge should be adjusted according to players' capabilities in order to not discourage them. Indeed, players should master the target skills step by step. They cannot be asked, for example, to become brilliant negotiators in just one session.

As noted earlier, when a game session starts, all players are informed of their role. This means that in different game sessions, within the same or other scenarios, they may be asked to play different roles implying various types of behaviour and goals, according to the individual player's story and specific skills to be developed. This ensures that individual learners' perception of their experience may vary as they explore different perspectives, while practising different roles.

Furthermore, people who usually have difficulties in paying attention or staying quiet during a traditional lesson may have fewer problems of concentrating during a game.

A scenario could also contain aspects that promote competitive elements among players—either acting in the same session or belonging to different groups of learners playing different sessions—that the trainer may decide to activate in order to encourage development of mutual agreements and collaborative strategies.

Finally, depending on the scenario and therefore the learning objectives, a game can include and alternate well-timed jokes and dramatic actions that trainers can decide to introduce, for example, to relax tense situations or disagreements or to solicit the expression of specific emotions.

For instance, *Young people on the interface*, developed in Eutopia-MT, represents a training scenario focused on intercultural communication and negotiation skills, particularly those related to active listening, empathising with and understanding others and developing mutually acceptable solutions. In Northern Ireland, interface areas are those along the boundary between Catholic and Protestant communities in urban regions. Participants were practitioners and trainers in Northern Ireland in the field of mediation and negotiation.

The general learning objectives identified by the trainer included the capability to engage with young people, explore the reasons for the violence, develop cultural identity and finally obtain local support for a regeneration project that would benefit young people. In preparing for the training, the participants were fully briefed about the scenario, the character's background and personality and what was therefore expected from them. Once logged in, participants were projected into an interface area heavily affected by the "Troubles" and where there had also been recent outbreaks of violence involving young people from the two communities. According to the scenario, Belfast City Council had recently announced that it would be

interested in supporting a funding proposal for sports-based regeneration of interface areas, provided that proposals had cross-community support. Interested parties
had then agreed to meet in order to engage in face-to-face negotiations or at least in
an initial meeting about young people's involvement in fights on the interface. This,
briefly, is the story described in the script and the starting point for the players.

The scenario involves eight roles, Billy (a middle-aged community activist),
Jimmy and Toker (two adolescents involved in rioting and antisocial behaviour in
the area), Gladys and Pauline (two young local councillors), Betty (a community
activist), Sergeant Wilson (a police officer) and Michael (a middle-aged community
worker). As noted before, according to the learning goals, the trainer assigns to each
participant a specific character, endowed with specific physical and psychological
aspects, with a personal story and set of specific individual tasks to accomplish.

Betty, for example, is a middle-aged long-standing community activist whose
husband was killed in the "Troubles". She would like to see her two grandchildren
growing up in an area free of conflict. She has extensive cross-community contacts,
is on the board of the local primary school and has been involved in running summer
schemes for younger children. Betty's specific tasks are identified as exploring the
reasons for the current cycle of violence and possible solutions which might involve
young people as well as work towards establishing a tentative dialogue with the
"other side" and turning that dialogue into something concrete.

The storyboard also includes events that can be activated by the trainer during the
gameplay such as, for example, the introduction of an accident involving one of the
adolescents during riots in the areas. This may introduce elements of understanding
personal responses to distressing events and the need to develop empathic responses
in order to manage the situation effectively.

An expressive comment made by one of the participants highlights how, through
an engaging scenario and contents, an online role play can help to elaborate personal emotions and experiences:

> The role-playing isn't always comfortable. It requires us to momentarily suspend our own
> reality and take on the reality of another. At times that discomfort may be due to feeling the
> pain of the role-play character because it has touched something deep in our own
> experience…

This poses the accent on the enormous value of the psychodramatic role-play
method used in group settings. Processes of observing and participating in each other's personal stories can facilitate feelings of deep understanding and trust among
group members. Expressing feelings and ideas in action is a natural tendency that
allows a physical experience of embodying a role, offering a greater degree of full-
ness and a stronger expression of will, as well as sense of self. As it operates in the
interpersonal field, when an idea is embodied so that it can be witnessed by the other,
it becomes more real. It operates in order to promote self-reflectiveness: through role
detachments participants can metaphorically step back and witness their own performances (Bromberg 1958; Fingarette 1969; Davies 1976).

4.3.2   Modelling of Relevant Psychological and Pedagogical Theories

Eutopia is not just a game but rather a platform with which it is possible to create an unlimited number of role-playing games. It is important to stress this when we come to the psychological and pedagogical grounds of Eutopia.

Of course, as we have pointed out in this chapter, the main framework behind Eutopia is that of role-play methodology as a psycho-pedagogical approach applied to MMORPGs and MUVEs. Thanks to the immersive features of such virtual worlds, it is possible to enhance the learning strengths of the psychodrama/sociodrama, as defined by Moreno (1946a, b). That is why we call Eutopia a Drama-Communication Technology-based Educational Role-Play Game (Drama-ComTech-based EduTech-RPG).

However, as a platform, Eutopia allows the creation of different games, and as such it requires a preliminary game design activity. This is an important aspect of Eutopia for two main reasons.

First, in the creation of each single game, the game designers can model the different aspects of a selected soft skills theory that encompass the description of the story and the characters, the attribution of specific features to the characters and the design of relevant events, documents and questionnaires. In other words, game designers can use Eutopia to address different soft skills and implement different theoretical frameworks in the form of a game scenario. Indeed, psychology and pedagogy provide a theoretical framework for the successful design, development and implementation of learning scenarios around a specific soft skill. Thanks to the Eutopia game editor, trainers can easily convert these scenarios into real-time sessions and play them.

Second, the game design activity in Eutopia is itself an important aspect of the learning process, which also provides advantages for trainers. Indeed, designing their own games enables trainers to discover a new way of working in which they can collaborate with researchers, other trainers and learners. Researchers, psychologists, educators and game developers have recognised the importance of working together for the design and use of games as effective learning tools. When this process is collaborative, trainers have the opportunity to be involved in a team and distribute work among themselves. Moreover, when a functional prototype of the game is available, it can be evaluated not only by the trainers that created it but also by other colleagues and experts in the field, who can provide feedback and contribute with new creative ideas.

Moreover, the game design process is usually considered challenging and fun by trainers and helps to keep their motivation high. It also allows them to reflect on the teaching process, because role-play games must be carefully designed to suit the learners' needs and goals. Game design can even offer trainers the possibility of learning new technologies and updating their knowledge in the ICT field.

4.3.3   Feedback, Debriefing and Back-Stage Agents

In Chap. 3, we discussed the importance of the evaluation layer in building an EduTech-RPG. Indeed, in order to correctly train the learners, it is necessary to firstly assess them to provide a teaching fitted to their level and needs. From this point of view, back-stage agents, who can observe learners and provide them with support and feedback when needed, have an important role to play.

In Eutopia, back-stage agents are controlled by human teachers/trainers. This choice was taken to allow players to express themselves freely, without constraints due to the use of automatic systems. For example, the use of natural language would entail great limitations for a virtual agent, because natural language processing is a complex problem that is still far from being completely understood and managed by automatic systems.

Therefore, the presence of human tutors is still a necessary constraint for this kind of educational systems. Their presence guarantees that learners receive correct feedback and guidance. Moreover, being online during real-time sessions, they can ensure that support and feedback are constantly accessible when needed by learners. Even if players do not see them during the game session, in that they have no physical avatar, they can "feel" their presence. Indeed, learners can ask questions to trainers or read their public comments at any time.

The use of feedback and debriefing mechanisms provided by the Eutopia platform also allows exploitation of all the potential of trainers' guidance, facilitation and support.

Trainers guide the learning process and may intervene as facilitators at any time during the simulation and on completion of activities. Trainers can observe and analyse the evolution of the simulation and learner's actual performances and monitor improvements, progress and/or difficulties. They can send messages and comments to players for soliciting an immediate reflection on the dynamics that have taken place.

They can also activate events to change the dynamics of actual interactions.

Moreover, they can be involved directly in the interaction, playing the role of one of the characters, as can happen in real face-to-face role-play activities. This represents the case in which the role of BSAs coincides with that of OSAs.

Trainers can record the training sessions for debriefing and feedback purposes in order to encourage the communication process, mutual sharing, self-reflection and self-discovery and help in identifying potential areas of personal development. The recording tool helps trainers to support participants in observing the dynamics they have played from a detached perspective and analyse the implication of personal actions and emotional attitude on the final decision.

The value of video recording simulations has been stressed by Ebner and Kovach (2011) as a tool that can help participants in a more accurate reflection on the dynamics that have taken place than within the feedback and debriefing processes. Indeed, reviewing the session from a different viewpoint represents a both physical and psychological space that enhances the self-discovery process, which increases self-awareness and helps to identify consequences of behaviour on other players and on the entire game, leading to individual changes. In the light of role-play principles and mechanisms discussed in Chap. 2, this is a tangible example of a tool available to learners to facilitate the exploration of their emotions, concepts and thoughts from a detached perspective, for the development of metacognitive capacity, empathy and self-awareness (Brown et al. 1987).

At the end of each session, trainers can solicit and provide feedback to participants and promote input for group discussion by analysing users' dominant playing strategy, behavioural patterns adopted, emotional reactions, communication and relational dynamics activated. On completion of the training phase, they also act as assessors by verifying and ensuring achievement of individual and collective learning objectives.

In summary, the trainer's role in the digital classroom evolves from instructor to flexible tutor and guide who gives learners appropriate feedback when needed.

The gaming experience also enables trainers to enter into the learners' culture and reality by using tools that fully integrate with their everyday environment. Employing digital tools is important for building a better relationship with learners, by moving closer to their language and interests.

4.3.4   Blended Methodology

Even though we have mainly discussed the technological aspects of the Eutopia platform so far in this chapter, it is important to note that it is not based exclusively on the use of software tools. Indeed, Eutopia is grounded on a blended methodology for soft skills training, which combines e-learning sessions based on online role-play games with traditional face-to-face delivery and material (Bonk and Graham 2012), such as workshops, lectures, reading material and questionnaires. This method is often used when personal contact is more critical, as in the case of soft skills training.

For all projects based on the use of the Eutopia platform that will be described in detail below, we have applied a blended learning methodology to train and develop soft skills, organised around the following key activities:

- Design of the simulation environment
- Training of tutors
- First face-to-face meeting, introducing goals, contents, methodologies and tools of the platform and finalising the "learning agreement" with participants
- Online simulations, using the software tools described in this chapter
- Second follow-up face-to-face meeting for a final evaluation test

Of course, this general structure can be adjusted and adapted to the specific context in which it is used. In the next paragraph, we will examine some experiences that have used Eutopia platform in different contexts and with different learning goals.

4.4 Results and Experiences

The rationale of Eutopia is to create immersive role-play simulation scenarios based on experiential and constructionist approaches which outline the use of the technology as an artefact for representing a model of the world, allowing meaningful investigations of a certain soft skill.

Since its first version in 2007, the Eutopia platform has accumulated many years of experience, underpinning several European projects. It has been used in different contexts, with different target groups and for the development of various soft skills. In order to produce successful learning scenarios, role-play game implementation and design for each project followed a series of steps established by game developers, learning suppliers and publishers that come together in order to integrate the model for transferring an effective immersive learning environment and correct application design. These steps can be summarised as follows:

1. Identification of target group
2. Identification of soft skills to be developed, according to a preliminary training need analysis
3. Definition of soft skills to be developed (theoretical psycho-pedagogical model)
4. Definition of learning goals and objectives
5. Scripting of role-play scenarios
6. Game designing, implementation and operationalisation of theoretical model

In the following paragraphs, we will describe how the aforementioned approach has been implemented in different projects, along with a summary of corresponding results and experiences.

4.4.1 Negotiation and Soft Skills in SISINE and SINAPSI

SISINE represents the embryonic version of the Eutopia platform that was developed within the Lifelong Learning Programme (2005 I/05/B/F/PP–154023) framework in 2007, with the primary objective of conducting online role-play simulations in negotiation. In this early version, players could benefit from two different interactive systems: multiplayer (as for Eutopia) and single-player environments (Miglino 2007; Miglino et al. 2007). The last system allowed learners to practise negotiation strategies through an offline exercise-game designed by trainers (the so-called gym), by interacting with a computer-controlled avatar (Bot), before the online group simulation session.

Online role-play scenarios were created in order to practise and apply negotiation skills in different contexts of target groups within the three countries involved in the project. More specifically, SISINE tools and methodology were tested in three tests in Italy, Poland and Slovakia. Each test focused on one specific kind of negotiation according to the target groups of the three partners involved:

1. Intercultural negotiation at school (Italy)
2. Commercial negotiation (Poland)
3. Negotiation as a part of human resources management in NGOs (Slovakia)

These three contexts of application were identified as particularly relevant for the three partners from an accurate *training need analysis*. In order to understand how target groups act in their peculiar employment-related situations, specific training needs, expected benefits for learners and organisations and the impact on social and economic systems were explored by using a series of psychosocial instruments, including questionnaires, behavioural interviews and check lists.

Each of the three tests involved roughly 20 learners aged between 20 and 60. All learners satisfied the following inclusion criteria: (a) professional involvement in negotiation and/or mediation and (b) basic knowledge of computers and web-based services.

The blended approach shared between the three courses was organised in the following steps:

1. An initial classroom session to present the goals, content, methodology and tools used during the test
2. Four offline single-player sessions with bots
3. Remote multiplayer sessions in which four to five learners simulated a negotiation under the supervision of a tutor
4. A second classroom follow-up session, including assessment

Experienced trainers were responsible for facilitating activities during the above steps, providing feedback on feelings experienced and behaviour during the role play and assessing progress towards relevant learning objectives.

While Sisine concentrated mainly on negotiation, an improved version of the SISINE platform was used some year later in the broader field of soft skills development, which included negotiation, leadership, team building, time management, motivation, decision-making and problem solving. Such a version was created within the LLP-funded SINAPSI project (LLP-LDV/TOI/08/IT/477), which started in 2009. During the project, online role-play scenarios were created in order to allow participants to master new skills which could complement professional and job-specific training.

More specifically, three target groups were used: university students in Italy, employees of public administration agencies in Slovakia and people working in small and medium enterprises in France.

Therefore, even though we will discuss the SISINE project and negotiation skills here, the main principles and methodological aspects also apply to other soft skills.

4.4.1.1 Definition of Soft Skills, Goals and Learning Objectives

Within the Sisine project, the TNA process has defined negotiation mainly as a communicational and relational event. Moreover, both communication and negotiation are considered as intercultural events because each individual, regardless of national and cultural belonging, holds a system of values and worldviews. Therefore, communication and negotiation cannot be considered as "objective processes" because they are expression of events that take place and that can be comprehended and appreciated within situational contexts. By situational event, we mean a process with its own history, reason, dynamics and context, without which it is not possible to understand any communication.

As a first consequence, we need to be aware of the ways in which relational events are perceived and interpreted by individual actors. The interest in communication and, specifically, negotiation as situational events is addressed not only to interindividual but also to trans- and intercultural differences. It is a common experience that understanding each other on the basis of shared meanings within the same culture is already a complex phenomenon in itself. This becomes even more complex when our personal and cultural worlds interact with systems of the same complexity belonging to people from different cultures.

The SISINE project aimed at developing participants' personal skills and behaviour in both their personal and professional lives in order to deal effectively with difficult situations and people and within conflicting situations involving intercultural issues.

Therefore, enhancing effective communication in order to be able to negotiate shared meanings and relationships dealing with interpersonal and intercultural conflicts was a key part of the course proposed.

In particular, our aim was that at the end of the SISINE course, participants should have been be able to master the principles of effective communication as crucial skills for successful negotiation and dealing with difficult people and situations.

4.4.1.2 Results/Feedback

Although SISINE has been our first experience in soft skills training by means of education role-play games, the overall feedback from evaluation reports in the three countries was very positive. Learners identified role-play games as a valuable tool for exercising and experiencing negotiation skills. The role of avatars as artefacts that encourage self-disclosure was particularly appreciated. On the other hand, trainers recognised the authoring system as an extremely flexible tool for scripting a potentially infinite range of scenarios, creating role-playing exercises tailored to the specific training needs of learners.

However, the project encountered also some difficulty, related to two main aspects: technical/usability issues and software limitations. For example, in some cases, local Internet providers had installed filters/firewalls which prevented the software from being installed or communicating with the central server. Furthermore, users often demanded more attractive graphics in order to strengthen the identification of players with their role/character, for example, by extending the range of emotions that could be expressed through avatars.

4.4.2 Conflict Management in Eutopia-MT

After SISINE, the Eutopia platform has since been adopted within the European Union's TOI Leonardo Project "Eutopia-MT" in 2008 (LLP-LDV/TOI/2007/IT/160) where MT stands for "Mediation Tool". The overall aim was to promote the development and acquisition of mediation competencies for the multitude of people dealing with conflict resolution and integration of differences (trainers, teachers, politicians, lawyers, local administrators, intercultural mediators, social affair officers, police forces, peace workers, etc.).

Indeed, Europe has been the theatre for a growing number of intercommunity conflicts related to poor integration of immigrant populations and new immigration from developing countries. In this situation, a steadily growing number of professionals come into contact with intercommunity conflict in their daily work but in many cases lack the skills to perform their work effectively.

The main objective of the Eutopia-MT project was to develop a training system that could facilitate the improvement of mediation skills (Miglino et al. 2010; Delli Veneri and Miglino 2010). This training system was based on the use of role-playing games at a distance, using the Eutopia platform.

The target group was composed of experienced professionals in mediation and negotiation, as well as trainers, academics and students, with different grades of interest and involvement in mediation topics.

More specifically, during the project, three learning experiences were organised across the project partner countries: Italy, Ireland and Cyprus. Three online role-play scenarios were developed in order to explore three different conflict contexts:

1. An urban immigration social conflict (Naples, Italy)
2. An ethnopolitical conflict (Belfast, Northern Ireland)
3. An international conflict acting on urban issues affecting a city area (Nicosia, Cyprus)

The training was delivered through a blended methodology, according to the steps previously described in section 3.4, in order to balance theoretical approach and relevant experience-oriented practice. In particular, four online sessions were scheduled, each one consisting of a simulation meeting and a follow-up meeting. Participants, who were divided into subgroups, simulated a conflict situation and the linked mediation process, supervised by their tutor. An experienced trainer facilitated all the above activities, providing feedback on feelings experienced and behaviour displayed and evaluating progresses towards relevant learning objectives.

4.4.2.1 Definition of Soft Skills, Goals and Learning Objectives

The definition of intercultural competence, informed by an accurate TNA of the target group involved, consists in the ability to communicate effectively and successfully with people from other cultures who reside in the same territory, which lies in the sphere of emotional competence and intercultural sensitivity.

It includes a subset of relational, cognitive and self-managing skills such as effective communication, cultural self-awareness, mental flexibility, active listening, problem solving, empathy and negotiation.

The aim of the project was to develop knowledge, skills and attitudes that foster understanding cultural differences in terms of values, beliefs and behaviour in order to encourage effective and appropriate interactions in a variety of cultural contexts. More specifically, our aim was that at the end of the course, participants would have been able to develop effective ways to communicate in order to foster mental flexibility for cultural awareness.

4.4.2.2   Results/Feedback

Eutopia-MT conducted two rounds of user tests in Belfast, Nicosia and Naples for testing the learning effectiveness of both the simulation scenarios and the overall training process.

Target group reports confirmed that a well-established tradition in mediation practice in Northern Ireland was supported by a large number of organisations and agencies devoted to the mediation cause at different levels. By contrast, in Cyprus and Italy, isolated initiatives related to conflict resolution issues, mostly regarding university courses and training programmes, were reported.

This finding also had an impact on the recruitment process. It was more difficult than expected and the dropout rate was higher, leading to smaller sample sizes that differed from those foreseen in the proposal. In short, due to organisational difficulties, it was not easy to reach the intended beneficiaries.

The Eutopia authoring system was a technical success. As already highlighted, it allows the design of potentially infinite training scenarios for role-playing exercises, according to the learning needs and personal experience of the end users.

The results demonstrated that the tools and methodology developed have a strong learning potential. The experience of Eutopia-MT confirmed the value of using role-play simulations games as tools that can help trainers to reach dispersed learners and improve their learning and not as an artificial replacement for a trainer. Eutopia placed the design of learning exercises firmly in the hands of trainers, while the dynamics that emerged in the game depend on learners. This strategy allows trainers to develop personalised scenarios for a specific target population, with specific learning needs.

Learners' and tutors' reports (questionnaires, interviews and debriefing sessions) from all three sites produced interesting findings. One advantage was that Eutopia-MT attenuated the physical distances and divisions between communities in conflict, and participants described the overall training experience through RPG games as emotionally engaging, as an opportunity to improve communication skills and finally as a flexible tool that can stimulate learning even in contexts different from mediation.

Data from the tests (questionnaire analysis and interaction observation) highlighted that almost all people lived strong emotions such as anger and frustration while playing the session and that they managed to learn new communication strategies.

From the tutors' point of view, the debriefing tool was found to be very useful (Susskind and Coburn 1999). Moreover, tutors stressed the beneficial possibility of using the platform according to different modalities, both at a distance (different geographical locations) and in the same place (safeguarding anonymity). Thus, this aspect can be well applied in the blended training class organisation, where both theory and practice play a role. Tutors believed that Eutopia works well in conflicting situations, where it could be especially useful to have a filter instead of direct contact. Finally, trying to achieve negotiation by working through an online tool could help people involved to cool their emotional dimension, while working around a table could sometimes exacerbate the discussion. In other words, what emerged was that distance (which initially seemed to be a barrier in relational dynamics) may function as a positive factor in a mediation skills learning process.

4.4.3 Proactive

Within the LLP KA3 Proactive project (505469-LLP-1-2009-1-ES-KA3-KA3MP), during 2010–2011, Eutopia was employed for supporting teachers and trainers in the design and delivery of online role-play scenarios tailored to primary, high educational and vocational learning contexts. Along with Eutopia, the E-adventure editor game was used for the design of training games addressing pupils of primary schools as well as students of high education schools.

The overall aim of Proactive was to create a learning contest for supporting teachers and trainers belonging to different learning sectors in the use of educational games and the design of learning scenarios tailored to the needs and learning styles of trainees, in order to encourage their implementation in traditional educational practice. Eutopia was used to design a variety of role-play scenarios focused on effective communication, negotiation, mobbing, sales and advertising skills, employee selection, group dynamics and doctor-patient relationships. More specifically, Proactive aimed at fostering teachers' and trainers' creativity through the design of educational games, by taking into account the five metaphors of learning as identified by Simons, who defines different learning styles and methods (Simons and Ruijters 2003, 2008; Simons 2004): acquisition (traditional transfer of learning), participation (learning by interacting), discovery (learning by doing), imitation (learning by example) and experimentation (hands-on context-related learning).

In essence, the overall goal of Proactive was to implement an approach for designing educational games with the support of the five metaphors applied in natural learning, in order to create learning environments tailored as much as possible to users' needs.

4.4.3.1 Definition of Soft Skills, Goals and Learning Objectives

As mentioned earlier, within the Proactive project, Eutopia was used by trainers for creating a variety of scenarios focused on the area of soft skills training and development. We will report here only one scenario example out of the 30 produced during the project, which focuses on critical thinking and self-reflection. The number of scenarios produced further emphasises how Eutopia places the design and control of learning exercises firmly in the hands of trainers, and therefore technology is a tool rather than a cheap replacement for a teacher or a trainer. Trainers can flexibly develop their own scenarios, personalising their work for specific target populations with specific learning needs. For example, Community of Philosophical Inquiry (COPI) is a role-play game aiming at training young teachers to foster critical reflection in a group class. It is especially referred to the awareness of collective realities in which we are immersed and with which we interact and pertains to all spheres of our life, including education (cosmopolitan challenge).

In the COPI scenario, critical thinking (Lipman 1988) is defined as "skilful responsible thinking that facilitates good judgment", where judgment is understood as "a determination of thinking, of speech, of action or of creation". The design of the scenario is based on the idea that any process of inquiry is intended as a continuous reflective process of self-discovery and self-awareness, which leads to growth and development for individuals, communities and societies.

In other words, critical thinking opens a space of reflection within which individuals have the opportunity to think critically about their own assumptions and beliefs and develop a new understanding based on the possibility of reconstructing and therefore redefining individual meaning schemes and perspectives. Thus, the feeling of being and thinking in a group experienced in games provides the opportunity to participate in the construction of a narrative that is the result and the synthesis of individual stories and develops in a qualitative unity of critical thinking (Striano 2009, 2012).

The learning objectives of the COPI scenario were (a) to broaden the conceptual reference frame regarding the cosmopolitan experience and (b) to develop philosophical inquiry skills.

Our aim was that at the end of the training course, participants would have been able to recognise the value of reflective process in the interaction between one's own culture and the culture of others and develop empathy and alternative perspectives by fully recognising reciprocal differences.

4.4.3.2   Results/Feedback

Teachers and trainers from 23 educational institutions were engaged in the codesign of different games and role-play learning scenarios dealing with a wide range of subject matters across primary, high educational and vocational learning contexts, in the areas of medical education, negotiation skills and forensic skills. A collection of materials comprising templates, libraries, tutorials and a handbook was provided to trainers in order to facilitate the use of the editors (Eutopia game editor and E-adventure), as well as the design and implementation of role-play scenarios.

Teachers and trainers from the four countries involved in the project (Italy, Romania, Spain and the United Kingdom) designed about 30 learning scenarios that were later tested in real educational settings. The feedback collected in the form of questionnaires and open group discussions reveals that the game design experience was considered extremely positive by the participants. On the one hand, they considered as very interesting the discovery of an innovative and flexible tool to be used for creating experiential activities in support of traditional training methods, thus providing a new appealing way of combining theory and practice. On the other hand, they really appreciated the integrative, collaborative and problem-solving approach to learning promoted by the rationale behind the platform. Indeed, they reported that students felt engaged in achieving the desired goals and the process produced increased collaboration and teamworking.

4.4.4 Entrepreneurship Training in S-Cube

The LLP TOI S-Cube project (UK/11/LLP-LdV/TOI-419) represents the most recent application of the Eutopia platform, which was used for designing role-play scenarios that promote the soft skills development of individuals working in and supporting social enterprises. The project brought together project partners from four countries: the United Kingdom, Ireland, Germany and Italy.

S-Cube project provided organisations with a dedicated online training service through which they could develop highly customised soft skills training scenarios that could be fine-tuned to any unique social enterprise situation.

Social enterprises have the dual purpose of producing a profit to achieve organisational sustainability while also fulfilling a social mission. Their activities often benefit groups of people who are disadvantaged including, for example, unemployed persons, ethnic minorities and people with disabilities. Existing research shows that social enterprises face a number of operating challenges, and in order for them to compete, upgrading the skills of their staff may be necessary. They are often small and work under condition of meagre resources. This can preclude them from developing or gaining access to educational, management, technical and training expertise. Many such enterprises can benefit from additional support in the development of skills critical to their success. In particular, soft skills appear to be particularly important for them.

To inform the design and development of the S-Cube Learning Programme for soft skills development, a systematic investigation and analysis of the training needs of social enterprises across three partner countries—the United Kingdom, Ireland and Germany—was conducted. The TNA research was designed to identify and categorise the soft skills needs of a range of social enterprises and was inclusive of other social enterprise stakeholders such as educators and trainers, as well as support organisations. To this end, multiple methods were used such as interviews, questionnaires, self-assessment exercises and case studies that involved a total of 200 pivotal social enterprise actors. The findings of the TNA were used to inform the design of a competency model (Goleman et al. 2002; Ridley-Duff and Bull 2011) for assessing a range of soft skills to be developed and trained. The model will be briefly presented in the following section.

More specifically, the blended methodological approach adopted for the design and evaluation of the training process consisted of the following steps:

- Training needs analysis
- Self-reflection stage (before online testing, to gain further information on personal experiences about soft skills)
- Two sessions of online testing
- Final self-reflection stage (after online testing to assess any improvement)
- Evaluation of testing stage

4.4.4.1   Definition of the Soft Skills, Goals and Learning Objectives

In a first phase of the project, we concentrated on the assessment of the soft skills capabilities of participants most likely to use S-Cube. To this end, multiple methods were used, such as interviews, questionnaires, self-assessment exercises and case studies. This work was fed into the creation of a special role-play scenario called *Future Positive*.

The second phase of the project consisted of both group-based and online software tests, conducted using the Future Positive scenario and the S-Cube version of the Eutopia platform.

Within the S-Cube project, the learning goal was to develop the work skills of social entrepreneurs, enabling them to contribute positively to the community, earn an income and gain a sense of purpose and direction.

More specifically, our aim was that at the end of the S-Cube training course, participants would have been able to effectively communicate the organisation's goals, cultivate a sense of self-awareness through identifying a leadership style and values and motivate and drive workers towards the organisation's vision and mission.

The results of 22 scoping interviews with stakeholders informed the game design of a social enterprise soft skills competency model, which resulted in 17 soft skills grouped into three clusters:

- Inter-/intrapersonal skills: resilience, active listening, flexibility, self-awareness, personal effectiveness, understanding relationships and judgement
- Communication skills: communication, consultation, ability to influence and being able to convince
- Total quality management: effective leadership, conflict resolution, creative problem solving, team building, strategic thinking and decision-making

For each soft skill, behavioural indicators were identified for a more accurate objective assessment process.

The use of those three clusters took inspiration from the model proposed by Whetten et al. (2000) that distinguished between (1) intrapersonal skills (self-awareness, managing stress and effective problem solving), (2) interpersonal skills (communication, motivation and conflict management) and (3) people management (empowerment, delegation, teamworking, leadership and management).

The same distinction between intrapersonal and interpersonal is used by both Goleman et al. (2002) and Gardner (1993a, b). Grouping of skills such as effective leadership, creative problem solving and strategic thinking into total quality management took inspiration from Bull (2006), whereas the communication skill cluster drew on the work of Goleman et al. (2002) and Ridley-Duff and Bull (2011).

4.4.4.2   Result/Feedback

The S-Cube project has again shown how important improvements in soft skills can be achieved by the use of role-play games in a virtual online environment. The development of the Eutopia platform and its dissemination have been an important mechanism to improve soft skills for social enterprises across the European Union, improving their ability to fulfil the economic, social and environmental goals which are at the heart of their mission.

Organisations really appreciated the use of the Eutopia game editor, because it enables the easy creation of role-play characters, 3D environments and storyboards for training their staff.

The learning process has proved to have the capacity to help develop the soft skills of members of the European social enterprise community, as shown by the impact evaluation of the training experience carried out after the testing phases. Successful testing with social enterprise stakeholders helped to validate the S-Cube learning programme and has set it on track for sustaining the soft skills enhancement training of social entrepreneurs. At project close, different organisations in the four countries involved in the project expressed serious interest in providing training and education using the S-Cube Learning Programme.

4.5   General Remarks

In a study (Dell'Aquila et al.), we have investigated the perception of experienced professionals (educators, trainers, psychologists and educationalists adopting role-play activities in traditional settings) on the use of Drama-ComTech-based role-play games in educational and training contests, with a specific focus on the Eutopia platform. The professionals involved in this study had experience of using the Eutopia platform within the several European projects mentioned above, such as SISINE, Proactive, Eutopia-Mt and S-Cube.

A group of eighteen professionals completed a questionnaire on their perception of how online role play can encourage and foster meaningful learning experiences among participants with respect to the following different dimensions:

- Common characteristics and main differences between traditional and digital role play
- Value of specific features and tools of online role play

- Specific learning mechanisms/means not occurring in face-to-face experiences
- Role of mechanisms of feedback and debriefing in online settings
- Type of skills targeted with online role-play activities
- Level of involvement, engagement and comfort experienced
- Limitations and strengths of using online role play in professional practice

With respect to methodological effectiveness online, 72 % of respondents recognise that Drama-ComTech-based EduRPGs have the same effectiveness as face-to-face experience, though no better than traditional face-to-face experiences. This is because it helps in mastering specific and similar skills as for face-to-face activities and makes it possible to apply typical role-playing principles (e.g. mirroring, double) and feedback processes. Therefore, the psychological mechanisms and means that make a meaningful learning experience for participants in online role plays are assessed as not being different from those occurring during face-to-face activities, that is, guidance, feedback, debriefing and attention to learners' needs. When looking at the specific features of Drama-ComTech-based role-play games that make them suitable or at least different from traditional settings, the most important element seems to be the possibility of relying on the safety net of anonymity for 73 % of respondents, as already noted in other studies (Bond 2002; Martino 2007; Van den Brekel 2007). The anonymity of players who act through avatars encourages self-disclosure and also seems to allow more effective detachment. On the other hand, it is interesting to note that, according to the opinions of professionals, the possibility of assuming specific emotional, behavioural and physical properties through the avatars does not seem to be a decisive factor for greater identification with the character to be played. This seems to be confirmed by the perception of 67 % of respondents that one of the main vulnerable points associated with online role play is related to a general decrease of role and emotional engagement. So we can conclude that while, on the one hand, the avatar helps participants to better approach the role to play and be more open to reveal personal emotions, on the other, it does not seem to be a decisive factor for boosting the emotional involvement of users in the role to be played. In fact, the lack of emotional involvement is considered the biggest weakness of Drama-ComTech-based role-play games and the reason for their failure.

A large consensus among the professionals and also one of the most cited difficulties in implementing Drama-ComTech-based RPGs such as Eutopia in training practice regards the provision of adequate training for the use of the online role-play methodology. Indeed, the perception of failure is often associated with the lack of familiarisation with the methodology. Moreover, professionals share the perception that inexperienced trainers can compromise the effectiveness of the process. In the same vein, another possible factor cited is the complexity of combining game design with training needs analysis; this is a factor that could affect the motivation and commitment of trainers.

A related problematic element that emerged concerns the role of trainer, which is considered particularly critical in Drama-ComTech-based EduRPGs, especially multiplayer games such as Eutopia. Indeed, the fact that in online sessions the trainer is especially important in facilitating the quality of interactions among participants, and the achievement of the learning objectives is acknowledged as one of the key differences between online and face-to-face activities. There is a general perception that, in order to achieve an acceptable level of training experience, trainers must be skilled in mastering different tasks at once. In fact, in addition to role assignments, feedback and debriefing delivery and management and analysis of dynamics, trainers need to ensure a correct use of the tool and its features in order to support the accomplishment of training needs. They seem to feel the discomfort of having too many variables to take into account, and they might need the intervention of other trainers for supporting game, observation and feedback processes.

Another interesting difficulty in implementing online role play is attributed to possible differences in technical skills and access to technical resources (among countries and age groups of people involved), which is an interesting side effect of the well-known social and economic digital divide.

With regard to the methodological effectiveness of using the Eutopia digital platform, online role play is considered by professionals as a valuable method to be employed for supporting participants in developing and mastering skills and competencies. However, this is subject to additional customised dedicated sessions to support professionals on how to apply the online methodology and familiarise themselves with the tool and its features.

In summary, with respect to role of the trainer, the results seem to mark the crucial role of the trainer through the entire process of role play: definition of the learning scenario environment, monitoring of role play, its course and dynamics and the assistance offered with feedback and debriefing in order to maximise learning (Dawson 1990; Thatcher 1990; Perry and Euler 1988; Glandon 1978; Shirts 1976; Hermann 2015). This again highlights the crucial role of a human trainer in managing and conducting online role play.

What emerges is that the figure of the trainer simultaneously represents a source of strength and of weakness for Drama-ComTech-based EduRPGs.

It is undeniable that the human trainer can enrich game performance by providing facilitation and adaptable performance feedback. On the other hand, this study shows that the need for fully skilled trainers may increase the cost and time of training. As we will see in the following dedicated chapters, in designing other Rule and Drama-Communication and Simulation Technology-based EduRPGs, the authors have explored the possibility of using intelligent tutoring systems and/or design more structured scenarios to control the effects of too many variables involved in the game which have to be observed and interpreted in the learning process. However, with regard to our experience, we consider that which type of tutor is superior with respect to higher learning gains is still an open question. As will see in later chapters, this will depend on situations, time and resources available.

Chapter 5
ENACT: Virtual Experiences of Negotiation

In this chapter, we will describe the methodology and the characteristics of an educational tool in the form of a 3D, single-player EduRPG to assess and train the user's negotiation and communication skills in realistic scenarios. The tool presented in this chapter has been created in the context of the European Union-funded ENACT project (543301-LLP-1-2013-1-UK-KA3-KA3MP). The acronym stands for Enhancing Negotiation skills through online Assessment of Competencies and interactive mobile Training, and it aims to cross the boundaries between educational games and ITSs, merging the importance of an online and dynamical learner assessment with the intrinsic and extrinsic motivating environment of serious games. ENACT is implemented by a consortium of six partners in four different countries: the United Kingdom, Italy, Spain and Turkey.

ENACT focuses on the simulation of a dialogue between two humans, in which behavioural characteristics such as the act of speech and some elements of body language play a fundamental role (Marocco et al. 2015; Pacella et al. 2015, Mazzucato and Marocco 2015). In this regard and according to the characteristics delineated previously, it can be seen as an implementation of *Drama-based* games. Moreover, given that ENACT is designed to be played by a single user over the Internet, the entire interaction of the user with a 3D artificial agent is simulated on the computer, according to well-defined psychological theories. This aspect characterises the platform as *SimTech*.

Here we will discuss the motivational background of ENACT, the characteristics of the soft skills involved in the assessment and training, the methodology and the technological implementation.

© Springer International Publishing Switzerland 2017
E. Dell'Aquila et al., *Educational Games for Soft-Skills Training
in Digital Environments*, Advances in Game-Based Learning,
DOI 10.1007/978-3-319-06311-9_5

5.1   Theoretical Background and Psycho-pedagogical Modelling

As we have extensively discussed throughout the entire book so far, a crucial feature of soft competencies is the fact that they can be developed through training, education and development programs. Besides the training, such competencies can also be assessed using quantitative methodologies. This is an aspect that has not been deeply explored in the tools discussed in other chapters, and it represents a central feature and one of the main motivations of ENACT.

The first chapter of the book clarified how and why the most effective training method for soft skills development is considered to be role playing, which is usually performed by trainees face-to-face with the guidance of a professional trainer, who acts as facilitator. But how can the benefits of role-playing simulations be applied to e-learning platforms without the requirement of direct interactions among people synchronously connected online? We have seen that the Eutopia platform aims to enhance classical role-play games with technological communication systems and ad hoc features specifically designed for tutors, in order to break the traditional constraint imposed on trainer and trainees to share the same physical space. The aim of ENACT is to push further the technological boundaries and enrich a *Drama-based* game like Eutopia with computer simulation and artificial intelligence.

Within the ENACT project, *negotiation* has been identified as crucial soft skill or learning and personal development, because it is a social intra-/interpersonal competence that can effectively and positively impact on people's personal and professional life. The specific idea of negotiation embraced within ENACT is a concept of negotiation primarily based on *effective communication*, which mainly concerns our way of communicating, as well as awareness of how we are perceived and understood by others. The basic assumption is that negotiation and effective communication can be effectively discovered, improved and developed through dedicated training courses and personal development programmes.

The European Commission's New Skills for New Jobs initiative, which has the specific goals of promoting better anticipation of future skill needs and developing better matching between skills and labour market needs, identifies negotiation as one of the main skills capable of improving both "social and civic competences" and a "sense of initiative and entrepreneurship", as also highlighted in The European Framework for Key Competences for Lifelong Learning (KCLL), which identifies and defines the key competences that citizens require for improving their social inclusion and employability. A common element of these competences is the need for enhancing good communication and negotiation skills. The project identifies the need for the development of social and entrepreneurial skills, with respect to negotiation in particular, given that the lack of negotiation skills is recognised as a missing key element in entrepreneurship and enterprise skills education (Frank 2007) and negotiation skills are known to be fundamental in order to obtain better social and economic inclusion (Turok and Taylor 2006), as well as better job performances (e.g. Baron and Markman 2003).

5.1.1   Negotiation Concept Adopted Within ENACT

Although it is extremely difficult to identify a unique and universally accepted formal definition of negotiation, because it often reflects the variety across disciplines in which the term has been defined and theorised—such as economics, law, international relations, psychology, sociology and conflict management—the project takes inspiration from the integrative approach (Walton and McKensie 1965; Fisher and Ury 1981; Zartman and Berman 1982) which is based on the idea of negotiation as a cooperative rather than competitive-distributive process, that is, an approach based on integration that involves "making concessions" to reach an agreement, and its specificity regards the searching for reciprocal mutually satisfying solutions. The integrative approach is often also referred as a win-win paradigm (Covey 1989). However, we prefer the term "integration" to "win-win" because of the misuse and overuse of the latter which, although it suggests some form of competition, is sometimes used to describe lack of conflict, sometimes a form of compromise between parties and other times is identified with the integrative style of handling conflict episodes. In particular, we are interested in the concept of negotiation as the process of effectively communicating back and forth (constructive feedback process), in order to identify a joint view or solution to differing needs or ideas. In this view, within a conflicting situation, it is also important to learn to adopt others' positions, by looking at the other side as a partner (rather than an opponent). By working together, parties have an opportunity to craft a solution that could be beneficial to both sides. This approach is different from the distributive approach to negotiation, where parties compete to get the best deal. That is, each party is battling for obtaining the greatest advantage and leaving the other side with the smallest possible outcome.

Effective negotiation processes involve effective communications skills and related self-awareness. In fact, there is a general consensus among authors and practitioners that negotiation is only possible through effective communication. For example, Fisher and Ury (1981) claim that feeling understood can be a key interest for both sides in a negotiation. Effective communication can change attitudes, prevent or overcome impasse and misunderstandings and help to improve relationships. Indeed, negotiation is frequently hampered by common communicational barriers. Listening provides important information about the other side and demonstrates that the other party is being attentive to the other side's thoughts and respectful of their concerns. The integrative approach focuses on building mutual trust relationships between parties, and this is exploited through an effective communication attitude.

5.1.2   Psychological Modelling

The negotiation model adopted in ENACT is based on the five styles of handling interpersonal conflict proposed by Rahim and Bonoma (1979) and Rahim (1983) which is the model most recognised by occupational psychologists. This model differentiates five styles based on two basic dimensions: *concern for self*, the degree

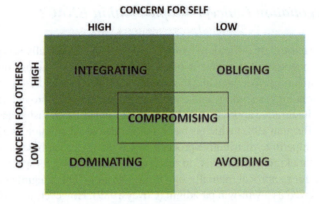

Fig. 5.1 Rahim and Bonoma's two-dimensional model of the five styles of interpersonal conflict management

(high or low) to which a person attempts to satisfy her own concern, and *concern for others*, the degree (high or low) to which a person attempts to satisfy the concern of others. The combination produces the following styles of conflict management, as shown in Fig. 5.1:

1. *Integrating* (high concern for self and others) involves openness, exchange of information and examination of differences to reach an effective solution acceptable to both parties.
2. *Obliging* (low concern for self and high concern for others) is associated with attempting to play down the differences and emphasise commonalities to satisfy the concern of the other party.
3. *Dominating* (high concern for self and low concern for others) has been identified with a win-lose orientation or with forcing behaviour to win one's position.
4. *Avoiding* (low concern for self and others) has been associated with withdrawal, buck-passing or sidestepping situations.
5. *Compromising* (intermediate in concern for self and others) involves give-and-take whereby both parties give up something to make a mutually acceptable decision.

Each style manifests itself in a pattern of observable behavioural indicators that we have identified in the communication model of assertiveness, passivity and aggression (Dryden and Constantinou 2004). For each of the styles, excluding compromising, we have distinguished three sets of variables, verbal (the words used in a sentence), paraverbal (how the verbal message is conveyed, tone, pitch and volume of the voice) and non-verbal (body language), grouped in the two dimensions proposed by Rahim, i.e. concern for self and concern for others. Those variables have been used to design the behaviour of the avatars, as discussed in the next section.

For the purpose of designing the training scenarios within ENACT, Rahim's model has been chosen for the following reasons:

1. It stresses the learning process and the idea of enabling people to learn the appropriate use of conflict styles depending on situations (Rahim 1983). In training

contexts, this implies that the appropriateness of a style depends on the specific situation and on the learning objectives. When facing conflict experiences, people might employ different conflict-handling styles, and not only one. Through the interactions within ENACT scenarios, learners can have the opportunity to reflect on the different styles employed during a conflict episode and of being aware of the most appropriate effective style for that specific given situation.

2. It is very positive about the idea of conflict proposed: every situation of conflict is an opportunity for people to grow, learn and work even more effectively. When conflict is handled appropriately, positive learning experiences may result in the development of individuals and teams. This hinges on how a conflict is managed and handled. Key aspects of conflict management start from being aware of oneself, understanding team dynamics and finally taking action. This reflects our challenge: giving users the opportunity to experience and being aware of personal and others' way of interacting and communicating by experiencing ENACT negotiation scenarios.

3. Rahim and Bonoma developed the *Rahim Organizational Conflict Inventory-II* (ROCI-II), for assessing the styles of handling interpersonal conflict (Rahim and Bonoma 1979). ROCI-II is currently the most widely used and rigorously tested conflict-handling psychometric instrument and has been used by many researchers throughout the years and not only by the original authors. It is available in three forms (A, B, C) for investigating respectively the five styles of handling interpersonal conflict with superiors, subordinates and peers. ROCI-II is used for assessment and feedback for the users and also for validating the model adopted within the software.

5.2   Design of the ENACT Platform

The software of ENACT is based on a web platform accessible through the Internet and has been designed to bring the model into a 3D virtual environment. The game is organised in scenarios, each independent from the others, where the user can play a different character and negotiate with various artificial agents in realistic and everyday life situations.

5.2.1   Psychological Model Implementation and Behavioural Indicators

On-Stage agents within ENACT are both the user and the artificial agent, the BOT, with which the user interacts with during the game. They are implemented as 3D avatars inside the game scenarios developed using the unity framework (https://unity3d.com/). Avatars are able to perform a range of basic expressions using verbal cues, such as vocal tone and structure of the sentence, and non-verbal indicators, such as facial expression, eye contact, body posture and gestures. Those indicators, in total 7, have been chosen for their relevance in the behavioural description of different communication styles, and they can be seen as indicators of specific behavioural traits that can be objectively observed and measured. Specifically, the variables are the following:

1. Structure of the sentence. *"I" statement*, that is, the way in which own ideas are communicated to others and how the term "I", as subjective element, is phrased in the sentence (e.g. "I would prefer....", "I must have...", "I am not sure...").
2. *Fact-opinions*, that is, the awareness shown by the speaker of the difference between owns opinions and objective facts (e.g. "I think that....", "it's all your fault....", "I may be wrong....").
3. *Enquiring*, that is, the level and value of inclusion of other's opinions, such as "How would you feel about that?" which is inclusive and open to discussion versus, e.g. "I don't mind what you think, just do it!" which is the opposite.
4. *Criticism*, which is the rate of constructive versus manipulative and/or self-destructive criticisms, e.g. "would you find it more helpful if..." versus "If I was you I would..." or "I am completely useless in doing...".
5. *Vocal tone* is represented as the callout's shape.
6. *Facial expressions are* represented as "idle" 3D animations of the avatars. These animations occur when the character does not perform any action (hence being idle) and awaits the interlocutor's answer.
7. *Body gestures are* represented as 3D animations that are activated while the avatars utter sentences.

5.2.2 User Representation and Avatars

In each scenario, two On-Stage agents are involved, represented by 3D avatars, one controlled by the user and the other by the computer (the BOT).

Figure 5.2 shows different implementation of the variables described in the previous sections. In particular, it is possible to note the vocal tones, implemented by callouts of different shapes, a variety of facial expressions and body gestures, because they are represented within the game by the avatars. The efficacy and unambiguousness of such variables and their graphical implementations were assessed during the demo sessions using data collected through online and paper questionnaires administered at the end of game sessions, as further explained in the chapter.

The gender of the characters is a variable related to the gender specified by the user at the registration, mandatory for accessing the platform. More specifically, the user's character has always the same gender of the user, and the BOT's gender can vary according to it, depending on the genders represented in a given scenario. As an example, if the user is a male, and the scenario is about a husband-wife discussion, the BOT will play the female character and the user the male, whereas if the user is a female, the BOT will be male and the user the female. In case of scenarios requiring the same gender for both characters, they both change accordingly to the user's gender.

Fig. 5.2 Graphic representation of avatars within the game. The image depicts four different styles. From *left* to *right*, *top* to *bottom*: integrating, avoiding, obliging and dominating

5.2.3 The Visual Interface and Game Dynamics

The interface is designed to be as intuitive as possible and only require minimal and simple interactions.

Each scenario starts with a brief text explaining the situation in which the user has to play the game, the role assigned to the user and her goal within the given scenario.

After the user has started the game by pressing the "play" button, the two characters, here from a different scenario than that of Fig. 5.3, are shown on the

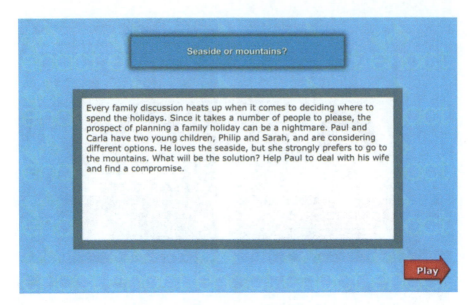

Seaside or mountains?

Every family discussion heats up when it comes to deciding where to
spend the holidays. Since it takes a number of people to please, the
prospect of planning a family holiday can be a nightmare. Paul and
Carla have two young children, Philip and Sarah, and are considering
different options. He loves the seaside, but she strongly prefers to go to
the mountains. What will be the solution? Help Paul to deal with his wife
and find a compromise.

Play

Fig. 5.3 Example of the start of a scenario within ENCAT game showing a brief text with expla-
nation of the situation in which the user has to play the game and the user's role and goal within
the scenario

screen along with their gestures, while the sentences are shown in bubbles over the
head of the avatars (Fig. 5.2). The BOT sits in front of the user and is the main character focused on by the camera. The user's avatar is also shown in a small window at
the left upper corner of the screen. When the mouse is over one of the user sentences
(on the left-hand side of the screen), the animation related to that sentence is shown in
the top-left window. In order to choose a sentence, the user needs to click on it (Fig. 5.4).

The game dynamics are based on the user-BOT interaction, which is divided into
states formed by one turn of speech for each party. In every state, the user can
choose one among 4 possible sentences, each of which is correlated to a gesture
and/or facial expression that shows the way the sentence will be told to the BOT, as
explained above. After the player's answer, the BOT computes the answer according to the embedded psychological model and the specific characteristics associated
to it within the scenario. That is, for example, a dominating BOT will show predominantly aggressive and authoritative behaviours. Conversely, an obliging BOT
will show an overall passive and submissive attitude towards the negotiation.

The game is fully cross-platform and is also available on mobile platforms.

When the game is loaded, it asks for the registration of the user, which is needed
to personalise the game according to individual parameters like gender and nation-
ality. For the purpose of the project, scenarios are available in four languages—
English, Italian, Turkish and Spanish—and include different situations and different
roles for the user.

The innovative aspect of the game is the assessment element, which implements soft
skills measurements with innovative methodology, yet with a rigorous psychometric

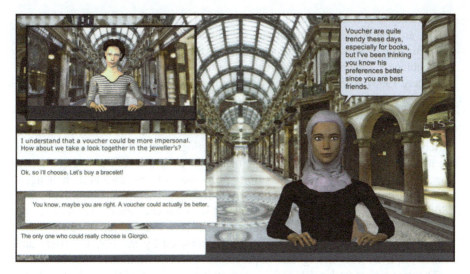

Fig. 5.4 The user interface of one scenario in assessment mode. The foreground avatar is controlled by the computer, and the avatar in the smaller window at the *top-left* corner represents the player avatar. Both avatars convey emotions and actions through facial and body animations. The sentences on the left represent the choices of the player in response to the actions of the BOT

approach. Training within the game can be implemented in many different ways and based on the psychometric profile of the user. In particular, thanks to a selection of scenarios from the assessment in which the user is guided through the recognition and self-reflections of various negotiation styles and accompanying behaviours. This will help the user to recognise situations and people's behaviour, as well as contextualise the negotiation in different realistic situations.

5.3   Assessment in ENACT

The final goal of the ENACT game is to return an assessment and provide training opportunities. The assessment of the player is based on the preferred negotiation styles used during a series of negotiation scenarios, based on the description of the five styles provided by Rahim. The assessment should be comparable to a professional assessment conducted with traditional "pen and pencil" methods. The assessment is also fundamental for automatic elaboration of a training strategy tailored to the specific development areas of the player, in order to create an effective learner-centred environment, where the user activity is focused on the areas of behaviour that mostly require improvements.

The process of assessment is validated by the use of the following five instruments: (1) the Rahim Organizational Conflict Inventory-II Form C (ROCI-II), (2) the specifically tailored Big Five personality test, (3) the Assertive efficacy scale, (4) the Self-efficacy scale and (5) the Coping scale. Both personality traits and self-efficacy are related to social skills and assertiveness. Personality traits, in particular, are one of the most important determinants of conflict management styles. The Big Five personality dimension consists of five traits: Extroversion, Agreeableness, Openness to experience, Emotional stability and Conscientiousness (Goldberg 1993). Administration of a tailored version of the Big Five aims to assess whether a model of personality has a direct impact on the preferences of conflict-handling style selection. The self-efficacy and assertive efficacy (Bandura 1977, 1986) scales aim to assess self-beliefs of an individual about the ability to handle a variety of difficult demands in life (e.g. conflicting situations) that are considered the most important determinants of the behaviour people choose to engage in and how much they persevere in their efforts in the face of obstacles and challenges. Finally, the coping scale assesses a range of thoughts and acts that people use to deal with the internal and/or external demands of stressful encounters. Therefore, it is possible to investigate possible relationships between high scores of self-efficacy and relevant personality traits with the style adopted by the ENACT users and related positive effect on negotiation processes observed within the game sessions.

The assessment within ENACT corresponds to the core of the evaluation layer discussed in Chap. 3 and is a playful way for the user to be assessed in a standardised manner according to the aforementioned Rahim model. The system collects the data about the user's behaviour and choices and creates a model of the player that will then be used for generating tailored information in the training session. The score and profile of the player's negotiation skills are actually calculated by summing the independent *concern for self* and *concern for other* variables accumulated during interactions, which are represented within every sentence that the user can choose. The assessment environment is composed of a series of eight different scenarios that concern a negotiation situation between two peers. The artificial agent's behaviour is static, not adaptive and reflects a specific negotiation style for each of the scenarios. For controlling the effect of possible cultural influences caused by avatar appearances, avatars are represented as female or male within the 20–40 years age range and of various ethnic groups, such as European, Asian, African and Arabic.

The user does not receive any feedback between scenarios, and there is no right or wrong answer.

There are three parameters according to which the scenarios were designed:

1. The negotiation style adopted by the BOT, respectively, integrating, dominating, obliging or avoiding.
2. If the player and the BOT have the same or opposite gender, the interactions can be male-male (or female-female) and male-female (or female-male).
3. If the negotiation concerns a decision about two different possibilities (divergence) or concerns a single object which must be exclusively assigned to one of the two characters (convergence).

It is worth noting here that the compromising style is not present among the negotiation styles shown by the artificial agents. This has been a methodological choice based on the dual concerns model of Rahim, because the compromising style is only represented by a moderate interaction of the 2 concern variables. Indeed, the

Table 5.1 The table shows a summary of the eight scenarios developed for the assessment session and their parameters

Title of scenario	Agent	Conflict	Gender
Who is going to take the motorbike?	Integrating	Convergence	Different
Pizza or Chinese?	Integrating	Divergence	Same
The disputed CD	Avoiding	Convergence	Same
A weekend in London	Avoiding	Divergence	Different
The contended parking space	Dominating	Convergence	Same
Question Time or Masterchef?	Dominating	Divergence	Different
Logo design	Obliging	Convergence	Same
Which present to buy?	Obliging	Divergence	Different

assessment of the user will still result in one of five styles, where the compromising one corresponds to a moderate interaction of the two variables, *concern for self* and *concern for other*. The user interacts with four distinctive styles, and the user's style will result by summing the independent variables, as described above, and by identifying the position of the user's profile within the graph depicted in Fig. 5.1. Table 5.1 shows a summary of the scenarios and their characteristics.

5.3.1   Tutoring System

The tutoring system is available only after the assessment has been completed; thus, it will intervene during the training scenarios and at the end of the game session in order to provide useful information to the user about her performance related to the BOT she is currently interacting with and to her general behaviour when managing conflicting situations. The user is given again a profile based on the Rahim model related to the specific situations she played, together with advice about how to improve the efficacy of her communication and the changes achieved since the assessment profiling. The profile emerges mainly through comparison of the behaviour of the user and the style of the artificial agent she interacted with. As with Eutopia, the user can revise the history of all the choices made during the scenario and is guided through the understanding of the possible hidden aspects of the negotiation.

5.4   Results

5.4.1   Training Need Analysis

In order to design and develop the ENACT learning scenarios for enhancing the negotiation skills of users, a systematic investigation and analysis of the training needs of target groups across three partner areas, Italy (secondary school students;

researchers/teachers), Spain (SME managers and employees) and Turkey (young people and athletes), was conducted. Multiple methods of data collection were used: (1) completion of a scoping questionnaire from nine pivotal group target stakeholders (to gather information regarding existing training policy and practices of soft skills), (2) completion of ten face-to-face semi-structured interviews (to identify different cultural definitions of the negotiation concept) and (3) utilisation of an online survey completed by 56 respondents (to elicit views and gain useful insights and nuanced opinions on the training needs). Results from scoping questionnaires in the three countries have consistently highlighted that there is a gap between (a) recommended educational practice of national guidelines and current practice in schools and training institution about soft skills-related subject and (b) national practice guidelines of technology application and the training provided to teachers in the use of technology. A few projects and training activities have been developed for promoting the use of computer games for soft skills development, with exception of Italy which, in the last decade, has been at the forefront of innovative role playing and simulation tools for soft skills training, as is thoroughly reported in this book. Results from interviews have shown that the definition of key elements related to the concept of negotiation varies among target groups and age range. In business, for example, where time is limited, problem solving and effective time management are the aspects most appreciated within negotiation. While teachers consider the ability to positively manage a conflict as essential, for students, interpersonal relationships are the key for a successful negotiation. Moreover, findings from the online questionnaires have identified the relational competencies considered to be more characteristic of negotiation:

- Spain: effective communication (90 %), empathy (70 %) and decision-making (65 %)
- Turkey: effective communication (80 %), problem solving (50 %), empathy (50 %) and creative thinking (50 %)
- Italy: critical thinking (64 %) and active listening (64 %)

The entire corpus of data recorded, as well as the analyses and a detailed description of the methodology, is available as deliverables of the ENACT project (under the section Materials, on the enactskills.eu website).

5.4.2   Pre-validation Testing Data

The platform underwent two full iterations of software development, and after every iteration, the software was tested in order to gain information about key elements: in particular, those elements that we believe can play the most prominent role in the efficacy and acceptability of the platform as a training and assessment tool. Iterations of development and testing are fundamental for assessing the development phase and make sure that the objectives are met to an acceptable extent. After the two iterations presented here, the platform was released for an extensive validation phase.

The first set of data was collected at the Sci-Tech Showcase 2014, held at Plymouth University in September 2014. The first demo of the ENACT game was presented, and feedback was collected in the form of questionnaires focused on the quality of the interface and of the BOT. The survey forms were administered right after the game sessions. The participant pool was composed of people between the ages of 6 and 60; the questionnaires were administered only to people who had reached at least the age of 11.

One hundred and fifty two subjects tested the game, of which 72 in the 6–10 age group. A total of 79 subjects between the ages of 11 and 60 completed the questionnaire, with a mean age $\approx$ 20.6, of whom 41 were males and 38 females. The questionnaire (see Table 5.2) was made up of eight questions about the game content and interface. The first seven items had five possible answers based on a 5-point Likert scale, where 1 stood for "extremely bad" and 5 "extremely good"; the last question, instead, asked the participant if she would have played the game again in different scenarios. Data showed that the overall feedback was positive. The average rating for each of the questions never scored below 3.5 points except for questions 2 (regarding the realism of the conversations) and 5 (about the game graphics) which scored a mean of 3.4 and 3.3; 95.3 % of the subjects answered "Yes" to question 8, showing an overall interest in future development of the game (as shown in Table 5.2).

The latest questionnaires about the newly released second demo interface and the full assessment system were collected at the British Science Week hosted at Plymouth University in March 2015, where subjects were asked to play four different scenarios and to provide feedback about the platform. The pool was composed of 39 people, in the 11–28 age group, of whom 18 were males and 21 females. The questionnaire was composed of 13 questions, of which 12 had a 5-point Likert

Table 5.2 Average scores for each of the questions in the questionnaire administered in September 2014

	Questions	Average pts/5
1	How appropriate and natural were the emotions expressed by the artificial BOT?	3.7
2	How much realistic did you find the conversation with our artificial BOT?	3.4
3	How would you rate the user interface (the controls, buttons, settings, etc.) of the ENACT game?	3.75
4	How interesting were the information and the profile given at the end of your game session?	3.77
5	How would you rate the graphics and video quality of the ENACT game?	3.29
6	How would you rate the usefulness of such game in dealing with real-life situations?	3.70
7	Can you rate your overall experience with the ENACT game?	3.91
8	Would you play this game again with different scenarios and characters?	95.3 % Yes. 4.7 % No

Table 5.3 Average scores for each of the questions in the questionnaire administered in March 2015

	Questions	Average pts/5
1	The conversation with the agents is realistic	3.59
2	The emotions expressed by the agents are appropriate and natural	3.9
3	The agents' movements and gestures are appropriate and natural	3.69
4	The emotions and gestures of the agents are useful for the comprehension of the speech	3.77
5	The graphics and video quality is modern and appropriate	3.41
6	The user interface (controls, buttons, settings) is intuitive and good-looking	3.87
7	The information and the profile given at the end are useful and clear	3.69
8	The scenarios deal about real-life situations	4.1
9	The agents are behaving differently in each scenario	3.72
10	I found it easier to negotiate with some agents than others	3.97
11	I am motivated to negotiate even with the toughest agent	3.97
12	I find the overall experience with the ENACT game positive	4.33
13	Would you play this game again with different scenarios and characters?	94.7 % Yes, 5.3 % No

scale as possible responses that ranged from "totally disagree" (represented as 1) to "totally agree" (represented as 5). All the questions asked in the previous event showed at least a slight improvement in their scoring, and in this case, only question 5, about how modern the graphics looks, scored less than 3.5. Two questions even scored above 4, and, in particular, the highest score was reached by question 12, which concerned whether the experience with the ENACT game was positive, while that same question had scored 3.9 on the previous demo; 94.7 % of the subjects answered that they would play the game again with different scenarios. The table below shows a summary of the average scores obtained by the platform (Table 5.3).

5.5   User-Centred Approach and Flexibility

The final aim of ENACT is twofold. On one hand, it is to apply role-playing techniques in a digital context in order to obtain comparable information provided by the administration of ROCI-II, as well as investigate possible relationships between the scores from the questionnaire about the different styles and the styles used by users during the interaction with the artificial agents. On the other hand, it is to provide a personalised, learner-centred and protected environment, where the user can build from the assessment and gain awareness of her own negotiation and communication style to a certain extent. It makes it possible to practise negotiation in context, therefore providing a constructive and experienced-based environment for soft skills development.

Besides the technical development, we are proposing a methodology that focuses on the complementarity with traditional assessment and training tools and offers inclusive training processes for soft skills that are alternative to the often expensive assessment centres provided by professional consultancy firms.

We believe that technology can offer a new and positive model for approaching the fundamental domain that involves the personal sphere of the individual, not only through well-known social networks dynamics that are often difficult to control but also thanks to a rational and scientific approach that does not dismiss the work done in the past but tries to bridge the past and the present with modern, accessible and effective tools that can be comparable with other assessment and training tools. This is the case of ENACT in comparison with the ROCI-II test.

Bearing this in mind, two general features of the proposed approach within ENACT can be highlighted. The first is that the user of the EduTechRPG is constantly at the centre of the assessment and training process developed within the software. The user can test her own natural attitude towards a given soft skill, can improve the understanding and the practice of that soft skill thanks to the tutoring system provided and can freely reassess the performances following the training. Therefore, it presents a complete and self-sustained training process.

Moreover, the ENACT approach presents a novel element of flexibility, both in delivery and practice of soft skills training for professionals. On one hand, it provides the possibility to broaden the practice of soft skills training outside the traditional classroom approach by leveraging Internet technologies.

On the other hand, which is even more interesting, the professional can be in total control of the model implemented, the assessment and the training process. In fact, what we have presented is a specific implementation of this approach to a widespread and well-renewed soft skill: negotiation. However, every soft skill that requires the exploitations of people's interactions can benefit from such realisation of an EduTechRPG. The reason is that, whatever interactions and soft skills have to be transferred in the role play, the *Drama-based* and *SimTech* dimensions represented within ENACT enable modification of the narratives and the psychological models underlining the assessment and training requirements, but the overall game dynamics based on interactions, situational learning and dramatisation remain untouched.

Chapter 6
DREAD-ED: Improving Communication Skills in Critical Situations

In this chapter, we will describe an example of ICT rule-based EduRPG designed to train soft skills in general and primarily focusing on communication in the context of disaster management.

It has been realised under the framework of the LLP-Information and Communication Technologies (ICT) (2007-3628/001-001) programme, supported by the European Commission. It involved a consortium of five partners from Finland, Italy, Germany and the United Kingdom. Two partners were involved in the game design and software implementation, whereas the others were involved as stakeholders given that they actually worked in an emergency context.

This description will encompass the results and practice of the EU project DREAD-ED, the objective of which was to improve the resiliency of local communities and emergency forces when responding to unexpected events and situations, particularly in the context of disaster (Haferkamp et al. 2011; Linehan et al. 2011). Effectively managing disasters requires close collaboration among many different actors: local and central government, emergency services, hospitals, schools, telecommunications operators, companies operating major plant in the area affected by the disaster and, of course, ordinary citizens. This collaboration often takes place against a background of inadequate and conflicting information. Sometimes mortality and damage could be drastically reduced if people were properly trained in some basic soft skills like communication and understanding of information under conditions of stress, problem solving with partial or contradictory information and decision-making in the face of competing demands. Planning and training are the two pillars which support people reacting to specific disaster events. To this end, DREAD applied a blended training methodology involving both classroom teaching and multiplayer role-playing games in a 2D interactive environment. The aim was to develop a new integrated model for training in the management of emergency situations. The model placed a strong emphasis on online activities and was designed to comply with the needs of professionals operating in the field.

© Springer International Publishing Switzerland 2017
E. Dell'Aquila et al., *Educational Games for Soft-Skills Training in Digital Environments*, Advances in Game-Based Learning,
DOI 10.1007/978-3-319-06311-9_6

6.1 A Game Designed to Teach Disaster Communication

Successful emergency management requires that key personnel involved should not only be trained to familiarise themselves with predefined plans, protocols and procedures for intervening effectively (what we have defined as hard skills in Chap. 1), but a good training in soft skills, communication in particular, should also be considered equally important.

In general, the management of natural disasters, industrial accidents or other kinds of catastrophes has always included a significant communication component in the form of warnings and risk messages (Reynolds and Seeger 2005). Different kinds of crises, however, involve different forms of threat and different communication exigencies (Pauchant and Mitroff 1992). In the past, various definitions of risk communication have been proposed. Reynolds (2002) defines crisis communication, risk communication, and crisis and emergency risk communication in ways that should be acceptable to most communication theorists and at the same time give the practitioner a firm foundation for discussing the differences and similarities among the fields of communication.

According to Reynolds (2002), *crisis communication* deals primarily with factual communication by an involved organisation to its stakeholders and the public. Crisis communication is simply the effort by community leaders to inform the public that they have to evacuate in advance of a disaster. In this definition, the organisation is not being overtly judged as a possible participant in the creation of the disaster, and the information is empirically sound, so the individual can judge its veracity without the help of an expert. The underlying thread in crisis communication is that the communicating organisation is experiencing an unexpected crisis and must respond. Crisis also implies lack of control by the involved organisation in the timing of the crisis event.

Risk communication is a field that has flourished in the area of environmental health (Reynolds 2002). Through risk communication, the communicator hopes to provide the receiver with information about the expected type (good or bad) and magnitude (weak or strong) of an outcome of a behaviour or exposure. Typically, it is a discussion about an adverse outcome and the probability of that outcome occurring. In some instances, risk communication has been employed to help an individual make a choice about whether or not to undergo a medical treatment, continue to live next to a nuclear power plant, pass on genetic risks or choose to vaccinate a healthy baby against whooping cough. In some cases, risk communication is used to help individuals adjust to the knowledge that something that has already occurred, such as exposure to harmful carcinogens, and may put them at greater risk for a negative health outcome, such as cancer, in the future. Risk communication would prepare people for that possibility and, if warranted, gives them appropriate steps to monitor the health risk, such as regular cancer screening.

Crisis and emergency risk communication comprises the urgency of disaster communication as well as the need to communicate risks and benefits to stakeholders and the public. Crisis and emergency risk communication differs from crisis communication—according to Reynolds (2002)—in that the communicator is not perceived as a participant in the disaster, except as an agent to resolve the crisis or

Fig. 6.1 Audience relationship to the event by Reynolds (2002)

emergency. Crisis and emergency risk communication is the effort by experts to provide information to allow an individual, stakeholder or an entire community to make the best possible decisions about their well-being within nearly impossible time constraints and ultimately help people. Crisis and emergency risk communication also differs from risk communication in that a decision must be made within a narrow time constraint, the decision may be irreversible, the outcome of the decision may be uncertain and the decision may need to be made with imperfect or incomplete information (Reynolds 2002). Crisis and emergency risk communication represents an expert opinion provided in the hope that it benefits its receivers and advances behaviour or an action that allows for rapid and efficient recovery from the event. In order to simplify the name of this communication form, we will just call it "disaster communication" in the following.

Figure 6.1 shows the different receivers of disaster communication according to Reynolds (2002). All of them must be considered in planning and training for disaster communication. For instance, the public's awareness of government is heightened during a disaster. A lack of continuity, control, adequate resources or full knowledge of the event can cause panic and threaten social unity. The audiences' needs can be judged in three ways:

1. Their relationship to the incident (e.g. are they directly involved in the disaster (persons concerned) or do they have to coordinate the emergency services?)
2. Their psychological differences (e.g. are they shocked because of the disaster, do they have to come to a decision in a stressful situation?)
3. Their demographic differences

According to Reynolds (2002), there are many different audiences that are involved in a disaster and are directly affected by disaster communication. The most important target groups are the following:

1. The public within the circle of a disaster or emergency for whom action messages are intended. The main concerns for this target group are personal safety, family safety, pet safety, stigmatisation, property protection.
2. The public which is immediately outside the circle of disaster or emergency for whom action messages are not intended. Their primary concerns are personal safety, family safety as well as the interruption of normal life activities.
3. Emergency medical services, fire fighters as well as policemen who have to care for the public within the circle of the disaster. Their concerns are resources to accomplish response and recovery, personal safety, family safety, pet safety.
4. Crisis management groups of a district or—in the case of an industrial accident—of a company which have to estimate the damage caused and then come to a decision about what information is to be published about the accident. Furthermore, they coordinate the emergency services, fire fighters and operation controllers on site. The latter inform citizens, teachers and school masters about what actions to take.
5. Public health and medical professionals who are involved in the disaster response. Their concerns refer to resources adequate to respond, personal safety, family safety and pet safety.
6. Healthcare professionals outside the response effort but who are next to professionals directly involved in the disaster situation. Their concerns are vicarious rehearsal of treatment recommendations, ability to respond to patients with appropriate information and access to treatment supplies if needed/wanted.
7. Civic leaders who are concerned with response and recovery resources, liability, leadership and quality of response and recovery planning and implementation. They have to think about opportunities for expressions of concern.
8. Media are interested in publishing information about the disaster. After receiving a press release, journalists of television channels or newspapers are sent to the site of an accident for reporting. They want to interview spokespersons and persons concerned. On the one hand, their reporting is important for publishing information about the danger of, for example, an industrial accident (dispersion of toxic substances); on the other hand, journalists might be a handicap for crisis management. In fact, media (e.g. television newscasts) may constrain disaster communication by publishing false reports or by handicapping the rescue services at the site of an accident.
9. Family members of victims and response workers are interested in the well-being of their acquaintances and relatives. Their concerns are personal safety, safety of victims and response workers.
10. Trade and industry have to calculate several business issues that are affected by the disaster (loss of revenue, liability, business interruption) and care for the protection of employees.
11. National community. Concerns: vicarious rehearsal, readiness efforts started
12. International community. Concerns: vicarious rehearsal, exploration of readiness

The DREAD-ED game is mainly concerned about communication within crisis management groups (point 4 in the above-mentioned list), but other audiences are also considered in the game. As we will see in the next paragraph, the public relation parameter is one of the main indicators of the disaster situation that players must consider when taking their decisions.

6.2   DREAD-ED Game Description

As mentioned at the beginning of the chapter, DREAD-ED is a rule-based game, and, as we will see next, its structure is very similar to a cardboard game (Fig. 6.2). A game of this type can soon become boring and repetitive, and for this reason, a great effort has been put into providing the game with powerful narrative elements. The game places players in a disaster situation that is described at the beginning of the game through a simulated TV news report that appears just before the game starts (see Fig. 6.3). Depending on the scenario selected by the trainer, the disaster can be an earthquake, a fire in a chemical plant or the flooding of a river. Players are member of a crisis management team that is dealing with an immediate and developing emergency. Each team member has a specific role with unique abilities and actions within the game. The information that is needed to mitigate the possible negative consequences of the situation is distributed among all game players in the form of resources assigned to single players. In order to successfully manage the situation, these resources must be managed among group members, and each player must effectively communicate her unique information to the others and appraise the many courses of action available before acting.

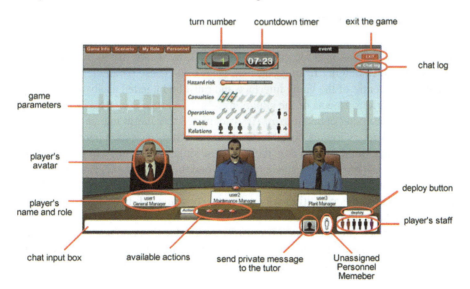

Fig. 6.2   DREAD-ED game interface

Fig. 6.3 Simulated TV news report shown at the beginning of the game

The DREAD-ED game interface, shown in Fig. 6.2, represents the visible layer of the game (representing what the user sees and acts upon) and will be described in the following sections.

6.2.1   Game Parameters

The emergency situation is represented in the game by means of four global parameters with values ranging from zero to six (Fig. 6.4). These parameters are always visible at the centre of the game interface and must be intended as abstract descriptions of the various aspects of the situation.

The first parameter called *hazard risk* is depicted as a thermometer. This parameter must be kept as low as possible to avoid casualties (see next parameter). The higher the value of the hazard risk, the worse the situation becomes. When the value of the hazard risk moves beyond six (goes beyond the end of the thermometer), it is reset to zero and the value of casualties increases by one point. This indicates that a potentially dangerous condition was not properly managed, triggering an incident that caused damages to people.

The parameter labelled *casualties* also consists of a six-point scale and is represented in the game as a series of stretchers. This parameter can only increase its value due to hazard risk overflow. It is not possible within the mechanics of the game to lower it. The casualties parameter is the main indicator of players' success in the game. Specifically, if the casualties parameter reaches six, and then the game

Fig. 6.4 Game parameters

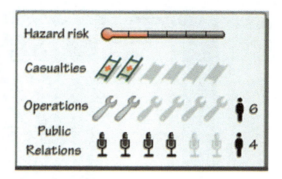

is over and players have lost. A team of players can be considered to be successful if they manage to keep the casualties parameter low for a long time during a game session.

The *Operations* parameter is represented in the game by a series of wrenches. The value of the Operations scale works in a different way with respect to the casualties and hazard risk parameters: the higher the value, the better the situation. As the value decreases, the situation becomes less positive. The Operations scale influences the deploy action (see below). The number of personnel objects required to carry out this action is dependent on the Operations parameter. Specifically, the number of personnel required increases as the Operations rating decreases and vice versa. This is represented by a small black man icon on the right side of the scale, with a number on the side. For example, when the operation is at level four, then five personnel objects are required to carry out a deployment.

The *Public Relations* parameter works in a similar way to the Operations parameter where a higher value represents a better situation. Public Relations is represented by a series of microphones. As for the Operations parameter, the level of this parameter affects the number of resources necessary to carry out some deployment actions which in this case are related to public relations.

6.2.2 Game Loops

The game is structured as a series of time-constrained turns (or game loops) that start with a multimedia content (video, audio file or picture) informing players that a new event occurred with negative consequences for the disaster situation (Fig. 6.5). During each game turn, players have a limited amount of time to evaluate the new situation expressed by the pattern of game parameters, communicate with each other and decide how to use their resources to perform the appropriate actions.

The duration of game turns is decided by the tutor during the creation of a game session and usually depends on the number of players (the more players the longer the length of each turn) and their training level.

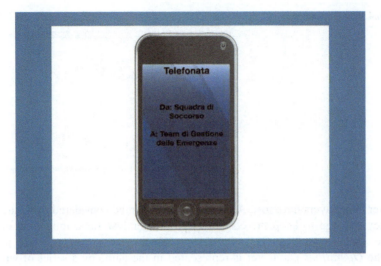

Fig. 6.5 Example of a multimedia content informing players about a new negative event at the beginning of a game loop. The screenshot from the Italian version shows a simulated phone call

Game loop duration can be set to become shorter and shorter as the game proceeds, creating a sense of time pressure. The current turn number and timer countdown is always visible on top of the game interface.

6.2.3   Avatars and Chat System

Each player in the game is represented by an avatar and can communicate with other players via a chat system. At the bottom of the game interface, there is a text input field that can be used to type in text messages. Pressing Enter makes the message visible to all players as a speech bubble on top of the head of the player avatar. The speech bubble disappears after a few seconds, but a copy of each message is permanently stored in the chat log window that can be visualised at any time during the game by pressing a little grey button at the top right of the game interface.

6.2.4   Resources

Most of the DREAD-ED game is about managing and exchanging personnel resources that can be deployed by each single player to carry out some operations. Each player has a group of people whom she is able to contact and coordinate with. The personnel resources available to each player are represented by six coloured men silhouettes on the bottom right of the game interface. Each player can only see her own personnel resources. Colours identify the area of competence of each staff member currently available to one player. There are nine types of personnel that can be used, but each player has only six staff members available at a time and cannot see another player's resources.

Players can affect the emergency situation by deploying teams of similarly skilled individuals (e.g. three medical staff). This has a direct effect in changing the emergency parameters. Depending on the type of personnel involved, the effect can be a reduction in the hazard risk, an increased operation or public relation level or a combination of these. The number of staff member required to perform a deployment action increases as the disaster situation worsens.

The unassigned personnel member (UPM), on the other hand, is a single-staff resource that all players can see and exchange with one of their six staff members. This is visible in the game interface as a coloured man on the left side of each player's personnel team.

6.2.5   Actions

Players can control the emergency situation by performing actions that allow them to influence the game parameters described above. The number of actions available in each game turn is limited to three. Actions are represented by three red lights positioned on the meeting table. Action lights are all turned on at the beginning of each game turn and progressively switch off as players perform actions.

As explained before, the most direct way of influencing the game parameters is through the *deployment action* that allows players to deploy teams of similarly skilled staff members. Since at the beginning of the game the six staff members are assigned randomly, it is improbable that players are ready for a deployment action. As noted earlier, players cannot see other players' resources, and so they are forced to communicate and share information. Therefore, during the game, players will try to communicate and exchange resources with each other in order to gather a uniform team of staff to carry out a deployment action.

The unassigned personnel member (UPM) is the only way players have to exchange members of their staff and costs two game actions. Suppose player 1 wants to obtain a medical staff member from the team of player 2. First, player 2 needs to exchange the medical staff member with the UPM to make it available to everyone. Then player 1 needs to exchange one of her unwanted staff members with the UPM (now a medical staff member).

The UPM can also be exchanged with a new one randomly drawn from a virtual pool of resources similarly to what happens in some card games. This provides a source of new resources but has a cost of one action and so cannot be repeated more than 3 times per game turn.

6.2.6 Roles

When creating a new game session, the tutor can assign one of six different available roles to each player. Playing a specific role in the game means having different powers when performing game actions. For example, some roles give extra effect when deploying a team of operations staff and then increasing the operation level of 4 instead of 2 levels. Some roles give an extra action per turn that can only be performed by the player who is playing that particular role. Some others give extra time in the next game loop. We will not go into details of each role here. What is important to highlight is that the game is designed so that the best group result is obtained if the right action is performed by the right role. Again, it is important that during the game, players communicate and share information with each other to fully express the potential of their own roles.

6.3 DREAD-ED Game Mechanics

The hidden layer of DREAD-ED is mainly constituted by the set of rules on which the game is based. Differently from other educational games described in this book, DREAD-ED's hidden layer is not based on artificial agents and it does not incorporate any scientific knowledge of some kind. The main purpose of DREAD-ED is to create a virtual setting in which some aspects of human communication and social interaction can emerge. As previously noted when describing the visible layer, the game design has been conceived to encourage communication among players and to improve resource management and decision-making under time pressure. So here we will describe the logic of the DREAD-ED game design, trying to highlight all these aspects.

6.3.1 Metaphor and Narrative

The structure of the DREAD-ED game is clearly the metaphor of a disaster situation. It is characterised by a degenerative process in which things can only get worse and the goal of the players is to minimise the negative consequences of new upcoming events. This is well exemplified by the fact that the casualties parameters, which is also the main indicator of team performance, can only increase, indicating that more and more damage and injured people are being pooled. The casualties parameter cannot be reduced but only kept under control by acting on the hazard risk, the value of which must be kept as low as possible.

From a training perspective, the goal is to mimic the dynamics involved in management of an emergency situation. Time pressure and chance play an important role in this context, and taking decisions often means striving for the least worst option. The countdown clock on top of the game interface signals that time is passing and that a bad event is next. Chance is present in many forms in the game mechanics.

Resources, for example, are assigned randomly at the beginning of the game, and the events at the beginning of each turn are generated in a random way, with unpredictable consequences for the situation.

The abstract structure of the game is "decorated" with a narrative structure that gives meaning to the parameters, resources and action that can be taken during the game. So, in the case of an earthquake disaster, the negative event producing more casualties at the beginning of a game loop can be described as an earth tremor of a certain scale or an explosion in a chemical plant.

6.3.2   Triggering Communication

Many elements of the DREAD-ED game mechanics have been designed to trigger communication among participants.

First of all, there is an inherent necessity to exchange information from the very beginning of the game. The random assignment of resources makes it very unlikely that one player is capable of performing any kind of action without communicating and exchanging resources with other players. Moreover, each player can see only her resources so what typically happens at the beginning of a game session is that players talk together in an attempt to have a picture of how resources are arranged across them.

Then as previously mentioned, each player—depending on her role—has particular characteristics, and some actions can have enhanced effect if performed by that role. It is important that each player is always aware of her role and must be able to effectively communicate it. So the very first reason for players necessarily communicating with each other is that it is a prerequisite for performing successful actions.

Usually, after players acquire a good understanding of how resources are distributed among them, they look at the disaster situation expressed by the game parameters and narrative description. Each participant then forms her own idea on how to proceed and what kind of action needs to be performed. At this point, everyone tries to explain their strategy and convince others that it is the best one. This is no more a simple exchange of information but involves something more. It is in this phase that group dynamics emerge and where the personality of players comes into place. However, this pattern of behaviour differs depending on the level of expertise of players. As we will see when discussing the results of the testing phase, experts first look at game parameters and then start looking for resources.

Once communication is established, there are no constraints on style and content. As explained previously, players can exchange public chat messages visible to all players as in a group discussion, but there are no filters or banned words (as in real life). All communications are available to the tutors for the debriefing phase. It has been pointed out many times in the past by DREAD-ED users that text messaging can hinder the spontaneity of the communication and it could sound strange that a game focusing on communication relies on a chat system instead of some kind of audio communication. This is partly due to technological constraints and limited budget at the time the game was developed. Sometimes, to overcome these limitations, the game has been played using third party VoIP solutions (e.g. Skype) to communicate in a faster and more spontaneous way. Whereas the text chat function may not be able to replicate all aspects of the communication typically available in a real-world emergency, this constraint itself increases the challenge of clear and organised communication.

6.4   DREAD-ED Evaluation Layer: Role of the Tutor

In DREAD-ED, the evaluation layer relies mainly on the work of a tutor/facilitator who plays a prominent role during all stages of a training session. A game session must be first prepared by the tutor deciding how many players, their roles in the game, the initial values of the game parameters and the number and length of game turns. After a game session is designed, the actual game can be planned by the tutor who will ask players to "meet" online at a certain time. The players and tutor first meet in the so-called pregame chat, and when all participants are ready, the tutor can launch the game session based on a previously created game session. So, a training game session cannot be started without a tutor.

Once in the game, the tutor has her own game interface which is slightly different from the interface of regular players as shown in Fig. 6.6.

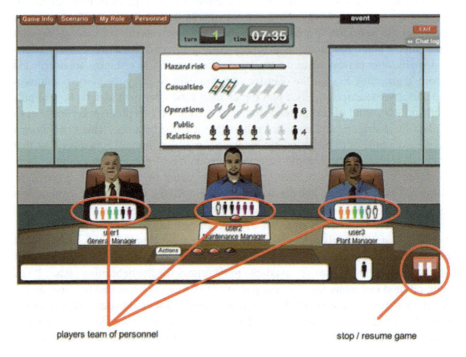

Fig. 6.6 Tutor game interface

The tutor can see all teams of personnel of other players to better supervise the game. She can stop the game for a while by pressing the stop/resume button on the bottom right. In this case, a message will inform all the players that the game has been paused. By pressing it again, the game will be resumed. When the game is paused, what actually happens is that the countdown timer stops.

The tutor can send private messages to each player by clicking on the avatars. As for the player interface, a private message window appears where the player can type private message text and send it. The player will receive the message with a pink background colour. The tutor can also send public messages to all other users in the same way as the player, by typing something in the input text box at the bottom of the interface and pressing Enter. The difference is that because the tutor does not have an avatar, the text bubble will be represented as a big rectangular square with a white background.

The tutor thus participates in the game as a backstage agent, an invisible entity, and can exchange messages with all other players, in both a private and public way. This is the first level of feedback that participants receive during the game. This kind of online feedback is very useful because learning becomes contextualised and learners can have real-time feedback on their emotional states.

The second level of feedback, which we call off-line feedback, is provided by tutor in the debriefing sections when the recorded game session is analysed in the presence of one or more players.

Every game session is automatically recorded on the server. The recording is not actually a video recording but an event recording. This means that only the main events of the game are captured. This includes chat messages, actions, game messages, starting turn, ending game turn, starting the game, game over, etc.

Once loaded, a recorded game session is similar to a real game session with the difference that the interface is from the point of view of the tutor (Fig. 6.7). On opening, the recorded session shows the first frame. A spin button (Fig. 6.8) makes it possible to step through all the successive frames. It is also possible to go straight to a certain frame by typing its number and pressing Enter.

All players participating can communicate through the floating chat window (Fig. 6.7). This is a rectangular frame that contains an input box (at the bottom) to type and send messages, a user list (on the right side) and a messages area where the messages of all users are displayed. The background of the window is semi-transparent in order to see what is happening behind. Two horizontal blue bars at the top and the bottom allow the players to move the chat window, positioning it where they prefer. Every player can manage her own window. This is to provide a basic mechanism of communication during the debriefing phase. Tutors can decide to use alternative ways of communication such as audio conference or a face-to-face meeting.

6.5   DREAD-ED as an Example of ICT and Rule-Based RPG

In this section, we will rapidly frame DREAD-ED within the taxonomy that we proposed in Chap. 3.

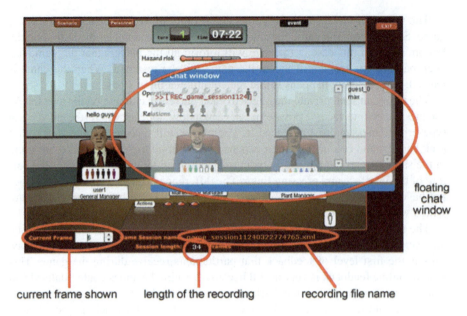

current frame shown   length of the recording   recording file name

Fig. 6.7 Debriefing phase using a recorded game session

Fig. 6.8 Frame selector   next frame

previous frame

From a technological viewpoint, it is in EduRPG where technologies allow for a virtual extension of the action space, the scene and of traditional psycho-pedagogic role-playing games to technologically enhanced stages, therefore ComTech.

Players interact by means of formal rules in an enhanced stage where the disaster narrative takes place.

From a psycho-pedagogical perspective, it is rule-based because the user is asked to perform abstract and strategic forms of decision-making. It is conceivable as a card game where the players interact, carrying out precise moves.

In the DREAD-ED game, the user plays with others, so it is a multiplayer game, the interaction of which is governed by formal rules. A fixed set of rules must be followed to reach specific goals by many OSAs (onstage agents). The main BSA (backstage agent) is the tutor who supervises all game phases.

We will now describe how this EduRPG was used as a training tool.

6.6   Testing DREAD-ED as a Training Tool

The DREAD-ED game was created in 2009, and since then it has been used and tested in several European projects. Some of the results of these tests have been published in scientific articles about training by means of serious games and virtual environments. Recently DREAD-ED became the starting point for a transfer of innovation project aimed at creating an innovative training methodology to teach decision-making to managers (DECIDE-IT project), and on this occasion, it was specifically tested as a training tool to teach decision-making in stressful situations. We will briefly summarise some of the results.

6.6.1   The First Testing of DREAD-ED

One of the first tests of the game occurred during the trial phase of the DREAD-ED project in 2009. The first version of the game was released in March, and the first testing occurred in June. After the first testing, some feedback was gathered by the partner in charge of the software development and was used to release the final version of the game that was used in the second trial phase which took place in December of the same year. The game was tested on two different samples which differed in the level of expertise in the field of emergency management.

The first sample was composed of members of the Academy for Crisis Management Emergency Planning and Civil Protection in Germany (five people with a mean age of 45 years). This academy is part of the Federal Office of Civil Protection and Emergency Aid of the German government. The academy has several tasks, including the training of crisis management units, research on new training simulations and analysis of disasters and development of prevention measures.

All five participants had a past experience as members of crisis units before becoming members of the academy. Therefore, this sample had high expertise in simulations and disaster training but was not very comfortable with gaming or virtual communication training.

On the other hand, the participants in the second sample (mean age: 24 years) were drawn from graduate and undergraduate media and computer science university courses. Subjects of this sample were very experienced with computer-mediated communication and virtual environments but had little or no experience in the training of soft skills or emergency management.

In both cases, the training phase was preceded by an introduction session in which the objectives of the study were described and the functioning of game was explained. Moreover, before the actual testing, all participants were left to familiarise themselves with the software in a series of free playing sessions. The actual training session (15 turns) lasted about two hours. Each participant had a personal computer and was able to communicate with the others only by using the text chat system of the game. After having played the game, the participants met with the tutor in a classroom for a debriefing session in which they discussed the main phases of the game, viewing the recorded game sessions. The results, which we will present below, are based on both the tutor's notes and the voice recordings of participant's responses during the feedback phase. As one would expect, the members of the academy outperformed the students. Although these participants did not have the same level of experience with computer-mediated communication as the sample of students, their style of communication was shorter and more efficient. Indeed, their decision-making process was based on efficient discussions made of short sentences. Moreover, the members of the academy were more focused on the parameters and their possible negative consequences, while the main concern of students was to collect personnel of the same colour without first analysing the values of the four parameters. With regard to the communication style, the tutors noted that students communicated more emotionally and exhibited more stress than people from the academy. This was confirmed by the students who admitted that they felt stressed during the game. The members of the academy, instead, reported that they "don't care about time pressure and the development of the crisis because we are used to these problems in reality" (male, 52 years). On the contrary, a 25-year female student stated that she became "impatient when the other users didn't respond to my comments. I wanted to scream 'hurry up'. It was really annoying". Academy members evaluated media inputs more positively than the students, because "these inputs are close to reality" (2 participants). These participants stated that the media inputs are important in order to obtain an understanding of the disaster situation: "The media events are a very interesting feature of the game, because they give us a better understanding of the whole disaster. For me, it's quite positive, that the game aspect became less important while the training aspect became more important" (male, 45 years). The students, on the other hand, reported that they did not focus on the media inputs, but rather on personnel and swapping of teams. "The media inputs constrained our discussion because we wanted to use the time between the turns to discuss the next steps" (female, 24 years). Another interesting difference between the two groups was their different ability in self-organisation. It must be recalled here that in the game there is no hierarchical organisation based on role and all participants were called with generic names (e.g. user1, user2, etc.). The academy evaluated the missing of specific coordination roles more positively than the students. "It was advantageous to leave out the roles due to the fact that we were all equal. This leads to a more democratised communication, in my opinion. It was not clear who of the guys had been my supervisor and this was quite good" (male, 40 years). As reported by tutors on the basis of game recording analyses, they showed a high capacity of self-organisation. The students, instead, missed the designation of a leader who assumed control over the situation. "Our performance would have been better if we had had a leader in our team who made the final decisions" (female, 23 years).

The comparison of emergency managers with naïve university students in terms of group performance clearly shows how possessing the target skills (effective communication and group decision-making) leads to success within the game, while poor use of these skills leads to failure within the game. Although the narrative of the game is rather specific, namely, disaster management, the game design itself could be helpful for training in general communicative behaviour based on a fictitious scenario.

6.6.2   DREAD-ED Potential as a Training Tool for Decision-Making

As mentioned at the beginning of this section, DREAD-ED has been chosen as the starting point in a European Transfer of Innovation (TOI) project called DECIDE-IT which is aimed at developing a new game-based methodology for training for decision-making under stress in the business environment. The adaptation of DREAD-ED for the new scope required two key aspects: context and target group. The context changed from emergency and disaster management to business decision-making. The target group changed from the crisis management group, which was quite heterogeneous comprising people from different institutions and competences to a group of managers of the same company, possibly with different roles and skills. Both aspects played a major role in the adaptation process. It is interesting here to describe the results of the pilot test conducted during that project in which managers of three big companies tested DREAD-ED as a potential tool in training for decision-making. This allows us to highlight strengths and weakness in comparison with other EduTechRPGs introduced in the other chapters of this book.

Fifteen managers from three big companies in Italy, Spain and Romania participated in the pilot test. Much data came from the focus groups in which participants were asked open-ended questions about their experience with the game and recommendation for future improvements and adaptation. The interactive nature of the focus groups made it possible to gather a richer amount of information than could have been obtained from a standard questionnaire. Participants had different levels of experience with digital training tools, from no experience at all to some experience with standard e-learning environments. As can be deduced from the small number of participants involved, the goal of this study was to gather qualitative information about the game. So the results will be presented in verbal form. In particular, we will summarise what managers said about the game in relation to some key area of group decision-making.

By playing the game, each participant experimented an interesting way of achieving *self-awareness*. The multiplayer feature of the game, together with the fast-paced interaction needed during the sessions, gave the players much feedback about their behaviour during a short space of time. This is quite unusual in real-life situations where experiences and interactions are spread out over a longer period. This enhanced effect of short feedback loops highlighted the self-knowledge potential of this kind of multiplayer game.

The game mechanics of DREAD-ED have been designed to force players to communicate and exchange information. Triggering *team communication* has been recognised as one of the most notable characteristics of DREAD-ED and has been ranked by participants at the top of the list of the skills needed in a group decision-making context. Moreover, team communication was evaluated as crucial for effective group performance.

One aspect experienced during the game was the efficacy of a far-sighted strategy in some circumstances, in other words long-term thinking. In the trials, the players realised after a few game sessions that a more forward-looking strategy was necessary to prevent the effects of unpredictable events on the game parameters. This revealed the potential of the game in teaching long-term thinking and planning.

The *teamwork style* of each participant also played an important role in group performance. Being aware of one's teamwork style has been identified as an important step towards a successful group decision-making process.

Multitasking was reported by players as a specific ability required in real-life working contexts. The DREAD-ED game design did not put particular emphasis on that, and the participants suggested it as a potential development in a new version of the game.

During the pilot test game sessions, some players adopted a rather autonomous behaviour contrasting with the collaborative strategy adopted by the rest of the group. This raised a discussion about the right balance between the *level of autonomy and cooperation*.

Risk management is an interesting skill that can be improved by means of a serious game. Training in risk management can be very difficult in the real working setting because of the potential negative consequences and high cost associated with it. On the contrary, serious games and simulation can provide a safe context in which to assess and train risk management skills.

Decisiveness is another quality that can be safely practised and improved in a game experience. Some negative consequences of not being decisive, both as an individual and as a group, can be learnt in the serious game context.

A key aspect of decision-making experienced during the pilot tests was the need for strong *organisational skills*. After a few game sessions, players realised that having a good organisation allowed the group to react quickly to upcoming events. One of the first things that started to become structured after a few game sessions was the communication pattern, given the importance in the game of quickly exchanging information about resources and roles.

Chapter 7
Learn to Lead: An Educational Game for Leaders to Be

In this chapter, we will describe Learn to Lead (L2L), an educational role-playing game to train about leadership. It has been realised within the framework of the Leonardo Lifelong Learning programme, supported by the European Commission (502903-LLP-1-2009-1-IT-LEONARDO-LMP). It involved a consortium of 6 partners from France, Italy, Spain and the United Kingdom with different expertise related to training in soft skills, cognitive technologies and artificial intelligence application to education, the use of ICT to affect behaviour, "serious gaming" and design of online games. Here, we will describe the design process that gave birth to Learn to Lead.

7.1 The Soft Skill to Be Transferred: Leadership

As shown in methodological Chap. 3, the starting point of the EduRPG design process is the soft skill to be transferred: in this case study, it is leadership.

This issue has raised much interest since ancient times, consider, for example, Plato and Plutarch writings about politics, through *The Prince* by Machiavelli to present-day literature which proposes many theoretical frameworks that address leadership in social sciences (e.g. psychology, anthropology, sociology), in humanities (e.g. history and philosophy), in professional and applied fields of study (e.g. management and education) and in organisational studies. Even if in this section we do not intend to propose an extensive review about this multifaceted theme, let us quickly outline the main theories about leadership, especially the theory that Learn to Lead is built on the full-range theory (Avolio and Bass, 1991).

© Springer International Publishing Switzerland 2017
E. Dell'Aquila et al., *Educational Games for Soft-Skills Training in Digital Environments*, Advances in Game-Based Learning, DOI 10.1007/978-3-319-06311-9_7

7.1.1   Theories About Leadership

Many definitions have been proposed about leadership: Chemers (1998) defines it as "a process of social influence in which a person can enlist the aid and support of others in the accomplishment of a common task"; Myers and Smith (2000) see it as a process thanks to which some people in a group mobilise or lead other group components to help them in reaching their objectives; Hollander (1985) underlines the aspect of influencing other people and assuming relevant roles in a hierarchy; Moscovici (1976) also introduces the theme of power, connecting it to influence.

Many approaches have also been adopted to deal with this theme. The first one is the *behavioural* one that considers leadership as a set of behaviours.

Some research indicates that specific behaviours can predict one's emergence as a leader, and these behaviours belong to two categories, task- and member-focused behaviour (Bales 1950; Taggar et al. 1999; Bales and Slater 1955).

Lewin, Lippitt and White (1939) recognise three leadership styles, democratic, authoritarian and laissez-faire, whereas Likert (1961) identifies two main leadership styles, job-centred and employee-centred.

The behavioural approach does not consider that even if some leadership traits and behaviours are commonly observed across a number of studies, a huge amount of evidence suggests that persons who are leaders in one situation may not necessarily be leaders in other *situations*. This idea has been adopted by Tannenbaum and Schmidt (1958) with the situational leadership continuum and Fiedler (1964) who proposes the contingency model. Tannenbaum and Schmidt sketch two dimensions to explain leadership patterns: boss-centred leadership and subordinate-centred leadership and underline that situational elements can orient style choice such as organisational culture and collaborators' features.

Blake et al. (1962) conceived a managerial grid which signals the link between leadership and change, proposing two dimensions, concern for people and concern for results, and leaders can choose between obtaining five leadership styles: impoverished management, country club management, authority compliance management, team management and middle of the road management.

The stress upon change led to conceiving transformational leadership, a style of leadership where the leader has the very relevant role in identifying the needed change and promoting it by creating a vision to guide the change that inspires group members. This concept, initially introduced by Burns (1978), was developed by Bass (1991) who proposed one of the most well-known *transformational leadership* models that has rapidly become the preferred approach in leadership theory.

This model is based on four elements, the four "Is": idealised influence, inspirational motivation, intellectual stimulation and individual consideration.

Idealised influence describes leaders who are exemplary role models for followers. They can be trusted and respected by followers to make good decisions.

Inspirational motivation refers to leaders who motivate followers to commit to the organisational vision. They encourage team spirit to reach ambitious goals.

Intellectual stimulation is the element regarding leaders who encourage innovation and creativity through challenging the normal beliefs or views of a group. They are able to promote critical thinking and problem solving.

Individual consideration is attributed to leaders who act as coaches and advisors to followers. They encourage followers to reach goals that help both the followers and the organisation.

This reflection on transformational leadership was the prerequisite for the comprehensive *full-range theory* (Bass 1991; Avolio and Bass 1991) that includes in a unique model transformational and non-transformational leadership styles, namely, transactional and laissez-faire. This theory, as hinted before, has received great attention in research and organisational contexts and has been extensively applied to dynamics in small groups.

As described above, *transformational* leaders are proactive; they raise followers' awareness in order to achieve better performance level and to reach collective interests, thus helping followers to achieve extraordinary goals. They exploit the four "Is", empathising with individual needs, making interpersonal connections with followers; encouraging continuous development and growth of followers (individualised consideration); stimulating followers' imagination and thinking outside of the box, challenging the old ways of doing things, looking for better ways to do things and favouring risk taking for potential gains (intellectual stimulation); inspiring, connecting individual and organisational needs (inspirational motivation); and demonstrating an inclusive vision, exhibiting commitment and persistence in pursuing objectives, expressing confidence in organisation vision and developing trust and confidence among followers (idealised influence).

Transformational leadership does not replace transactional leadership, but it augments it in achieving leader, associate, group and organisation objectives. Although transformational leaders can be transactional when appropriate, transactional leadership often leads to low-performance or non-significant change.

In fact *transactional* leaders focus on standard organisational goal fulfilment and on setting objectives while monitoring outcomes by followers. They apply constructive transactions, make clear the expectations of outcomes and rewards, actively monitor employees' progress and provide supportive feedback.

Transactional leadership is also known as managerial leadership because it is focused primarily on the role of supervision, organisation and group performance; it is a style of leadership in which the leader promotes compliance of her followers through both rewards and punishments, not looking to change the future but to make things work the way they are. Leaders with transactional leadership style pay attention to followers' work in order to find faults and deviations, but do not promote followers' fulfilment. This type of leadership is effective in many situation such as crisis and emergency situations, as well as for projects that need to be carried out in a specific way.

A *Laissez-faire leader* avoids making decisions, abdicates responsibility and does not use her authority; this is therefore considered the most passive and ineffective form of leadership because the leader does not respond to situations and problems systematically and avoids specifying agreements, clarifying expectations and providing goals and standards to be achieved by followers who do not give any feedback or support. This leadership style has a negative effect on desired outcomes.

Within the full-range theory (FRL) model, three important outcomes can be achieved as an effect of leadership: extra effort, group effectiveness and satisfaction. Moreover, this model can be easily integrated with other models or theories pointing to personal characteristics of the leader, such as McClelland's motives (McClelland 1987), as well as to situational factors and their interaction with leaders and followers characteristics.

A key point in the FRL model is that every leader displays each style to some extent in different moments and contexts and has to govern changes within team dynamics. Effective team leaders can manage these dynamics in ways that help the team to meet its objectives.

7.2   Learn to Lead Game Description

Leadership is a key competence that can be acquired through adequate training which is crucial in every kind of organisation. In SMEs, non-profit organisations and work groups (Yukl and Van Fleet 1992; Storey 2004), many training programmes are devoted to teaching effective leadership.

In these programmes, role playing is often introduced (e.g. see Yukl 2002; Yukl and Van Fleet 1992 describing exercises and role-playing activities), because it is a fruitful training method. In recent years, Agboola Sogunro (2004) analysed the efficacy of role-playing pedagogy in training leaders. In this chapter, it is underlined that the traditional pedagogical techniques of training leadership lack the potentiality to teach quickly the critical thinking and interpersonal skills that are relevant for effective leadership transfer. Traditional pedagogical techniques are less dynamic, less learner-centred and less experiential. On the contrary, the role-playing method induces participants to quick understanding, and it has the potential to transform theoretical concepts into an experiential format. It is concluded that role playing has presented itself as one of the most promising training techniques for leadership.

In the context of Learn to Lead (L2L) project, the case study we are dealing with in this chapter, the goal was to design, implement and test a novel, online approach to training in team leadership, suitable for use in SMEs, small government offices, NGOs, etc. The training provided by L2L is based on an online game (Di Ferdinando et al. 2015; Gigliotta et al. 2014). In the game, each learner manages a simulated team of employees (e.g. a team of workers in a bank agency, a post office or a local government office) which competes against other teams to maximise its objectives (e.g. profit, volume of services delivered, customer satisfaction). The L2L research project was funded by the European Agency for Education, Culture and Audiovisuals.

Let us now follow, step by step, the design process of L2L as we have outlined in Chapter 3, starting from the visible layer.

Fig. 7.1 The firm's office where the game takes place at level 1

Learn to Lead (L2L) is a digital virtual role-playing setting, an online serious game where a user, acting as a leader, learns by governing a team of artificial agents, followers. It is a point-and-click online game in a 2D environment which takes place in a firm's office, which can be inferred from some decorative elements: desks, chairs, PCs and furniture, stacks of paper, etc. (Fig. 7.1). This physical setting varies across all game levels, becoming increasingly attractive as the player advances in her career.

In L2L, the RPG dyad is made up of the player acting as a leader and the follower, an artificial agent in a hierarchical interaction. This game is therefore single player because one human player is involved in the game at a time: we have a single human OSA (on-stage agent) interacting with one or more (up to 10) artificial agents.

Each learner manages a simulated team of agents representing, for example, a team of workers in a bank agency, post office or local government office. This simulated team competes against other teams to maximise its objectives (e.g. profit, volume of services delivered, customer satisfaction).

It represents a digital virtual role-playing setting where the user acts as a leader and can affect the behaviour of artificial agents by manipulating psychological and environmental variables.

What narrative does L2L rely on? The player is hired to work in a large corporation. The CEO has picked the player out as a future leader and has arranged for her to follow a programme of on-the-job training, where she will learn all that is necessary to become a great leader. The game is played across a number of levels. Across those levels, the player will lead teams in a number of different corporation departments, from catering to research and development.

During the game, the player has two goals:

1. Ensure that the company runs efficiently and productively.
2. Ensure that her followers develop appropriately, as outlined by the full-range leadership (FRL) model (see above).

The third outcome of leadership, satisfaction of followers, has not been implemented, because this requires a value judgement, something that is not feasible yet in a game context.

Day-to-day running of the department involves dealing with jobs that have specified deadlines and workloads and assigning staff to work on those jobs. The basic challenge is to ensure that followers finish all jobs in time. The leader is in control of assigning followers to work on jobs.

With a smart management, it is possible to finish a respectable number of jobs within their deadlines. However, leadership involves more than management, and if the player uses a strategy for developing her followers, she will gain an effective advantage in the game. In fact, each follower has an ability level and a motivation level: these two variables combined define the amount of work the follower can do in any given day.

The player can consider her followers' workloads, abilities, stress levels and personalities in assigning players to jobs, a typical management task, and this will improve performance with respect to a leader who limits herself to standard managing. In this optic, the player has the option of running workshops, organising team-building events, performing one-to-one coaching, getting involved in day-to-day work, sending memos, proposing training courses, giving lectures about poor performance, delivering evocative speeches at staff meetings, etc., thus helping her followers' development in ability and intrinsic motivation. More developed followers can complete more jobs; thus spending time on developing staff helps the player to reach both efficiency and development, the goals that players should be aiming for, according to the FRL model. Followers experience stress, which affects their ability to work. Stress can be caused by demanding more work of the follower than their level of ability allows and is also naturally increased by imminent deadlines. The work has also a competitive side: the player must compete with other groups to achieve goals: manage workloads, stress and employees' motivations in order to increase profit, create new services and improve customer satisfaction. The system allows users to experiment different approaches before competing with other players.

At the beginning of the game, the player is explicitly introduced in the narrative with a specific description of what the game will be like (Fig. 7.2 reports a part of the message from the CEO at level 1).

The player has different learning chances during the game, and it is possible to follow tutor's suggestions or study the provided materials besides playing the game.

L2L is divided into 5 levels, which are increasingly complex and articulated (Fig. 7.3). At the beginning of each level, reading material, tutorials and mini-games are provided about some theories and principles of leadership, such as path goal theory and full-range leadership (see the first section for details).

After the player has completed the theoretical part, she is able to practice it in a safe environment (the player is not fired if she fails), where the level of acquired knowledge is evaluated. In order to surpass a level, it is necessary to study leadership theory and apply it to the virtual environment as required by the game.

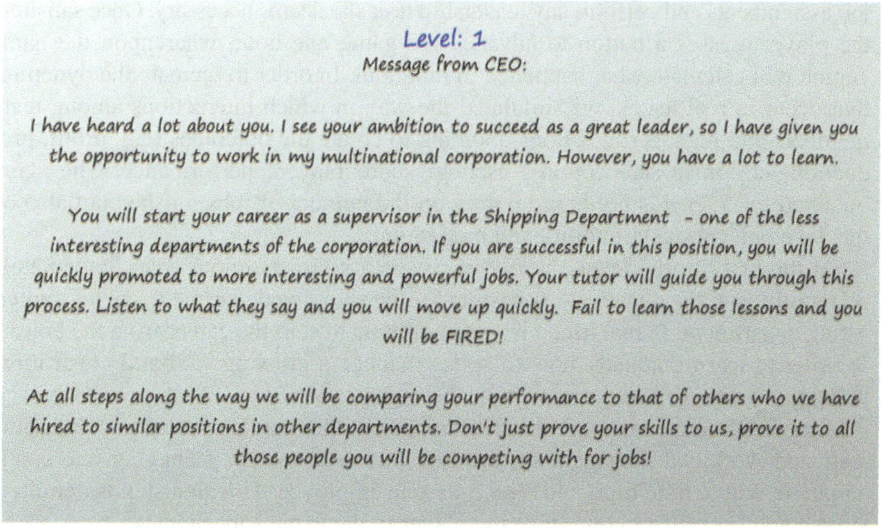

Level: 1
Message from CEO:

I have heard a lot about you. I see your ambition to succeed as a great leader, so I have given you the opportunity to work in my multinational corporation. However, you have a lot to learn.

You will start your career as a supervisor in the Shipping Department – one of the less interesting departments of the corporation. If you are successful in this position, you will be quickly promoted to more interesting and powerful jobs. Your tutor will guide you through this process. Listen to what they say and you will move up quickly. Fail to learn those lessons and you will be FIRED!

At all steps along the way we will be comparing your performance to that of others who we have hired to similar positions in other departments. Don't just prove your skills to us, prove it to all those people you will be competing with for jobs!

Fig. 7.2 Message from CEO at level 1 that introduces the player in the narrative

Fig. 7.3 Game scenario at level 5

Each level or tutorial is played across a number of weeks; each made up of five days and 8 hours per day. During each hour of that week, the player will have the opportunity to view the performance and progress of her team, make any changes to job assignments and perform any leadership task she deems necessary. Once satisfied, the player presses a button to advance the game one hour, whereupon the game engine will calculate what happened in that hour. In order to recreate the dynamics that occur in real teams, we simulated the way in which interactions among team members and managerial actions combine to create the outcomes (e.g. profit, production, customer satisfaction), used to score players performance. The score obtained for a level is not based purely on the number of jobs finished but also on the development of staff ability and motivation.

At the first tutorial level, the player covers a non-prestigious role: immediately on recruitment, the player is responsible for the shipping department, the least interesting department. In real life, it is quite common to start the career from the bottom in order to learn gradually how to better manage a growing staff and cover more prestigious roles of greater impact for the organisation.

After reading the instructions which represent the first theoretical part regarding staff and workload management, the first task is assigned: managing one single shipment with a time limit and with only one employee. This first step is definitely simple and is needed to introduce the player to the game's mechanics.

As the game proceeds, levels become more difficult, roles more complex and ambitious, the workload increases and personnel is larger and characterised by subjective and distinctive peculiarities: each single employee has her own personality, strengths and weaknesses, and the leader has to take these features into account to efficiently monitor the task and achieve it within the pre-established time limit.

The team is formed by brilliant and motivated employees as well as by agents who need to be motivated. In order to achieve newer and more complex goals, it is therefore necessary to manage employees' workload and tasks, without ignoring their stress and satisfaction levels.

Verifications or weekly checks must be run to support and provide feedback, rewarding or punishing for the job done.

Players who complete the game have performed an effective training session, learning about leadership theories on the theoretical side and useful psychosocial dynamics to manage teams, motivational strategies, the importance of human resources management, workloads and respecting deadlines on the practical side. These strategies constitute important expertise for the manager as well as for the employee.

Learning to recognise and deal with stress, divide workloads, set goals for each employee based on strengths and weaknesses and how to collaborate with employees undoubtedly improves working performance in real life.

7.3   Learn to Lead Game Mechanics

The L2L hidden layer contains the game engine which defines the game operation. In game space terms, L2L is a logical structure in which an asynchronous interaction takes place between the leader and the followers.

Playing is based on a turn-based structure so that players always have an unlimited amount of time to consider their actions carefully and consult reference material about FRL if necessary before making a decision.

The player acts on the work environment and team dynamics by setting the work plan of each follower.

There are three main types of interaction between the leader and the followers:

- Stimulation: the leader stimulates a follower, by talking to her or in some other way.
- Punishment: the leader gives a punishment to a follower.
- Reward: the leader gives a reward to a follower.

Leader choices influence the psychology of followers, in particular their motivation, and thus their contribution to the team.

These are the moves that change the problem state. The player interacts with followers and artificial agents with their own psychological state that the player has to monitor carefully if she wants to advance successfully in the game.

The psychology of followers (artificial) is composed of three variables taken from the cited McClelland theory:

(a) Achievement: followers have a disposition for excellence in performance, a continuing concern for doing better all the time. This motive concerns achieving excellence through one's individual efforts.
(b) Affiliation: followers have a concern for establishing, maintaining and restoring close personal relationships with others.
(c) Power: followers have a concern for acquiring status and having an impact on others. High power motivation induces highly competitive behaviour.

It is important to stress that followers with different personalities should be managed in a different way to obtain optimal results.

Each follower is represented by an animated character sitting at the desk and typing in front of a computer. The character is animated and conveys important information about followers' internal states. Typing speed is proportional to follower motivation and the face changes from normal to stressed when the stress level approaches a dangerous level.

Each follower has to accomplish a task allocated by the leader, in different kinds of environments. The maximum workload is determined by two variables: ability and motivation. The player/leader can vary those variables through a series of possible actions (e.g. by sending the follower to a training course or by stressing them). Leaders obtain a score on the basis of the motivational and skill development of the followers. The team spends 30 days in accomplishing a task, and each day a measure of outcome is computed, based on each follower. Each day the leader can make just one action with respect to a selected follower. At the end of the specified time lapse, the final work outcome is computed and a leadership profile is created.

The idea underlying this general framework is that in some given conditions, the leader (i.e. the player) has to take some decision about one or more followers (moves).

The player must feel that her actions do have reliable and realistic consequences on followers' behaviour and development.

The teamwork is constituted by a set of artificial agents, as already noted, and each agent is controlled by a neural network implementing a specific theory about leadership.

To represent the FRL theory in the L2L hidden layer, an agent-based approach joined with connectionist networks was adopted: every agent is modelled by a connectionist network or controlled by a human being. In particular, the user takes the role of one of the agents, more specifically the leader, whereas the followers are artificial players, artificial agents. In other words, a combination of two techniques was used: agent-based modelling and artificial neural networks in order to combine social and cognitive factors (Sun 2006). Agent-based simulations are extensively used in many branches of natural and social sciences to study complex phenomena that are not safely reducible to a set of mathematical equations (Borshev and Filippov 2004) and that typically emerge from the interaction among individual entities. For more details about agent-based modelling in EduRPG, see Chap. 3.

When the leader agent (i.e. the user) takes decisions about one or more followers (the moves), these decisions are encoded in the follower's network as a combination of inputs. Based on the inputs received from the leader, and those from the environment, the agent's internal states will change and influence her contribution to the team job.

The followers' network represents the way the FRL theory is implemented inside the L2L game. (Fig. 7.4).

An agent-based simulation of the FRL theory allows us to create an infinite number of specific contexts in which knowledge can be experienced and practised. Artificial agents are essentially input-output systems with an internal state that changes over time depending on the external input and some internal variables. Every follower has some internal variables that affect the final contribution in getting through the jobs assigned. The most relevant to the FRL theory is motivation. The motivation level is affected by three subcomponents: intrinsic, reward and fear. The intrinsic component models the dynamics of intrinsic motivation, and it is related to the transformational leadership style, while the reward and fear components model extrinsic motivation and are related to the transactional leadership style. What differs among the three is time dynamics and specifically their decay. For example, the intrinsic component has a slower decay than reward and fear, but can be activated only by appropriate leader behaviours (typically pertaining transformational style).

The stress variable is linked to some external inputs such as social interaction, workload and deadlines. It affects the contribution and is an important aspect to keep under control during the game. Stress also has a modulator effect on leader motivation-oriented behaviour. Personality and ability try to capture what the FRL theory says about individual consideration. Ability level is linked to follower performance. Personality is conceived as a modulator for leader behaviour so that the same leader action may have a different impact on followers with different personalities. On the contrary, the leader who aims at raising the motivation of the team as high as possible needs to perform some individualised considerations.

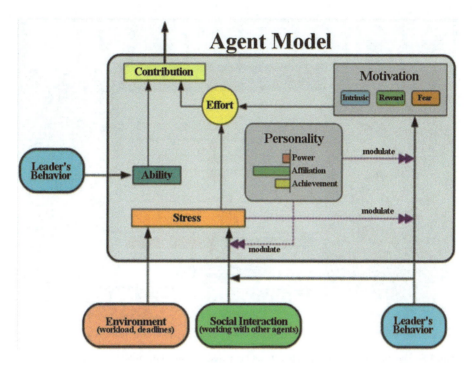

Fig. 7.4 L2L Game model. According to FRL theory, each agent's behaviour is guided by a set of external variables such as leader's behaviour, workload, etc., and a set of internal variables related to personality, motivation, ability and stress. The agent model in L2L has been implemented exploiting neural nets

7.4 Learn to Lead Evaluation Layer

In L2L, the evaluation layer is implemented in different ways. First of all, we have the feedback that is provided immediately throughout the game by the described computerised model to each action performed by the player.

In fact, the decisions the player takes influence the effectiveness and efficacy of teamwork and, thanks to the response of the virtual platform, the player will be able to immediately realise the mistakes made in the game and fix them by replaying the same level. The interface has a warning button that appears when there are some hints the player can read to improve her performance.

The player can monitor the psychology of followers, in particular their level of stress, motivation and satisfaction. Moreover, the player can monitor some data about her management, workload management, ability and personality management, leadership style and conflict management. At the end of each level or tutorial, the player receives a comment regarding the way in which she has played, some overall statistics and, in case of failure, feedback about this failure. At the end of the entire level, the player receives a general comment about her progress. Let us show in more detail what kind of feedback the player receives from her team by statistics, graphs (Figs. 7.5 and 7.6) and follower information and animations (Fig. 7.7).

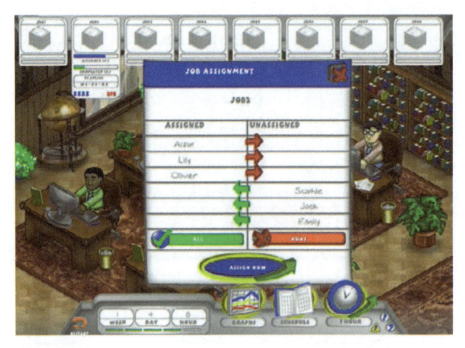

Fig. 7.5 The player can monitor job state and can assign jobs to the members of her team based on their ability

Fig. 7.6 Graphs representing the varying levels of stress and motivation of team members

Fig. 7.7 Monitoring the psychological state of followers

Figure 7.5 shows the job panel. It indicates the job name, amount of workload to complete (pile of paper), assignment and amount of completed work. It also makes other information available, such as the deadline, the follower this work is assigned to and if there is a conflict among followers.

Figure 7.6 shows the graph panel. On the horizontal axis, we have the single hour in a week, whereas the vertical axis reports motivation and stress level.

In Fig. 7.7, it can be seen that, in the interface, a single hour can be highlighted by a transparent square: this indicates that a leader has performed a task that permits connecting the internal states of followers and leader actions.

Figure 7.7 displays the follower panel. This appears when the mouse is placed on the animated follower character and indicates the following information: ability (skill level—a more skilled follower works more than a less skilled one), workload (how a follower is working with respect to her ability), personality (achievement, affiliation or power), motivation (motivated followers are more efficient; motivation increases when the leader takes care of her followers), stress level (stressed followers are less efficient than unstressed ones, and stress increases with too much work, approaching deadlines and when there is conflict with others), and satisfaction (reflects the judgement on the leader; more motivated followers tend to be more satisfied, but this also depends on their motivation).

The reward offered is to see one's social status within the company increasing.

The player will be able to compare herself with other players, evaluating both their score and their strategies when playing simultaneously.

Moreover, we have a contribution to learning analytics from the BSAs (backstage agents) ruled by intelligent tutor systems: interactions between followers and the leader are monitored by an artificial evaluator which, based on the user's behaviour and decisions, creates a user's profile, according to the leadership literature. In particular, the profile is built on FRL theory, its concepts and its structures.

During the game, because many important aspects of player leadership are involved, at the end of each level or tutorial, a summary of these aspects is proposed. In more detail, the following information is shown:

- Workload management: shows how the followers are busy doing their work; this affects stress level.
- Followers' stress.
- Followers' motivation.
- Leadership style: gives the player feedback about the style used when performing a leadership task—transactional, transformational or mixed.
- Ability management: shows how the player took into account follower ability when performing leadership tasks.
- Personality management: shows how the player took into account follower personality when performing leadership tasks.
- Conflict management: shows how the player took into account follower personality to avoid conflicts in the team while assigning jobs to members.

L2L also provides another feedback through a ranking among players, as is common in mainstream games, in order to compare users' performances. This ranking can be tuned according to different levels and sublevels and a podium pictures the best players (Fig. 7.8).

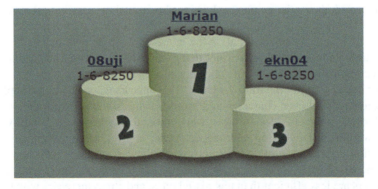

Fig. 7.8 The L2L podium. It shows the best players in ranking for a specified level and sublevel

7.5 Learn to Lead as an Example of Computational and Rule-Based RPG

In this section, we will frame L2L within the taxonomy we have proposed in Chapter 3, highlight values and shortfalls and describe how the game was tested during the project.

From a technological viewpoint, it is an EduRPG whose technologies build an "artificial" micro-world based on simulated formal models about psychological issues, therefore *SimTech*. Because of these features, it was feasible to foresee an artificial player interacting with the human user. Artificial intelligence therefore plays a central role in this game. It resides inside followers who are artificial agents controlled by a connectionist network and between followers whose dynamics are modelled using a computational approach. L2L exploits technologies to build an "artificial" micro-world based on computer-simulated, formal models about leadership. From a psycho-pedagogical perspective, it is *Rule-based* because the user is asked to perform abstract and strategic forms of decision-making.

In the L2L game, the user plays individually, so we have a single player interacting with artificial OSAs (on-stage agents), whose behaviour is based on formal rules. A fixed set of rules must be followed to also reach specific learning goals by different moves. The BSAs (back-stage agents) implement learning analytics, collect data about user interaction (behaviour and decisions) and create a user's profile, according to the leadership literature.

It is worth stressing that the L2L engine is modelled according to a specific leadership theory: the action exchange is modelled according to FRL theory, so, while training the user about the selected soft skill, she also learns about the theory itself. The game becomes a role-playing setting where the user can test what she has learnt in theory, intervening on specific variables. In fact, the human behaviour is properly modelled in this agents' simulator, and learners can observe how agents' behaviour changes according to a set of psychological variables. In other words, observation takes place in an artificial scenario rather than in a natural context. This is surely a distinctive feature of this kind of game compared with the other EduTechRPGs we have described in the previous chapters that do not exploit this kind of game as a powerful way to implement psychological theory and thus allow its effective acquisition.

Leaders, along with technical skills related to their area of business, must have competencies in people management, resource management and organisation. Effective leadership is obviously strongly demanded in an organisational context, but becoming a good leader is not an easy task: it is necessary to study psychology intensively, attend very costly MBA courses and observe human behaviour as much as possible. This latter solution is very time and resource demanding but can be potentially the best way in the education of leaders.

L2L offers a clear advantage instead: programmes about leadership are very expensive and time demanding, whereas playing L2L can constitute an effective training that is much less expensive and can be managed individually and autonomously.

Although L2L could not substitute lengthy professional training, it is an implementation of psychological theory in an agents' simulator and can therefore be used as a powerful supporting tool in teaching how to successfully manage a group of followers (Di Ferdinando et al. 2011).

L2L's particular game design facilitates the adaptation of the game to different work environments. It is fit for training in many different context, from SMEs to no-profit organisation up to public administration. Moreover, using the game is effective either in self-teaching or tutored conditions, thus making it a very versatile tool.

However, the game also has some drawbacks. The game is currently based on a quite limited model with a team of 11 individuals: 1 leader and 10 followers. The user takes the role of the leader, whereas the followers are controlled by a connectionist network. In the future, the goal is to increase model complexity: the user will be able to play in different ways: she will eventually take the role of one of the agents, not only the leader role; she will be able to be just a visitor, observing model dynamics, thus becoming a backstage agent; she will also be able to observe her behaviour on another level, by training an artificial BOT to imitate her behaviour style and then observe BOT behaviour and decisions.

This first version of L2L has been used in several European vocational courses about leadership and human resources management. Beside the game, a Moodle portal has been released for managing the learning path on leadership skills in a self-learning mode.

The L2L project lasted for 24 months. The work began with a study of user requirements, followed by the definition of the training methodology, definition of the underlying team dynamics model, "game design" and implementation of the necessary software components.

The project starting point was the need analysis, which included a review of literature review in order to provide an extensive overview of current practices in leadership training in Europe and especially in Italy, Spain and France, interviewing stakeholders and process owners (human resources managers, training managers, policy makers) among the different targets of the L2L project, namely, SMEs, small government offices and NGOs. Questionnaire and interview templates were designed with the purpose of collecting data in Italy, Spain and France; user needs collection from the target groups and potential beneficiaries who were involved in the pilot trials in order to understand and collect their learning strategies and needs was made; analysis of current practice in leadership training, a benchmark analysis of the state of the art of the training in leadership and team management were run.

The next step was to define the training methodology used in the pilot study and in large-scale trials.

As foreseen in the proposal, L2L reached three targets through the trials: individual users, who took advantage from the development of the L2L training programme, small organisations and NGOs, and private and public organisations.

In the first and second target group, the beneficiaries accessed the L2L training programme for free and improved competencies, given that it is usually very rare for them to get involved. In the case of the third target group, employees were involved in a personalised training programme, again for free, since the experimentation foresaw two modes: a blended tutored programme and an online programme.

The direct beneficiaries of the L2L project were in total 100 people, 28 taking part in the pilot study and 72 in the large-scale trials. A total of about 2500 hours of training were delivered if we consider the face-to-face training, the online platform with its exercises and hands-on and finally practice with the L2L game.

With the L2L game having been presented during exhibits and festivals, the estimated number of users is larger than that reported, as is the number of training hours delivered. Moreover, two training companies belonging to the partnership used the game to offer tutor-supported training to their commercial customers.

In parallel with this effort, the partnership provided free access to the stand-alone (non-tutored) version of the game, through servers maintained by one of the partners. These servers have been maintained in operation so far. Large-scale use of the system has been encouraged by using online and traditional media (e.g. online publicity, use of popular "social networking sites", distribution of CDs via newspapers and magazines, etc.).

With regard to indirect beneficiaries, the number of user who had used the L2L game at least once by the end of the project was more than 1000, with the number of visitors to the website continuously increasing, especially after release of the final version of the game.

To conclude this chapter, we would like to report some data about a pilot study that was conducted using the L2L game on a sample of university students.

Participants were enrolled in the third year of the "Psychological Science and Techniques" bachelor's degree and attending a "Work and Organisational Psychology" course, which covered leadership and motivational topics. In terms of gender, 57 % of the participants were female (16 out of 26 subjects) and the remaining 43 % were male. The average age was 21. Participants were randomly divided into two different samples with an equal number assigned to two different conditions.

A structured questionnaire was used to obtain data on possessed knowledge regarding the topics covered in both L2L and the course simultaneously, namely, a structured questionnaire formed by 30 multiple choice questions. It was used during both the pretreatment and post-treatment phases.

The first group attended the Work and Organisational Psychology course and had access to additional theoretical material: they followed a classic learning method. In this group, the treatment did not differ from classic lecture teaching.

The second group accessed the L2L virtual online platform. In this group, participants also had simultaneous access to the Work and Organisational Psychology course. The didactic material and the guidelines to access L2L were delivered on the Facebook social network, where a "virtual focus group" emerged. The participants within both groups were free to choose whether to use the theoretical material and the virtual platform or not.

Moreover, a game satisfaction questionnaire was administered to the second group. The questionnaire comprised 11 items which, using a Likert scale, permitted expression of users' opinion about some aspects of L2L.

At the end of the questionnaire, two open-ended questions were inserted in order to evaluate the strengths and the weaknesses of L2L, according to participants.

Data analysis was run both on quantitative and qualitative data and indicated that knowledge about leadership was noticeably increased in both conditions, and in the group that played with the game, the knowledge level was more homogenously distributed.

Moreover, it can be said that L2L had a great reception, with quite high overall satisfaction among participants. It was not only important for them to combine an EduRPG with the Work and Organisational Psychology course in order to improve their knowledge, but it was equally important to consider the learning process from a different point of view. Subjects showed great interest in technological tools to enhance learning, particularly L2L. The game pushed them to "go further", to "experiment new strategies in order to solve problems", and it kept their attention and motivation high. Combining game practice with theory greatly involved the participants, who felt "safe" and free to learn and experiment. Moreover, immediate feedback allowed the users to focus on their mistakes while playing the game.

Conclusions

The advent of e-learning technologies has been challenging the acquisition and the development of many traditional competences, as well as professional practices. The book has presented some empirical and theoretical experiences in using new technology in education and professional training practices, through the interdisciplinary nature of experiences gained via a variety of European projects based both on software development and soft skills training practice.

The rationale of the book is based on how to apply and migrate psycho-pedagogical role-playing methodology to educational online role-playing games for soft skills training. We have drawn attention to the fact that soft skills are interpersonal and intrapersonal dimensions and involve a combination of emotional, behavioural and cognitive components that are expression of how people know and manage themselves, as well as their relationships with others. We have seen soft skills are in everyday use, and essentially defined them as behaviourally based competencies, complementary to hard skills and goal-directed behaviours. We have affirmed that soft can be learnt and developed through personal experience, interaction, disclosure, feedback and reflection, as they can be exercised within "learning-by-doing" environments, enabling opportunities for practice and ongoing and constructive feedback. We have therefore explored the reasons for researching training on soft skills in the application of the role-play methodologies and principles in digital virtual environments.

We have also outlined similarities and differences between traditional settings and new technologies for role-play implementation, as interactive training method proved especially effective at enhancing transversal soft competences such as cognitive, affective and skill-based outcomes of interpersonal skills. Therefore, role play can be considered as the crucial method to realise the link between training of soft skills and enhancement of individuals' relationships with others.

Chapter 3 of the book is particularly relevant from a methodological point of view, as we have outlined a tentative of a general taxonomy for describing the approaches used by the authors to design the so-called Technologically Enhanced

© Springer International Publishing Switzerland 2017

E. Dell'Aquila et al., *Educational Games for Soft-Skills Training in Digital Environments*, Advances in Game-Based Learning, DOI 10.1007/978-3-319-06311-9

Educational Role-Playing Game for soft skills training (EduTechRPG) along with different EU-funded projects resulting in two main dimensions: psycho-pedagogical and technological. The first dimension refers to the psycho-pedagogical background for the learning approach adopted and identifies two main categories of EduTechRPGs: drama based and rule based. The technological dimension explains how the psycho-pedagogical approach can be exploited through the use of Communication Technology, allowing a virtual extension of traditional face-to-face psychodramatic mechanism and experiences, and Simulation Technology systems, producing "artificial" worlds based on computer-simulated, formal models about the social and psychological phenomena intended to investigate. The dedicated chapters to the EU projects have been aimed to support both the choice of the most appropriate game/scenarios to implement in a specific domain of practice, as well as the design of tailored role-playing games for different training purposes and context of application.

In particular, we have seen how drama-based EduRPGs represented by Eutopia and ENACT respectively multiplayer and single-player systems allow users to experience direct involvement with the learning objectives through the dramatisation of personal aspects by acting out roles and competences within a virtual environment that augment players' sense of self-disclosure though this is does not seem to be related to the identification with the character to be enacted. On the other hand, we have seen how rule-based EduRPGs such as DREAD-ED and Learn to Lead, respectively, multiplayers and single-player environments, result crucial for assessing, learning and practicing skills involved in logical reasoning and thinking critically performances. We have also highlighted how a set of formal rules and guidance for users to follow embedded in the game is functional to learner's performance in this direction.

Either the psycho-pedagogical or technological dimensions should not be considered as mutually exclusive, but rather as complementary aspects. Indeed, the ability of integrating such dimensions in a single game implementation contributes to the design of an educational tool to create meaningful learning.

The experiences of the EU projects confirmed the value of using information technology as a tool placed in the hands of a trainer for the development of controlled ad hoc learning exercises, rather than being considered a simple replacement for trainers and learners.

With regard to the EduTechRPGs such as the software developed on the Eutopia platform (Eutopia-MT, Sisine, Sinapsi, Proactive and S-Cube), we have seen how dynamics of the game play depend on learners, rather than on any form of artificial intelligence; therefore, participants are offered a far richer, more open, learning experience than would have been possible, if they had to interact with an artificial trainer or computer-controlled players. There is certainly a gain in terms of learners' potential richness and dynamics of their learning experience. This fact has induced professionals to consider the advantages of introducing game technology less dependent on the supervision of real facilitators. On the other hand, although trainers consider those kinds of online role plays methodologically as effective as traditional face-to-face experiences, the critical element is related to the trainers/teachers' role in managing the online role plays. In fact the disadvantages of this method are represented by high cost and time consumption in organising and managing the complexity on the virtual learning scenarios, as well as interactions among participants. Experienced trainers in order to achieve an appropriate level of training experience must be skilled in mastering different tasks at once. In addition to the role-play management and facilitation (scripting, role assignment, feedbacks and debriefing), trainers need to ensure a correct use of the tool and its features in order to support the accomplishment of training needs. They require to be trained on the use of the tool to get the most of the experience, as they feel that for effective learning to take place, familiarity with the methodology and the tool is essential. Those limits have induced the authors to consider the advantages of introducing game technology less dependent on the supervision of real facilitators. We have seen as for rule-based EduRPGs (Learn to Lead and DREAD-ED) and in the case of Drama-Simtech EduRPG as ENACT that when the complexity of the dynamics and interactions between players is limited by the rule of the game to a certain number of actions, the responsibility of the trainer for managing emergent dynamics is certainly reduced. Therefore, the assessment and observation of learning experience is less subjected to the influence and interpretation of many other potential interfering variables.

This brings us to another aspect of our experience that is the appropriateness of the use of EduTechRPGs. The methods you decide to use depend largely on the skills to be developed, as well as resources and the time allocated for achieving the learning objectives. For instance, if our learning objective is a job-related training from the cognitive domain, and involves people who attend training within their work hours, the training approach is more likely to be SimTech and rule-based EduTechRPG. The educational resources and learning path that learners follow is easily accessible at anytime from anywhere and even more manageable, as it does not depend necessarily on the presence of a real trainer or teacher. Yet, when the priority is making players to rapidly learn and asses specific skills or behaviours (e.g. problem solving or decision-making requiring immediate actions), rule-based EduTechRPG is the most ideal methodology. The set of formal rules and interactions to be followed to achieve the relevant learning objectives are embedded in the software and do not require a constant presence of experienced external guidance. This can drive the player to a stable training outcome more rapidly than in open dynamic situations. Therefore, the advantage of this method lies in the fact that is very low cost, as after an initial phase to familiarise users with the system, it can be used without the guidance of a trainer, as the system is self-regulated and enables learners to achieve objectives rapidly and at the same time strongly as it is based on experience, observation, reflection about themselves and in relation with the social environment. Conversely if the soft competences we mean to develop are more related with aspects of emotional awareness, self-assessment and self-confidence, we think that a situation methodologically closer to the traditional role play is the most appropriated. For all the software presented, we can acknowledge that the strengths to provide the software with authoring systems have been valued an extremely beneficial aspect as it allows trainers to rapidly develop their own scenarios, personalising their work for specific target populations with specific learning needs. In the last analysis, what the different EduTechRPG presented offers is a way for learners to practice and improve their ability to interact with others, in the area of soft skills. Seen in this light, there are many possible and potential areas of application. We have seen as in management training, education, personal development, business, organisational and training contexts an increasing emphasis on soft skills such as interpersonal communication, negotiation and decision-making.

In whatever area we work—and we are not limited to e-learning—we see computers, not as a replacement for human beings but as tools. Computers are tools that can be shaped through the collaboration of game designers, teachers, trainers, pedagogists to reach more learners, improve their learning and make "human agents" more effective. Yet we believe that experiences from Eutopia-MT, Proactive, S-Cube, ENACT, Learn to Lead and DREAD-ED have shown that they can make a real contribution to the development of soft skills.

References

Admiraal, W., Wubbels, T., & Pilot, A. (1999). College teaching in legal education: Teaching method, students' time-on-task, and achievement. *Research in Higher Education, 40*(6), 687–704.

Agboola Sogunro, O. (2004). Efficacy of role-playing pedagogy in training leaders: Some reflections. *Journal of Management Development, 23*(4), 355–371.

Aldrich, C. (2005). *Learning by doing: A comprehensive guide to simulations, computer games, and pedagogy in e-learning and other educational experiences.* San Francisco, CA: Wiley.

Aldrich, C. (2009). Virtual worlds, simulations, and games for education: A unifying view. *Innovate: Journal of Online education, 5*(5), n5.

Altschuler, C. M., & Picon, W. J. (1980). The social living class – a model for the use of sociodrama in the classroom. *Group Psychotherapy Psychodrama & Sociometry, 33,* 162–169.

Amory, A., Naicker, K., Vincent, J., & Adams, C. (1999). The use of computer games as an educational tool: Identification of appropriate game types and game elements. *British Journal of Educational Technology, 30*(4), 311–321.

Aronson, E. & Carlsmith, J. M. (1968). Experimentation in social psychology. *The Handbook of Social Psychology, 2*(2), 1–79.

Ashton, F. (1994). The other managers' competencies. *Training Officer, 30*(1), 15–16.

Avolio, B. J., & Bass, B. M. (1991). *Full-range training of leadership. Manual.* Binghamton, NY: Bass/Avolio & Associates.

Aylett, R., Figueiredo, R., Louchart, S., Dias, J., & Paiva, A. (2006). Making it up as you go along–improvising stories for pedagogical purposes. In *International Workshop on Intelligent Virtual Agents* (pp. 304–315). Berlin/Heidelberg: Springer.

Bacolod, M., Blum, B. S., & Strange, W. C. (2009). Urban interactions: Soft skills versus specialization. *Journal of Economic Geography, 9*(2), 227–262.

Bales, R. F. (1950). *Interaction process analysis: A method for the study of small groups.* Chicago, IL: University of Chicago Press.

Bales, R. F., & Slater, P. E. (1955). Role differentiation in small decision-making groups. In T. Parsons & P. E. Slater (Eds.), *The family, socialization and interaction processes* (pp. 259–306). Glencoe, IL: Free Press.

Bandura, A. (1977). Self-efficacy: Toward a unifying theory of behavioral change. *Psychological Review, 84*(2), 191.

Bandura, A. (1986). *Social foundations of thought and action* (pp. 5–107). Englewood Cliffs, NJ: Prentice Hall.

© Springer International Publishing Switzerland 2017
E. Dell'Aquila et al., *Educational Games for Soft-Skills Training in Digital Environments*, Advances in Game-Based Learning,
DOI 10.1007/978-3-319-06311-9

Bar-On, R. (1992). The development of a concept and test of psychological well-being. Unpublished manuscript. Tel Aviv: Reuven Bar-On.

Bar-On, R. (1997). *EQ-i BarOn emotional quotient inventory: A measure of emotional intelligence: Technical manual*. Toronto, ON: Multi-Health Systems.

Baron, R., & Markman, G. (2003). Beyond social capital: The role of entrepreneurs. Social competence in their financial success. *Journal of Business Venturing, 18*, 41–60.

Barthes, R. (1977). *Introduction to the structural analysis of narratives*. London: Fontana.

Bass, B. M. (1991). From transactional to transformational leadership: Learning to share the vision. *Organizational Dynamics, 18*(3), 19–31.

Bass, B. M., & Avolio, B. J. (1990). Developing transformational leadership: 1992 and beyond. *Journal of European Industrial Training, 14*(5).

Bedwell, W. L., Salas, E., & Fiore, S. M. (2011). Developing the 21st century (and beyond) workforce: A review of interpersonal skills & measurement strategies. In *National Research Council: Assessment of 21st century skills*. Washington, DC: The National Academies.

Bell, M. (2001). Online role-play: Anonymity, engagement and risk. *Educational Media International, 38*(4), 251–260.

Betts, K., Lewis, M., Dressler, A., & Svensson, L. (2009). Optimizing learning simulation to support a quinary career development model. *Asia-Pacific Journal of Cooperative Education, 10*(2), 99–119.

Bienkowski, M., Feng, M., & Means, B. (2012). *Enhancing teaching and learning through educational data mining and learning analytics*. Washington, DC: USA Department of Education: Office of Educational Technology. Retrieved April 11, 2012, from http://ctl2.sri.com/eframe/wp-content/uploads/2012/04/EDM-LA-Brief-Draft_4_10_12c.pdf

Bjork, S., & Holopainen, J. (2006). Games and design patterns. In *The game design reader* (pp. 410–437). Cambridge, MA: MIT.

Black, R. A. (1978). Psychodrama in classroom teaching. *Improving College and University Teaching, 26*(2), 118–120.

Blake, R. R., Mouton, J. S., & Bidwell, A. C. (1962). The managerial grid. *Advanced Management Office Executive, 1*(9), 12–15. Society for Advancement of Management and National Office Management Association, 1962–1963, New York.

Blatner, A. (1995). Drama in education as mental hygiene: A child psychiatrist's perspective. *Youth Theatre Journal, 9*(1), 92–96.

Blatner, A. (1996). *Acting-in: Practical applications of psychodramatic methods* (3rd ed.). New York, NY: Springer.

Blatner, A. (2000). *Foundation of psychodrama: History, theory and practice* (4th ed.). New York, NY: Springer.

Blatner, A. (2006). Enacting the new academy: Sociodrama as a powerful tool in higher education. *ReVision: A Journal of Consciousness & Transformation, 28*, 30–36.

Boggs, J. G., Mickel, A. E., & Holtom, B. C. (2007). Experiential learning through interactive drama: An alternative to student role plays. *Journal of Management Education, 31*(6), 832–858.

Bollens, J. C., & Marshall, D. R. (1973). *A guide to participation: Field work, role playing cases, and other forms*. Englewood Cliffs, NJ: Prentice-Hall.

Bonabeau, E. (2002). Agent-based modelling: Methods and techniques for simulating human systems. *Proceedings of the National Academy of Sciences, 99*(suppl 3), 7280–7287.

Bond, K. (2002). Perceptions of anonymity in a language learning text chat room. *CALL-EJ Online, 3*(2).

Bonk, C. J., & Graham, C. R. (2012). *The handbook of blended learning: Global perspectives, local designs*. Pfeiffer, San Francisco, CA.

Borshev, A., & Filippov, A. (2004). From system dynamics and discrete event to practical agent based modeling: Reasons, techniques, tools. In *Proceedings of the 22nd International Conference of the System Dynamics Society*.

Boyatzis, R. E. (1973). Affiliation motivation: A review and a new perspective. In D. C. McClelland & R. S. Steele (Eds.), *Human motivation: A book of readings* (pp. 252–276). Morristown, NJ: General Learning Press.

Boyatzis, R. E. (1982). *The competent manager: A model for effective performance*. New York, NY: Wiley.

Boyatzis, R. E. (2007). *Competencies in the 21st century*. Cleveland, OH: Case Western Reserve University.

Boyatzis, R. E., & Goleman, D. (2001). *The emotional competence inventory: University edition.*

Boyatzis, R. E., Goleman, D., & Acquisition, H. (2007). *Emotional and social competency inventory.* Boston, MA: Hay Group Social intelligence.

Boyatzis, R. E., Goleman, D., & Rhee, K. (2000). Clustering competence in emotional intelligence: Insights from the Emotional Competence Inventory (ECI)s. In R. Bar-On & J. D. A. Parker (Eds.), *Handbook of emotional intelligence* (pp. 343–362). San Francisco, CA: Jossey-Bass.

Boyatzis, R. E., Stubbs, E. C., & Taylor, S. N. (2002). Learning cognitive and emotional intelligence competencies through graduate management education. *Academy of Management Learning & Education, 1*(2), 150–162.

Boyce, G., Williams, S., Kelly, A., & Yee, H. (2001). Fostering deep and elaborative learning and generic (soft) skill development: The strategic use of case studies in accounting education. *Accounting Education, 10*(1), 37–60.

Bray, D. W., Campbell, R. J., & Grant, D. L. (1979). *Formative years in business: A long-term AT & T study of managerial lives*. New York: RE Krieger Publishing Company.

Bredemeier, M. E., & Greenblat, C. S. (1981). The educational effectiveness of simulation games: A synthesis of findings. *Simulation and Games, 12*(3), 307–332.

Brehmer, B., & Dörner, D. (1993). Experiments with computer-simulated microworlds: Escaping both the narrow straits of the laboratory and the deep blue sea of the field study. *Computers in Human Behavior, 9*(2), 171–184.

Bromberg, W. (1958). Acting and acting out. *American Journal of Psychotherapy, 12*(2), 264.

Brown, H. J. (2014). *Videogames and education*. New York: Routledge.

Brown, A. L., Weinert, F. E., & Kluwe, R. H. (1987). *Metacognition, motivation, and understanding*. Hillsdale, NJ: Lawrence Erlbaum Association.

Bruckman, A. (1999). Can educational be fun? In *Game developer's conference,* San Jose, CA.

Bull, M. (2006). *Balance: Unlocking performance in social enterprise*. Manchester: Centre for Enterpris., Manchester, Metropolitan University.

Burgoon, J. K., & Dunbar, N. E. (2000). An interactionist perspective on dominance-submission: Interpersonal dominance as a dynamic, situationally contingent social skill. *Communications Monographs, 67*(1), 96–121.

Burns, J. M. (1978). *Leadership*. New York, NY: Harper Collins Publisher.

Carbonell, J. (1970). AI in CAI: An artificial intelligence approach to computer aided instruction. *Science, 167*, 190–202.

Carr, D., Oliver, M., & Burn, A. (2010). Learning, teaching and ambiguity in virtual worlds. In *Researching learning in virtual worlds* (pp. 17–30). London: Springer.

Casti, J. L. (1997). *Would-be worlds: How simulation is changing the frontiers of science*. New York, NY: Wiley.

Catania, A. C. (1998). *Learning*. Englewoods Cliffs, NJ: Prentice Hall.

Caudron, S. (1999). The hard case for soft skills. *Workforce, 78*(7), 60–64.

Chemers, M. M. (1998). *An integrative theory of leadership, 1997*. Santa Cruz, CA: Library of the Congress.

Chia, M. Y. (2005). Job offers of multi-national accounting firms: The effects of emotional intelligence, extra-curricular activities, and academic performance. *Accounting Education, 14*(1), 75–93.

Clark, T. (1995). *Managing consultants: Consultancy as the management of impressions*. McGraw-Hill International.

Conati, C. (2009). Intelligent tutoring systems: New challenges and directions. In: *IJCAI* (Vol. 9).

Connelly, M. S., Gilbert, J. A., Zaccaro, S. J., Threlfall, K., Marks, M. A., & Mumford, M. D. (2000). Exploring the relationship of leadership skills and knowledge to leader performance. *The Leadership Quarterly, 11*(1), 65–86.

Conrad, C. A. (1999). *Soft skills and the minority work force*. Washington, DC: Joint Center for Political and Economic Studies.

Coppard, L. C., & Goodman, F. L. (Eds.). (1979). *Urban gaming/simulation: A handbook for educators and trainers*. Ann Arbor, MI: School of Education, University of Michigan.

Core, M., Traum, D., Lane, H. C., Swartout, W., Gratch, J., Van Lent, M., & Marsella, S. (2006). Teaching negotiation skills through practice and reflection with virtual humans. *Simulation, 82*(11), 685–701.

Covey, S. R. (1989). *The 7 habits of highly effective people*. New York, NY: Free Press.

Csikszentmihalyi, M. (2014). Intrinsic motivation and effective teaching. In *Applications of flow in human development and education* (pp. 173–187). Dordrecht, The Netherlands: Springer.

Davies, M. H. (1976). The origins and practice of psychodrama. *The British Journal of Psychiatry, 129*(3), 201–206.

Dawson, R. (1990). But soft, we are observed: The skills of observation. *Simulation/Games for Learning, 20*(4), 360–367.

de Freitas, S. (2008). Serious virtual worlds. *A scoping guide. JISC e-Learning Programme, The Joint Information Systems Committee (JISC), UK.*

de Freitas, S., & Griffiths, M. (2007). Online gaming as an educational tool in learning and training. *British Journal of Educational Technology, 38*(3), 535–537.

de Freitas, S., & Oliver, M. (2006). How can exploratory learning with games and simulations within the curriculum be most effectively evaluated? *Computers & Education, 46*(3), 249–264.

De Gloria, A., Bellotti, F., & Berta, R. (2014). Serious games for education and training. *International Journal of Serious Games, 1*(1).

Dede, C., & Swigger, K. (1988). The evolution of instructional design principles for intelligent computer-assisted instruction. *Journal of Instructional Development, 11*(1), 15–22.

Deepa, S., & Seth, M. (2013). Do soft skills matter? Implications for educators based on recruiters' perspective. Implications for educators based on recruiters' perspective. *The IUP Journal of Soft Skills, 7*(1), 7–20.

Delli Veneri, A., & Miglino, O. (Eds.). (2010). Teaching mediation. Eutopia-mt: conflict management through digital worlds. Napoli: Fridericiana Editrice Universitaria.

Dewey, J. (1938). *Experience and education*. New York, NY: Collier Macmillan.

Dewey, J. (1966). *Democracy and education*. New York, NY: The Free Press.

Dhaliwal, K., Gillies, M., O'Connor, J., Oldroyd, A., Robertson, D., & Zhang, L. (2007). eDrama: Facilitating online role-play using emotionally expressive characters. In P. Olivier & R. Aylett (Eds.), *Proceedings of the AISB workshop on language, speech and gesture for expressive characters*. Leeds, UK: The Society for the Study of Artificial Intelligence and the Simulation of Behaviour.

Di Ferdinando, A. (2002). Simulare la mente. In A. Borghi & T. Iachini (Eds.), *Scienze della mente* (pp. 121–139). Bologna: Il Mulino.

Di Ferdinando, A., Schembri, M., Nigrelli, M. L., Linehan, C., & Miglino, O. (2011). Learn to lead a web based game to teach leadership theories in vocational courses. In: *Games and creativity in education and training*. Naples, Italy: Fridericiana Editrice Universitaria.

Di Ferdinando, A., Schembri, M., Ponticorvo, M., & Miglino, O. (2015). Agent based modelling to build serious games: The learn to lead game. In J. M. Ferrández Vicente, J. R. Álvarez-Sánchez, F. de la Paz López, F. J. Toledo-Moreo & H. Adeli (Eds.), *Bioinspired computation in artificial systems* (pp. 349–358). Springer, Switzerland.

Dickey, M. D. (2007). Game design and learning: A conjectural analysis of how massively multiple online role-playing games (MMORPGs) foster intrinsic motivation. *Educational Technology Research and Development, 55*(3), 253–273.

Dondlinger, M. J. (2007). Educational video game design: A review of the literature. *Journal of Applied Educational Technology, 4*(1), 21–31.

Dreyfus, H. L., & Dreyfus, S. E. (1989). *Why computers may never think like people* (pp. 125–143). MIT, MA, USA.

Dryden, W., & Constantinou, D. (2004). *Assertiveness step by step*. London: Sheldon Press.

Dubois, D. D. (Ed.). (1998). *The competency casebook: Twelve studies in competency-based performance improvement*. Human Resource Development, Press, Inc, MA, USA.

Duffy, F. D., Gordon, G. H., Whelan, G., Cole-Kelly, K., & Frankel, R. (2004). Assessing competence in communication and interpersonal skills: The Kalamazoo II report. *Academic Medicine, 79*(6), 495–507.

Dziabenko, O., Pivec, M., Bouras, C., Igglesis, V., Kapoulas, V., & Misedakis, I. (2003). A web-based game for supporting game-based learning. In *Proceedings of 4th Annual European GAME-ON Conference (GAME-ON 2003)*, London, UK, 19–21 November 2003, pp. 111–118.

Ebner, N., & Kovach, K. K. (2011). Simulation 2.0: The resurrection. *Re-thinking Negotiation Teaching Series 2*, 245.

Egenfeldt-Nielsen, S. (2005). *Beyond edutainment exploring the educational potential of computer games.*

Egenfeldt-Nielsen, S. (2007). Third generation educational use of computer games. *Journal of Educational Multimedia and Hypermedia, 16*(3), 263–281.

Ferber, J. (1999). *Multi-agent systems: An introduction to distributed artificial intelligence* (Vol. 1). Reading: Addison-Wesley.

Ferster, C. B., & Skinner, B. F. (1957). *Schedules of reinforcement.*

Fiedler, F. (1964). A Contingency model of leadership effectiveness. In L. Berkowitz (1969). *Advances in experimental social psychology*(Vol. 1). New York, NY: Academic.

Filsecker, M., & Hickey, D. T. (2014). A multilevel analysis of the effects of external rewards on elementary students' motivation, engagement and learning in an educational game. *Computers & Education, 75*, 136–148.

Fingarette, H. (1969). Self-deception. In *Studies in philosophical psychology*. New York, NY: RF Holland.

Fisher, R., & Ury, U. (1981). *Getting to yes: Negotiating agreement without giving in*. New York, NY: Penguin Books.

Fleming Seay, A., & Kraut, R. E. (2007). Project massive: Self-regulation and problematic use of online gaming. In *Proceedings of the SIGCHI Conference on Human Factors in Computing Systems* (pp. 829–838). New York, NY: ACM.

Foster, J. L., Lachman, A. C., & Mason, R. M. (1980). Verstehen, cognition, and the impact of political simulations. *Simulation & Games, 11*, 223–241.

Frank, A. I. (2007). Entrepreneurship and enterprise skills: A missing element of planning education? *Planning, Practice and Research, 22*(4), 635–648.

Fredrick, W. C., & Walberg, H. J. (1980). Learning as a function of time. *The Journal of Educational Research, 73*(4), 183–194.

Freedman, R. (2000). What is an intelligent tutoring system? *Intelligence, 11*(3), 15–16.

Gaffney, C., Dagger, D., & Wade, V. (2009). Soft skill simulation authoring tools: A state of the art survey. WWW 2008, April 21–25, 2008, Beijing.

Gao, F., Noh, J. M., & Koehler, M. J. (2009). Comparing role-playing activities in second life and face-to-face environments. *Journal of Interactive Learning Research, 20*(4), 423–443.

Gardner, H. (1983). *Frames of mind: The theory of multiple intelligences*. New York, NY: Basic Books.

Gardner, H. (1993a). *Multiple intelligences: The theory in practice*. New York, NY: Basic Books.

Gardner, H. (1993b). *Creating Minds*. New York, NY: Basic Books.

Gardner, H. (2006). *Multiple intelligences: New horizons*. New York, NY: Basic Books. 1st ed. 1993.

Gardner, M., Gánem-Gutiérrez, A., Scott, J., Horan, B., & Callaghan, V. I. C. (2011). Immersive education spaces using Open Wonderland from pedagogy through to practice. In *Multi-user virtual environments for the classroom: Practical approaches to teaching in virtual worlds* (pp. 190–205).

Gardner, H., & Hatch, T. (1989). Educational implications of the theory of multiple intelligences. *Educational Researcher, 18*(8), 4–10.

Gardner, L., & Stough, C. (2002). Examining the relationship between leadership and emotional intelligence in senior level managers. *Leadership & Organization Development Journal, 23*(2), 68–78.

Garris, R., Ahlers, R., & Driskell, J. E. (2002). Games, motivation, and learning: A research and practice model. *Simulation & Gaming, 33*(4), 441–467.

Garrison, D. R., & Anderson, T. (2003). *E-learning in the 21st century: A framework for research and practice*. New York, NY: Routledge/Falmer.

Gee, J. P. (2003). What video games have to teach us about learning and literacy. *Computers in Entertainment (CIE), 1*(1), 20–20.

Gee, J. P. (2005). Why video games are good for your soul: Pleasure and learning. Australia: Common Ground PTY Ltd.

Gee, J. P., & Shaffer D. W. (2010). *Looking where the light is bad: Video games and the future of assessment* (Epistemic Games Group Working Paper No. 2010-02). Madison, WI: University of Wisconsin-Madison. Available at www.epistemicgames.org.

Giessen, H. W. (2015). Serious games effects: An overview. *Procedia-Social and Behavioral Sciences, 174,* 2240–2244.

Gigliotta, O., Miglino, O., Schembri, M., & Di Ferdinando, A. (2014). Building up serious games with an artificial life approach: Two case studies. In S. Cagnoni, M. Mirolli, & M. Villani (Eds.), *Evolution, complexity and artificial life* (pp. 149–158). London: Springer.

Gillard, S. (2009). Soft skills and technical expertise of effective project managers. *Issues in Informing Science and Information Technology, 6*(2009), 723–729.

Gillies, M., & Ballin, D. (2004). Integrating autonomous behavior and user control for believable agents. In *Proceedings of the Third International Joint Conference on Autonomous Agents and Multiagent Systems-Volume 1* (pp. 336–343). IEEE Computer Society.

Giloth, R. P. (2000). Learning from the field: Economic growth and work-force development in the 1990s. *Economic Development Quarterly, 14*(4), 340–359.

Glandon, N. D. (1978). The hidden curriculum in simulations: Some implications of our application. In *Perspectives on academic gaming and simulation* (Vol. 3, pp. 125–130). Aberdeen, Scotland: Kogan Page.

Goldberg, L. R. (1993). The structure of phenotypic personality traits. *American Psychologist, 48,* 26–34.

Goleman, D. (1995). *Emotional intelligence: Why it can matter.* New York, NY: Bantham.

Goleman, D. (1998). *Working with emotional intelligence.* Chicago, IL: Random House LLC.

Goleman, D., Boyatzis, R., & Mckee, A. (2002). *Primal leadership: Realising the power of emotional intelligence.* Boston: Harvard Business School Press.

Gonzalez, M. A. G., Abu Kasim, N. H., & Naimie, Z. (2013). Soft skills and dental education. *European Journal of Dental Education, 17*(2), 73–82.

Gratch, J., DeVault, D., Lucas, G. M., & Marsella, S. (2015). Negotiation as a challenge problem for virtual humans. In *Intelligent virtual agents* (pp. 201–215). Springer, Switzerland.

Gregory, S., & Masters, Y. (2012). Real thinking with virtual hats: A role-playing activity for preservice teachers in second life. *Australasian Journal of Educational Technology, 28*(3), 420–440.

Habgood, M. P. J., & Ainsworth, S. E. (2011). Motivating children to learn effectively: Exploring the value of intrinsic integration in educational games. *Journal of the Learning Sciences, 20*(2), 169–206.

Haferkamp, N., Kraemer, N., Linehan, C., & Schembri, M. (2011). Training disaster communication by means of serious games in virtual environments. *Entertainment Computing, 2*(2), 81–88.

Hankinson, H. (1987). The cognitive and affective learning effects of debriefing after a simulation game (Doctoral dissertation, Indiana University). *Dissertation Abstracts International,* 49, 04A.

Hawkes, W. L, Sharon, J. D., Kandel, A., & Taps Project Staff. (1986). *Fuzzy expert systems for an intelligent computer-based tutor* (Technical Report No: 86-5). Learning Systems Institute, Centre for Educational Technology, Florida State University.

Hayes, J. (2002). *Interpersonal skills at work.* NY: Routledge.

Heermann, D. W. (1990). *Computer-simulation methods* (pp. 8–12). Berlin/Heidelberg: Springer.

Helbing, D. (2012). Agent-based modeling. In *Social self-organization* (pp. 25–70). Berlin/Heidelberg: Springer.

Henneman, E. A., & Cunningham, H. (2005). Using clinical simulation to teach patient safety in an acute/critical care nursing course. *Nurse Educator, 30*(4), 172–177.

Hermann, K. (2015). Field theory and working with group dynamics in debriefing. *Simulation & Gaming, 46*(2), 209–220.

Herrnstein, R. J. (1961). Relative and absolute strength of response as a function of frequency of reinforcement 1, 2. *Journal of the Experimental Analysis of Behavior, 4*(3), 267–272.

Hochwarter, W. A., Witt, L. A., Treadway, D. C., & Ferris, G. R. (2006). The interaction of social skill and organizational support on job performance. *Journal of Applied Psychology, 91*(2), 482–489.

Hogarth, R. M. (2001). *Educating intuition.* University of Chicago Press, Chicago, USA.

Hollander, C. E. (1978). Psychodrama, role playing and sociometry: Living and learning processes. In D. W. Kurpius (Ed.), *Learning: Making learning environments more effective* (pp. 168–241). Muncie, IN: Accelerated Development, Inc.

Hollander, E. P. (1985). Leadership and power. In G. Lindsey & E. Aronson (Eds.), *The handbook of social psychology*. New York, NY: Random House.

Hollander, C. E., & Hollander, S. L. (1978). *The social atom and sociometry in education*. Denver, CO: Privately Published, Snow Lion Press.

Hurrell, S., Scholarios, D., & Thompson, P. (2012). More than a 'humpty dumpty' term: Strengthening the conceptualization of soft skills. *Economic and Industrial Democracy, 34*(1), 161–182.

Hussain, T. S., & Coleman, S. L. (Eds.). (2014). *Design and development of training games: Practical guidelines from a multidisciplinary perspective*. UK: Cambridge University Press.

Hut, P. (2008). Virtual laboratories and virtual worlds. *Proceedings of the International Astronomical Union Symposium, 246*, 90–99.

Hutchinson, K., & Brefka, D. (1997). Personnel administrators' preferences for resume content: Ten years after. *Business Communication Quarterly, 60*(2), 67–75.

Jackson, D. (2010). An international profile of industry-relevant competencies and skill gaps in modern graduates. *The International Journal of Management Education, 8*(3), 29–58.

James, R. F., & James, M. L. (2004). Teaching career and technical skills in a "mini" business world. *Business Education Forum, 59*, 39–41. National Business Education Association.

Jeuring, J., Grosfeld, F., Heeren, B., Hulsbergen, M., IJntema, R., Jonker, V., … van Zeijts, H. (2015). Communicate! — A serious game for communication skills. In *Design for teaching and learning in a networked world* (pp. 513–517). Springer, Switzerland.

Jeyaraj, A. (2010). Business process elicitation, modeling, and reengineering: Teaching and learning with simulated environments. *Journal of Information Systems Education, 21*(2), 253–264.

Johnson, W. L. (2014). Using virtual role-play to prepare for cross-cultural communication. In *Proceedings of the 5th International Conference on Applied Human Factors and Ergonomics AHFE 2014*, Poland.

Joseph, D., Ang, S., Chang, R. H., & Slaughter, S. A. (2010). Practical intelligence in IT: Assessing soft skills of IT professionals. *Communications of the ACM, 53*(2), 149–154.

Kantrowitz, T. M. (2005). *Development and construct validation of a measure of soft skills performance* (unpublished doctoral dissertation). Georgia Institute of Technology, Atlanta, GA.

Kerawalla, L., & Crook, C. (2005). From promises to practices: The fate of educational software in the home. *Technology, Pedagogy and Education, 14*(1), 107–125.

Kim, J. M., Hill, R. W., Jr., Durlach, P. J., Lane, H. C., Forbell, E., Core, M., & Hart, J. (2009). BiLAT: A game-based environment for practicing negotiation in a cultural context. *International Journal of Artificial Intelligence in Education, 19*(3), 289–308.

Kirriemuir, J. (2008). *Measuring the impact of Second Life for educational purposes*. Eduserv Foundation. Available from http://www.silversprite.com/?page_id=431

Klaus, P., Rohman, J., & Hamaker, M. (2007). *The hard truth about soft skills: Workplace lessons smart people wish they'd learned sooner*. HarperCollins e-books, NY.

Klein, C. R. (2009). *What do we know about interpersonal skills? A meta-analytic examination of antecedents, outcomes, and the efficacy of training*. ProQuest, MI, USA.

Klein, C., DeRouin, R. E., & Salas, E. (2006). Uncovering workplace inter-personal skills: A review, framework, and research agenda. *International Review of Industrial and Organizational Psychology, 21*, 79.

Klemp, G. O., & McClelland, D. C. (1986). What characterizes intelligent functioning among senior managers. In *Practical intelligence: Nature and origins of competence in the everyday world* (pp 31–50).

Kognito Interactive. (2009). *At-risk: Identify and refer students in mental distress: Results from a national study in 42 leading universities in the U.S.*. New York, NY: Kognito Interactive.

Kolb, D. A. (1984). *Experiential learning: Experience as the source of learning and development*. Englewood Cliffs, NJ: Prentice-Hall.

Kolb, D. A., & Fry, R. E. (1974). Toward an applied theory of experiential learning. In C. Cooper (Ed.), *Theories of group process* (pp. 33–58). London: Wiley, MIT, Alfred P. Sloan School of Management.

Kollöffel, B., & de Jong, T. (2015). *Can performance feedback during instruction boost knowledge acquisition? Contrasting criterion-based and social comparison feedback.* Interactive Learning Environments. UK: Taylor Francis Online.

Koster, R. (2013). *Theory of fun for game design.* O'Reilly Media, Inc, USA.

Kozma, R. B., Belle, L. W., & Williams, G. W. (1978). *Instructional techniques in higher education.* Englewood Cliffs, NJ: Educational Technology Publications.

Ladousse, G. P. (1987). *Role play.* UK: Oxford University Press.

Larkin, J., & Chabay, R. (Eds.). (1992). *Computer assisted instruction and intelligent tutoring systems: Shared goals and complementary approaches.* Hillsdale, NJ: Lawrence Erlbaum Associates.

Latham, A., Crockett, K., McLean, D., & Edmonds, B. (2012). A conversational intelligent tutoring system to automatically predict learning styles. *Computers & Education, 59*(1), 95–109.

Laurillard, D. (2001). *Rethinking university teaching: A framework for the effective use of learning technologies.* NY: RoutledgeFalmer.

Lee, T. (1991). The sociodramatist and sociometrist in the primary school. *Journal of Group Psychotherapy, Psychodrama & Sociometry, 43*(4), 191–196.

Lepper, M. R. (1985). Microcomputers in education – motivational and social issues. *American Psychologist, 40*(1), 1–18.

Lewin, K., Lippitt, R., & White, R. (1939). Patterns of aggressive behaviour in experimentally created social climates. *Journal of Social Psychology, 10,* 271–299.

Likert, R. (1961). *New patterns of management.* New York, NY: McGraw-Hill.

Lim, M. Y., Aylett, R., Enz, S., Kriegel, M., Vannini, N., Hall, L., & Jones, S. (2009). Towards intelligent computer assisted educational role-play. In *Learning by playing. Game-based education system design and development* (pp. 208–219). Berlin/Heidelberg: Springer.

Lim, M. Y., Dias, J., Aylett, R., & Paiva, A. (2008). Improving adaptiveness in autonomous characters. In *Intelligent virtual agents* (pp. 348–355). Berlin/Heidelberg: Springer.

Lindsley, O. R. (1992). Why aren't effective teaching tools widely adopted? *Journal of Applied Behavior Analysis, 259,* 21–26.

Linehan, C., Kirman, B., Lawson, S., & Chan, G. (2011). Practical, appropriate, empirically validated guidelines for designing educational games. In *Proceedings of the SIGCHI Conference on Human Factors in Computing Systems* (pp. 1979–1988). NY: ACM.

Linehan, C., Lawson, S., Doughty, M., Kirman, B., Haferkamp, N., Krämer, N. C., Nigrelli, M. L., & Schembri, M. (2011b). Teaching decision making skills to emergency managers via digital games. In A. Lugmayr, H. Franssila, P. Näränen, O. Sotamaa, J. Vanhala, & Z. Yu (Eds.), *Media in the ubiquitous era: Ambient, social and gaming media.* New York, NY: IGI Global.

Lipman, M. (1988). Critical thinking: What it can be? *Educational Leadership, 46*(1), 38–43.

Livingston, S. A. (1970). *Simulation games as advance organizers in the learning of social science materials.* Experiments 1-3, Report No . 64. Baltimore: Center for Social Organization of Schools, The Johns Hopkins University.

Loftus, G. R., & Loftus, E. F. (1983). *Mind at play: The psychology of video games.* New York, NY: Basic Books.

Lombardi, M. (2006). Ancient spaces: University of British Columbia. *ELI Innovations & Implementations: Exemplary Practices in Teaching and Learning (EDUCAUSE June 2006).* http://www.educause.edu/ir/library/pdf/ELI5012. pdf

Malone, T. W. (1981). Toward a theory of intrinsically motivating instruction. *Cognitive Science, 5*(4), 333–369.

Malone, T. W., & Lepper, M. R. (1987). Making learning fun: A taxonomy of intrinsic motivations for learning. *Aptitude, Learning, and Instruction, 3*(1987), 223–253.

Marlowe, H. A. (1986). Social intelligence: Evidence for multidimensionality and construct independence. *Journal of Educational Psychology, 78*(1), 52.

Marocco, D., Pacella, D., Dell'Aquila, E., & Di Ferdinando, A. (2015). Grounding serious game design on scientific findings: The case of ENACT on soft skills training and assessment. In G. Conole, T. Klobučar, C. Rensing, J. Konert, & É. Lavoué (Eds.), *Design for teaching and learning in a networked world, Lecture notes in computer science* (Vol. 9307, pp. 441–446). Springer, Switzerland.

Martens, A., Diener, H., & Malo, S. (2008). Game-based learning with computers–learning, simulations, and games. In *Transactions on edutainment I* (pp. 172–190). Springer, Switzerland.

Martin, R., Villeneuve-Smith, F., Marshall, L., & McKenzie, E. (2008). *Employability skills explored*. London: Learning and Skills Network. http://www.lsneducation.org.uk

Martindale, C. (1991). *Cognitive psychology: A neural-network approach*. Thomson Brooks/Cole Publishing Co.

Martino, J. (2007). *The avatar project: Connected but not engaged—the paradox of cyberspace*. Retrieved May 22, 2008, from http://art.tafe.vu.edu.au/avatar/wp-content/uploads/AvatarLitReview-revision%202.doc.

Maslow, A. H. (1970). *Motivation and personality*. New York: Harper & Row.

Mayer, J. D., & Salovey, P. (1993). The intelligence of emotional intelligence. *Intelligence, 17*(4), 433–442.

Mayer, J. D., Salovey, P., & Caruso, D. R. (2004). Emotional Intelligence: Theory, findings, and implications. *Psychological Inquiry, 15*(3), 197–215.

Mayo, M. J. (2007). Games for science and engineering education. *Communications of the ACM, 50*(7), 30–35.

Mazzucato, A., & Marocco, D. (2015). *Enhancing negotiation skills through on-line assessment of competencies and interactive mobile training*, Open Education Europa. http://www.openeducationeuropa.eu/

McClelland, D. C. (1973). Testing for competence rather than for "intelligence". *American Psychologist, 28*(1), 1.

McClelland, D. C. (1987). *Human motivation*. CUP Archive. UK: Cambridge University Press.

McClelland, D. C. (1998). Identifying competencies with behavioural-event interviews. *Psychological Science, 9*(5), 331–339.

McCulloch, W. S., & Pitts, W. (1943). A logical calculus of the ideas immanent in nervous activity. *The Bulletin of Mathematical Biophysics, 5*(4), 115–133.

McGill, I., & Beaty, L. (2001). *Action learning: a guide for professional, management & educational development*. Psychology Press. London: Kogan Page.

Michael, D. R., & Chen, S. L. (2005a). *Serious games: Games that educate, train, and inform*. NY: Muska & Lipman/Premier-Trade.

Michael, D., & Chen, S. L. (2005b) *Proof of learning: Assessment in serious games*. http://www.gamasutra.com/view/feature/130843/proof_of_learning_assessment_in_.php

Miglino, O. (2007). The SISINE project: Developing an e-learning platform for educational role-playing games. *ERCIM News, 71*, 28–29. ERCIM, 2007.

Miglino, O., Di Ferdinando, A., Rega, A., & Benincasa, B. (2007). SISINE: Teaching negotiation through a multiplayer online role playing game. In D. Remenyi (Ed.), *Proceedings of the 6th European Conference on E-Learning* (pp. 439–448). Reading, UK: Academic Conferences Limited.

Miglino, O., Pagliarini, L., Cardaci, M., & Gigliotta, O. (2008). TeamSim: An educational microworld for the teaching of team dynamics. In *New directions in intelligent interactive multimedia* (pp. 417–425). Berlin/Heidelberg: Springer.

Miglino, O., Venditti, A., Delli Veneri, A., & Di Ferdinando, A. (2010). Eutopia-Mt. teaching mediation skills using multiplayer on-line role playing games. *Procedia - Social and Behavioral Sciences, 2*(2), 2469–2472.

Miller, A., Allison, C., McCaffery, J., Sturgeon, T., Nicoll, R., Getchell, K., & Oliver, I. (2010). Virtual worlds for computer science education. In *11th Annual Conference of the Subject Centre for Information and Computer Sciences* (p. 239).

Moberg, P. J. (2001). Linking conflict strategy to the five-factor model: Theoretical and empirical foundations. *International Journal of Conflict Management, 12*(1), 47–68.

Moreno, J. L. (1934). *Who shall survive?: A new approach to the problem of human interrelations*. (XVI, pp. 2–20). Washington, DC, US: Nervous and Mental Disease Publishing Co.

Moreno, J. L. (1946a). *Psychodrama and sociodrama*.

Moreno, J. L. (1946b). *Psychodrama, first volume, fourth edition with new introduction*. Beacon NY: Beacon House Inc. 1977.

Moreno, J. L. (1953). *Who shall survive? Foundations of sociometry, group psychotherapy and socio-drama.*

Moreno-Ger, P., Martinez-Ortiz, I., Freire, M., Manero, B., & Fernandez-Manjon, B. (2014). Serious games: A journey from research to application. In *Frontiers in Education Conference (FIE), 2014 IEEE* (pp. 1–4). IEEE.

Moscovici, S. (1976). *Social influence and social change.* London: Academic.

Moss, P., & Tilly, C. (1996). "Soft" skills and race: An investigation of black men's employment problems. *Work and Occupations, 23*(3), 252–276.

Mullen, J. (1997). Graduates deficient in soft skills. *People Management, 6*, 18.

Murata, A. (2008). Human error management paying emphasis on decision making and social intelligence-beyond the framework of man–machine interface design. In *Proceedings: Fourth International Workshop on Computational Intelligence & Applications* (Vol. 2008, No. 1, pp. 1–12). IEEE SMC Hiroshima Chapter.

Muzio, E., & Fisher, D. (2009). Soft skill quantification (SSQ): Human performance vs. metric. *Cost Engineering, 51*(3), 26–31.

Muzio, E., Fisher, D. J., Thomas, E. R., & Peters, V. (2007). Soft skills quantification (SSQ) for project manager competencies. *Project Manager Journal, 38*(2), 30–38.

Myers, D. G., & Smith, S. M. (2000). *Exploring social psychology.*

Nahodil, P., Kadleček, D., Kohout, K., & Svrček, A. (2003). Artificial life simulation. In *Proceedings of WORKSHOP 2003* (pp. 364–365), Praha, Česká Republika, February 10–12, 2003.

Newell, D. (2002). The smarter they are the harder they fail. *Career Development International, 7*(5), 288–291.

Nkambou, R., Mizoguchi, R., & Bourdeau, J. (2010). *Advances in intelligent tutoring systems.* Heidelberg: Springer.

Nwana, H. S. (1990). Intelligent tutoring systems: An overview. *Artificial Intelligence Review, 4*, 251–277.

Olsen, J. K., Belenky, D. M., Aleven, V., Rummel, N., Sewall, J., & Ringenberg, M. (2014). Authoring tools for collaborative intelligent tutoring system environments. In *Intelligent tutoring systems* (pp. 523–528). Springer, Switzerland.

Ong, J., & Ramachandran, S. (2005). An intelligent tutoring system approach to adaptive instructional systems. United States Army Research Institute for the Behavior and Social Sciences, September 2005. Contract or Grant Number DASW01-00-C-3015.

Oppenheimer, L. (1989). The nature of social action: Social competence versus social conformism. In *Social competence in developmental perspective* (pp. 41–69). Amsterdam: Springer.

Ostrom, T. M. (1988). Computer simulation: The third symbol system. *Journal of Experimental Social Psychology, 24*(5), 381–392.

Pacella, D., Di Ferdinando, A., Dell'Aquila, E., & Marocco, D. (2015). Online assessment of negotiation skills through 3D role play simulation. In C. Conati, et al. (Eds.), *Proceedings of the Artificial Intelligence in Education: 17th International Conference, AIED 2015, Madrid, Spain* (Vol. 9112, pp. 921–923), June 22–26, 2015. Springer

Palmer, B., Walls, M., Burgess, Z., & Stough, C. (2001). Emotional intelligence and effective leadership. *Leadership & Organization Development Journal, 22*(1), 5–10.

Pant, I., & Baroudi, B. (2008). Project management education: The human skills imperative. *International Journal of Project Management, 26*(2), 124–128.

Parisi, D. (2001). *Simulazioni. La realtà rifatta nel computer.* Bologna: Il Mulino.

Parker, L. E., & Lepper, M. R. (1992). Effects of fantasy contexts on children learning and motivation: Making learning more fun. *Journal of Personality and Social Psychology, 62*(4), 625–633.

Pate, J., Martin, G., & Robertson, M. (2003). Accrediting competencies: A case of Scottish vocational qualifications. *Journal of European Industrial Training, 27*(2/3/4), 169–176.

Pauchant, T. C., & Mitroff, I. I. (1992). *Transforming the crisis-prone organization.* San Francisco: Jossey-Bass Publishers.

Paviotti, G., Rossi, P. G., & Zarka, D. (2012). Intelligent tutoring systems: An overview. Pensa Multimedia (iTutor project). Lecce: Pensa Multimedia, Italy.

Perkins, D. N., & Salomon, G. (1992). Transfer of learning. In *International encyclopedia of education* (2nd ed.).

Perreault, H. (2004). Basic business-business educators can take a leadership role in character education. *Business Education Forum, 59*, 23–25.

Perrenoud, P. (1997). *Construire des compétences dès l'école* (3rd ed.). Paris: ESF éditeur.

Perry, C., & Euler, T. (1988). Simulations as action learning exercises: Implications for conducting and evaluating business and economic simulations. *Simulation/Games for Learning, 18*(3), 177–187.

Petranek, C. F., Corey, S., & Black, R. (1992). Three levels of learning in simulations: Participating, debriefing, and journal writing. *Simulation & Gaming, 23*, 174–185.

Pierfy, D. A. (1977). Comparative simulation game research, stumbling blocks, and stepping stones. *Simulation and Games, 8*(2), 255–268.

Pink, D. (2005). *A whole new mind: Why right-brainers will rule the world.*

Plass, J. L., & Schwartz, R. N. (2014). Multimedia learning with simulations and microworlds. In *Cambridge handbook of multimedia learning* (pp. 729–761).

Polson, M. C., & Richardson, J. J. (Eds.). (2013). *Foundations of intelligent tutoring systems.* Psychology Press. NJ: Lawrence Erlbaum Publisher.

Popescu, E. (2010). Adaptation provisioning with respect to learning styles in a Web-based educational system: An experimental study. *Journal of Computer Assisted Learning, 26*(4), 243–257.

Pratt, J. A., Hauser, K., & Ross, S. C. (2010). IS staffing during a recession: Comparing student and IS recruiter perceptions. *Journal of Information Systems Education, 21*(1), 69–84.

Prensky, M. (2001). *Digital gamebased learning.* New York, NY: McGraw-Hill.

Prensky, M. (2005). Computer games and learning: Digital game-based learning. In *Handbook of computer game studies* (Vol. 18, pp. 97–122).

Proctor, R. W., & Dutta, A. (1995). *Skill acquisition and human performance.* CA: Sage Publications, Inc.

Rahim, M. A. (1983). A measure of styles of handling interpersonal conflict. *Academy of Management Journal, 26*, 368–376.

Rahim, M. A., & Bonoma, T. V. (1979). Managing organizational conflict: A model for diagnosis and intervention. *Psychological Reports, 44*, 1323–1344.

Rainsbury, E., Hodges, D., Burchell, N., & Lay, M. (2002). Ranking work-place competencies: Student and graduate perceptions. *Asia-Pacific Journal of Cooperative Education, 3*(2), 9–18.

Ranade, S., Tamara, C., Castiblanco, E., & Serna, A. (2010). Mapping competencies. *Mechanical Engineering, 132*(2), 30–34.

Randel, J. M., Morris, B. A., Wetzel, C. D., & Whitehall, B. V. (1992). The effectiveness of games for educational purposes: A review of recent research. *Simulation & Gaming, 23*, 261–276.

Reynolds, B. (2002). *Crisis and emergency risk communication.* Atlanta, GA: Centers for Disease Control and Prevention.

Reynolds, B., & Seeger, M. (2005). Crisis and emergency risk communication as an integrative model. *Journal of Health Communication, 10*, 43–55.

Ridley-Duff, R., & Bull, M. (2011). *Understanding social enterprise: Theory and practice.* London: Sage.

Rieber, L. P. (1996). Seriously considering play: Designing interactive learning environments based on the blending of microworlds, simulations, and games. *Educational Technology Research and Development, 44*(2), 4358.

Rieber, L. P. (2005). Multimedia learning in games, simulations, and microworlds. In *The Cambridge handbook of multimedia learning* (pp. 549–567).

Riemer, V., & Schrader, C. (2015). Learning with quizzes, simulations, and ad-ventures: Students' attitudes, perceptions and intentions to learn with different types of serious games. *Computers & Education 88*, 160–168.

Robbins, S. P., Judge, T. A., & Sanghi, S. (2008). *Organizational behavior.* India: Pearson Education.

Robles, M. M. (2012). Executive perceptions of the top 10 soft skills needed in today's workplace. *Business Communication Quarterly, 75*(4), 453–465.

Rogers, C. R. (1983). Freedom to learn for the 80's. In L. Stenhouse (Eds.) *An Introducrion to Curriculum Research and Development.* Columbus, OH: Charles E. Merrill.

Rosas, R., Nussbaum, M., Cumsille, P., Marianov, V., Correa, M., Flores, P., ... Salinas, M. (2003). Beyond Nintendo: Design and assessment of educational video games for first and second grade students. *Computers & Education, 40*(1), 71–94.

Ruben, B. D. (1999). Simulations, games, and experience-based learning: The quest for a new paradigm for teaching and learning. *Simulation & Gaming, 30*(4), 498–505.

Saarni, C. (1990). Emotional competence: How emotions and relationships become integrated. In R. A. Thompson (Ed.), *Nebraska Symposium on Motivation* (Vol. 36, pp. 115–182).

Sadler-Smith, E. (2011). The intuitive style: Relationships with local/global and verbal/visual styles, gender, and superstitious reasoning. *Learning and Individual Differences, 21*(3), 263–270.

Sadler-Smith, E., & Shefy, E. (2010). Intuitive intelligence. In J. Gold, A. Mumford, & R. Thorpe (Eds.), *Gower handbook of leadership and management development* (pp. 387–403). London, UK: Gower Publishing, Ltd.

Sadler-Smith, E., & Shefy, E. (2004). The intuitive executive: Understanding and applying 'gut feel' in decision-making. *ACAD MANAGEMENT Academy of Management Executive, 18*(4), 76–91.

Salen, K., & Zimmerman, E. (2003). *Rules of play: Game design fundamentals.* MIT, MA, USA.

Salovey, P., & Mayer, J. D. (1990). Emotional intelligence. *Imagination, Cognition and Personality, 9*(3), 185–211.

Schlanger, P. H., & Birkmann, M. H. (1978). *Role playing used to elicit language from hearing impaired children. Journal of Group Psychotherapy Psychodrama & Sociometry, 31*, 136–143. American Society of Group Psychotherapy and Psychodrama, Heldref Publications, UK.

Schonke, M. (1975). Psychodrama in school and college. *Group Psychotherapy and Psychodrama, 28.*

Seeney, M., & Routledge, H. (2011). Drawing circles in the sand: Integrating content into serious games. In *Instructional design: Concepts, methodologies, tools and applications* (Vol. 288).

Shaftel, F. R., & Shaftel, G. A. (1967). *Role-playing for social values.* Englewood Cliffs, NJ: Prentice-Hall.

Shaftel, F. R., & Shaftel, G. (1982). *Role playing in the curriculum.* Englewood Cliffs, NJ: Prentice-Hall.

Sharma, M. (2009). How important are soft skills from the recruiter's perspective. *The Icfai University Journal of Soft Skills, 3*(2), 19–28.

Shaw, M. E., Corsini, R. J., Blake, R. R., & Mouton, J. S. (1980). *Role playing: A practical manual for group moderators.* San Diego, CA: University Associates.

Shiflet, A. B., & Shiflet, G. W. (2014). *Introduction to computational science: Modeling and simulation for the sciences.* Princeton University Press, Princeton, NJ.

Shirts, R. G. (1975). Ten "mistakes" commonly made by persons designing educational simulations and games. *SAGSET Journal, 5*(4), 147–150.

Shirts, R. G. (1976). Simulation games: An analysis of the last decade. *Programmed Learning and Educational Technology, 13*(3), 37–41.

Siemens, G., & Baker, R. S. J. (2012). Learning analytics and educational data mining: Toward communication and collaboration. In S. B. Shum, D. Gasevic, & R. Ferguson (Eds.), *Proceedings of the 2nd International Conference on Learning Analytics and Knowledge* (pp. 252–254). New York, NY: ACM.

Simons, R. J. (2004). *Metaphors of learning at work and the role of ICT.* London: Workshop Learning and Technology at Work.

Simons, R. J., & Ruijters, M. P. C. (2003). Differing colours of professional learning. In L. Mason, S. Andreuzza, B. Arfè & L. Del Favero (Eds.), *Improving learning, fostering the will to learn. Proceedings of the Biennial Conference EARLI* (p. 31). Padua: Cooperativa Libraria Editrice Università di Padova.

Simons, R. J., & Ruijters, M. P. C. (2008). Varieties of work-related learning. *International Journal of Educational Research, 47*, 241–251.

Sitzmann, T. (2011). A meta-analytic examination of the instructional effectiveness of computer-based simulation games. *Personnel Psychology, 64*(2), 489–528.

Sjöberg, L. (2001). Emotional intelligence: A psychometric analysis. *European Psychologist, 6*(2), 79.

Skinner, B. F. (1938). *The behavior of organisms: An experimental analysis.*

Skinner, B. F. (1953). *Science and human behavior*. The free press, Simon and Schuster Inc, NY.

Skulmoski, G. J., & Hartman, F. T. (2010). Information systems project manager soft competencies: A project-phase investigation. *Project Management Journal, 41*(1), 61–80.

Sleeman, D. H., & Brown, J. S. (Eds.). (1982). *Intelligent tutoring systems*. London: Academic.

Smith, D. A., Kay, A., Raab, A., & Reed, D. P. (2003). Croqueta collaboration system architecture. In *Proceedings of the First Conference on Creating, Connecting and Collaborating Through Computing, 2003. C5 2003*. (pp. 2–9). IEEE.

Snyder, A. V., & Ebeling, H. W., Jr. (1992). Targeting a company's real core competencies. *Journal of Business Strategy, 13*(6), 26–32.

Spearman, C. (1904). "General intelligence", objectively determined and measured. *The American Journal of Psychology, 15*(2), 201–292.

Squire, K. (2003). Video games in education. *International Journal of Intelligent Simulations and Gaming, 2*(1).

Sternberg, R. J. (1985). *Beyond IQ: A triarchic theory of human intelligence*. New York, NY: Cambridge University Press.

Sternberg, R. J., Forsythe, G. B., Hedlund, J., Horvath, J. A., Wagner, R. K., Williams, W. M., Snook, S. A., & Grigorenko, E. L. (2000). *Practical intelligence in everyday life*. New York, NY: Cambridge University Press.

Sternberg, P., & Garcia, A. (2000). *Sociodrama: Who's in your shoes?* Westport, CT: Praeger Publisher/Greenwood Publishing Group.

Storey, J. (Ed.). (2004). *Leadership in organizations: Current issues and key trends*. Psychology Press, Routledge, NY.

Strebler, M. (1997). Soft skills and hard questions. *People Management, 3*(11), 20–24.

Striano, M. (2009). Managing educational transformation in the globalized world: A Deweyan perspective. *Educational Theory, 59*(4), 379393.

Striano, M. (2012). Philosophy as education for thinking: A pedagogical conversation with Matthew Lipman. In *Educating for complex thinking through philosophical inquiry* (pp. 519–525).

Sukhoo, A., Barnard, A., Eloff, M. M., Van der Poll, J. A., & Motah, M. (2005). Accommodating soft skills in software project management. *Issues in Informing Science and Information Technology, 2*, 691–703.

Sultana, R. G. (2009). Competence and competence frameworks in career guidance: Complex and contested concepts. *International Journal for Educational and Vocational Guidance, 9*(1), 15–30.

Sun, R. (Ed.). (2006). *Cognition and multi-agent interaction: From cognitive modeling to social simulation*. Cambridge: Cambridge University Press.

Susskind, L. E., & Coburn, J. (1999). *Using simulations to teach negotiation: Pedagogical theory and practice* (Working Paper 99-1). Cambridge, MA: Program on Negotiation, Harvard Law School.

Sutcliffe, M. (2002). Simulations, games and role-play. In *The handbook for economics lecturers* (pp 1–26).

Svetličič, M., & Kajnč, S. (2009). Small States Presidency Competences; the case of Slovenian EU Council 'Presidency'in 2008. Forthcoming in Halduskultuur–Administrative Culture, Tallinna Tehnikaülikool/Tallinn University of Technology.

Swartout, W., & Van Lent, M. (2003). Making a game of system design. *Communications of the ACM, 46*, 32–39.

Taggar, S., Hackett, R., & Saha, S. (1999). Leadership emergence in autonomous work teams: Antecedents and outcomes. *Personnel Psychology, 52*, 899–926.

Tannenbaum, A. S. & Schmidt, W. H. (1958). *How to choose a leadership pattern*. Harvard Business Review, MA, USA.

Thatcher, D. C. (1990). Promoting learning through games and simulations. *Simulation & Gaming, 21*(3), 262–273.

Thorndike, E. L. (1920). Intelligence and its uses. *Harper's magazine, 140*, 227–225.

Torrance, E. P., & Myers, R. E. (1973). *Creative learning and teaching*. New York: Dodd, Mead.

Trushell, J., Burrell, C., & Maitland, A. (2001). Year 5 pupils reading an "interactive storybook" on CD-ROM: Losing the plot? *British Journal of Educational Technology, 32*(4), 389–401.

Turner, D. A. (1992). *Roleplays: A sourcebook of activities for trainers*. London: Kogan Page.

Turok, I., & Taylor, P. (2006). A skills framework for regeneration and planning. *Planning Practice and Research, 21*(4), 497–509.

van den Brekel, A. J. P. (2007). Get your consumer health information from an avatar!: Health and medical related activities in a virtual environment. In *European Association for Health Information & Libraries Workshop* (pp. 12–15).

Van Der Hoek, W., & Wooldridge, M. (2008). Multi-agent systems. *Foundations of Artificial Intelligence, 3*, 887–928.

Van Ments, M. (1999). *The effective use of role-play: Practical techniques for improving learning.* London: Kogan Page Publishers.

Van Sickel, R. (1986). A quantitative review of research on instructional simulation gaming: A twenty-year perspective. *Theory and Research in Social Education, 14*(3), 245–264.

VVAA. (2011). Usage of second life applications in education and distance education. *Turkish Online Journal of Distance Education, TOJDE, 12*(3), 2.

Wagner, R. K., & Sternberg, R. J. (1985). Practical intelligence in real-world pursuits: The role of tacit knowledge. *Journal of Personality and Social Psychology, 49*(2), 436.

Walton, E. R., & McKersie, R. B. (1965). *A behavioral theory of labor negotiations: An analysis of a social interaction system.* Ithaca, NY: Cornell University Press, Sage House.

Warren, S., & Dondlinger, M. J. (2008). Designing games for learning. In *Handbook of research on effective electronic gaming in education.* Hershey, PA: Idea Group Reference: IGI Global.

Warren, S., Dondlinger, M. J., Stein, R., & Barab, S. (2009). Educational game as supplemental learning tool: Benefits, challenges, and tensions arising from use in an elementary school classroom. *Journal of Interactive Learning Research, 20*(4), 487–505.

Watson, C. M. (1983). Leadership, management, and the seven keys. *Business Horizons, 26*(2), 8–13.

Weber, M. R., Finley, D. A., Crawford, A., & Rivera, D. (2009). An exploratory study identifying soft skill competencies in entry-level managers. *Tourism and Hospitality Research, 9*(4), 353–361.

Weinert, F. E., & Kluwe, R. (1987). *Metacognition, motivation, and understanding.* Hillside, NJ: Lawrence Erlbaum Publisher.

Wellington, J. K. (2005). The "soft skills" of success. Vital speeches of the day, *71*(20), 628. New York, The City News Pub. Co.

Whetten, D. A., & Cameron, K. S. (2001). *Developing management skills.* Upper Saddle River, NJ: Prentice Hall.

Whetten, D., Cameron K., & Woods, M. (2000). *Developing management skills for Europe.* Upper Saddle River, NJ: Prentice Hall.

Wills, S., Leigh, E., & Ip, A. (2010). *The power of role-based e-learning: Designing and moderating online role-play.* UK: Taylor & Francis.

Woodruffe, C. (1993). What is meant by a competency? *Leadership & Organization Development Journal, 14*(1), 29–36.

Yardley-Matwiejczuk, K. M. (1997). *Role play: Theory and practice.* London: Sage.

Yukl, G. A. (2002). *Leadership in organizations.* Upper Saddle River, NJ: Prentice Hall.

Yukl, G., & Van Fleet, D. D. (1992). *Theory and research on leadership in organizations.* Palo Alto, CA: Consulting Psychologists Press.

Zanardo, A. (2011). Regia formativa: dinamiche di ruolo e metodologia della formazione, in Dialoghi. Rivista di studi sulla formazione e sullo sviluppo organizzativo (1).

Zartman, W., & Berman M. R. (1982). *The practical negotiator.* New Haven, CT: Yale University Press.

Zhang, L., Gillies, M., Dhaliwal, K., Gower, A., Robertson, D., & Crabtree, B. (2009). E-drama: Facilitating online role-play using an AI actor and emotionally expressive characters. *International Journal of Artificial Intelligence in Education, 19*(1), 5–38.

Zhang, L., Jiang, M., Farid, D., & Hossain, M. A. (2013). Intelligent facial emotion recognition and semantic-based topic detection for a humanoid robot. *Expert Systems with Applications, 40*(13), 5160–5168.

Zigler, E. F. (1972). Project head start: Success or failure? *Children Today, 2*(6), 2–7.

Index

A
Adaptation
  flexibility and creative, 21
  purposive/successful, 7
Agent-based modelling (ABM)
  description, 54
  in EduRPG, 53–54
  methodology, 55
  SimTech EduRPGs, 54
Agents, 53–54
  ABM (*see* Agent-based modelling (ABM))
  artificial, 38, 52
  BSA, 54–55
  computerised AI-guided, 35
  OSA, 54–55
  virtual, 37
Ancient Spaces, 30
Artificial environments, 26
Artificial intelligence (AI)
  and advanced 3D graphic techniques, 37
  applications, 27–28
  and learning analytic techniques, 47
  OSA and BSA behaviour, 54
  virtual tutor, 59
Artificial Intelligence in Education (AIED), 59
Artificial reality, 43, 53
Assessment
  organisational contexts, 26
  performance, 45
  skill, 27
Assessment design and techniques,
        EduTechRPGs
  AIED, 59, 60
  applications, 60
  BSA, 58

CAI, 60
  debriefing, 58, 59
  distributed learning, 60
  domain model, 60
  e-learning, 60
  feedback, 58
  ITSs, 60, 61
  pedagogical model, 61
  student model, 60
  user interface component, 61
  visible and external layer, 57
Attention
  care professions, 24
  EI, 4
  engaging and immersive principles
        of games, 26
  and motivation, 46
  object, 21
  from skills, 8
Avatars, 30–32, 34, 35

B
Backstage agents (BSA), 54–55, 118
Blended learning approach, 33
Bodily-kinaesthetic intelligence, 6
Body gestures, 94
BOT, 31, 58, 94

C
Casualties, 110
Characters
  AI, 36
  3D animated, 34, 35

Characters (*cont.*)
  E-adventures, 32
  EI, 5
  hard and soft skills, 10
  human-controlled, 36
  management skills, 17
  nonplayer character speakers, 29
  personal, 13
  and personal attributes, 2
  soft skills, 13
  street smarts/common sense, 8
  tacit quality of knowledge, 8
  training context, 43
  videogames, 55
  virtual, 33, 36
Chat
  live, 29
  online group/individual chats, 38
  text, 34
  windows for text messages, 30
Chocolate-covered broccoli approach, 48
Classical Moreno psychodrama, 23
Communication skills, 36
  basic, 13
  EI, 3
  soft skills, 14–16
Communication Technology (ComTech), 37,
    50, 52, 54, 55, 59, 61, 65–71
  client/server architecture, 65
  development, 65
  Eutopia (*see* Eutopia-MT)
  learners, 69–71
  trainers, 65–69
Community of Philosophical Inquiry (COPI), 83
Competency
  building mental flexibility and creative
    adaptation, 21
  and competence, 2, 9
  concept, 2
  critical differentiator of performance, 2
  description, 2
  encompasses, 10
  foreign language learning, 30
  managerial, 1, 9
  mapping, 15
  person-based concept, 2
  profiling, 14
  in skill performance, 17
  social, 1, 3, 9
  team building, 33
  transversal, 10
Compromising, 92
Computational approach, ABM, 53

Computer simulations, psychological and
    pedagogical modelling, 55–57
Computer-assisted instruction (CAI), 60
Conflict management, 80–82
Cooperation, 16
Crisis communication, 106
Criticism, 94
Croquet, 29, 30

D
Deal-breakers, 13
Debriefing processes, 21, 25, 34, 38
DECIDE-IT, 121
Decision-making, 2, 25, 26, 50
Deployment action, 113
Digital environments, role-play, 27–38
  and artificial, 26
  definition of game, learning purposes, 27
  digital role playing, 26
  domain, 27
  e-educational RPG, 27
  growth of online games, 26
  Internet, 26
  learning games, 26
  MMORPG, 27
  multimedia and simulation-based training
    systems, 26
  online games, 26
  personal computers, 26
  RPG (*see* Digital RPG)
  symbolic modelling, 26
Digital RPG
  advantages, 31, 37
  Ancient Spaces, 30
  artificial micro-worlds, 37
  At-risk E-Adventure, 31, 32
  BOT, 31
  communication skill, 36
  ComTech, 37
  Croquelandia, 29
  Croquet, 29, 30
  3D animated characters, 35
  domains, 27
  DREAD-ED, 37
  3D virtual environments, 29
  3D virtual world, Second Life-Scilands, 28
  each module (mini-game), 34
  E-adventure, 32
  E-circus project, 33
  E-drama, 34–36
  EduTechRPG, 37, 38
  e-learning environments, 28, 30, 31

EMMA, 35
EMORG, 31
EMORPG, 30, 31, 34
ENACT, 37
face-to-face psychodramatic mechanism, 37
factors, 27, 28
Fear-Not, 33
Igrishe, 30
implementations, 28
Infiniteams, 34
learning purposes, 28
MORPGs, 28
Open Wonderland, 29, 30
OpenSim, 29
open-source platforms, 29
ORIENT, 33
platform BiLAT, 37
players, 29
psychodrama, 27
psycho-pedagogical methodology, 38
Qwaq forums, 29
Second Life, 28
Secondhealth, 28
SimTech, 37
sociodrama, 27
squeak language, 29
TPLD, 34
Unigame, 33
in virtual environments, 30
VirtualPREX, 29
Dominating, 92
Drama-based training environments, 37
Drama-based games, 52
DREAD-ED game
    in 2009, 119
    Academy for Crisis Management
        Emergency Planning and Civil
        Protection in Germany, 119
    actions, 113
    actual training session, 119
    audiences, disaster, 108, 109
    avatars and chat system, 112
    capacity of self-organisation, 120
    casualties, 110
    crisis and emergency risk communication,
        106
    crisis communication deals, 106
    decision-making, 121–122
    description, 109–114
    disasters, 105
    emergency managers, 120
    evaluation layer, 116, 117
    hazard risk, 110

ICT, 105, 117–118
    loops, 111–112
    mechanism, 114–116
    metaphor and narrative, 114–115
    operations, 111
    parameters, 110–111
    participants, 120
    planning and training, 105, 107
    public relations, 111
    resources, 112–113
    risk communication, 106
    roles, 114
    rule-based RPG, 117–118
    teach disaster communication, 106–109
    testing, 119–122
    triggering communication, 115–116
Dream Factory, 35
3D virtual environments
    Ancient Spaces, 30
    avatars, 35
    characters, 35
    Fear-Not, 33
    flash interface, 34
    multi-user, 29
    open-source platforms, 29
    Second Life-Scilands, 28

E
Each module (mini-game), 34
E-adventure, 32
E-circus project, 33
E-drama, 30, 34–36
Education
    and development programmes, 4
    and learning, 7
    programme, 15
    training, 7
Educational Multiplayer Online Role-play
        Game (EMORPG), 30, 31, 34
Educational role-play game (EduRPG), 37
EduTechRPGs. *See* Technologically Enhanced
        Educational Role-Playing Game
        (EduTechRPGs)
E-learning
    and distributed learning, 60
    environments, 28
    e-UCM, 32
    platforms, 30
    technologies, 31
Emotional intelligence (EI), 1, 24
    ability, 3
    characterization, 5

Emotional intelligence (EI) (*cont.*)
  competencies, 4
  complexity, person's capabilities, 4
  construction, 4
  definition, 4, 5
  description, 4
  expressions, 15
  factors, 4
  family of soft skills, 3
  growing interest and research, 3
  high degree, 16
  human talent, 4
  leadership performance, 4
  social, 1–3, 9
  soft skills, 14, 16, 17
  taught and developed over time, 5
Emotion, metaphor and affect (EMMA), 35
Emotions
  disturbances, 24
  EMMA, 35
  and feelings, 24
  integration, 4
  interactions, 1, 22
  learners to explore, 20
  and memories, 33
  personal, 24, 25
  skills and capabilities, 19
  uncontrolled, 20
  virtual character, 36
ENACT project, 37, 52, 53
  advantages, 91
  artificial agents, 52
  assessment, 97–99
  behavioural indicators, 93–94
  design, 93–97
  drama-based games, 89
  The European Commission's New Skills
        for New Jobs initiative, 90
  Eutopia platform, 90
  feedback element, 58
  game, 51
  KCLL, 90
  "making concessions", 91
  negotiation processes, 90, 91
  parameters, 98
  pre-validation testing data, 100–102
  psychological modelling, 91–94
  in realistic scenarios, 89
  SimTech, 89
  training, 90, 99–100
  tutoring system, 99
  user-centred approach and flexibility, 102–103
  user representation and avatars, 94
  visual interface and game dynamics, 95–97

Enactment
  nurtures, 19
  personal terms and group experiences, 21
  and principal psychodramatic
        methodologies, 22
  role-play, 21
  sociodramatic, 24
  successful, 16
  tools facilitate, 20
Enquiring, 94
Entertainment games, 49–50
European Transfer of Innovation (TOI)
        project, 121
Eutopia, 37, 52, 63–79, 82
  Avatar control, 70
  communication (*see* Communication
        Technology (ComTech))
  ComTech games, 59
  conflict management, 80–82
  Drama-ComTech-based EduRPGs, 87
  Drama-ComTech-based role-play games, 86
  and DREAD-ED, 52
  entrepreneurship training, S-Cube, 84–86
  implementation, 87, 88
  inspiration, multiplayer games, 63
  intelligent tutoring systems, 88
  learning approach, 63, 88
  learning experiences, 86
  methodology
    back-stage agents, 75
    blended, 76
    digital classroom, 76
    feedback and debriefing mechanisms, 75
    gaming experience, 71–73
    psychological and pedagogical theories,
        74
    psycho-pedagogical principles, 71
    technological dimension, 71
    video recording simulations, 75
  multiplayer (*see* Multiplayer)
  negotiation (*see* Negotiation and soft
        skills)
  online role play, 86–88
  opinions of professionals, 87
  proactive (*see* Proactive, Eutopia)
  soft skills, 63
  steps, 77
  target groups, 77
  trainer, 88
  tutor version, 68
Eutopia-MT
  definition, 80
  development and acquisition, mediation
        competencies, 80

intercommunity conflicts, 80
learning experiences, 80
objectives, 80
outcomes/feedback, 81–82
relational, cognitive and self-managing
    skills, 81
target group, 80
training, 80
Evaluation and job performance, 22
Experience, 71–73
and academic background, 15
gaming, Eutopia
    avoid distractions, 72
    design of learning scenarios, 71
    difficulties, 72
    emotions, 72
    goals and objectives, 71
    group settings, 73
    learning process, 71
    middle-aged long-standing community,
        73
    mutual agreements and collaborative
        strategies, 72
    negotiations, 73
    and personal emotions, 73
    sessions, 72
    trainer, 72
    "Troubles", 73
hard/technical, 15
individual and group, 25
interactive, 33
learning, 19, 28
narrative, 31
and perceptions, 25
personal, 18
personal terms and group, 21
phenomenon of role distance, 21
and practice, 13
psychodramatic method, 23
role-play, 34
self and others, 7
training, 10, 30
and traits, 9
unspoken and unaccepted, 20
users, 35
within our environment, 8

F
Face-to-face, 46, 47
activities, 19, 22
learning activities, 33
psychodramatic mechanism, 37
settings, 18

Facial expressions, 94
Fact-opinions, 94
Feedback, 5, 17, 18, 21, 23, 26–27, 29, 31, 36–38
*Frames of the Mind: The Theory of Multiple
    Intelligences*, 1983, 6
Full-range theory (FRL) model, 126, 132

G
Game design principles, 49–50
Game loops, 111–112
Gamification, 42
Gaming experience and education, 40–41
Group dynamics, 22, 31, 46

H
Hard skills, 1, 2
concept of competence, 2
domain and discipline specific, 15
goal-directed behaviours, 10
in job success, 4
reciprocal relationship, 1
and soft (*see* Soft skills)
strategy, systems and structure, 6
technical ability and factual knowledge, 16
Hazard risk, 110

I
Immersive, 26, 28–30
Infiniteams, 34
Integrating, 92
Intelligence
artificial, 27, 28, 37
EI, 3–5, 24
factors, 4
interpersonal skills, 3, 4
intrapersonal, 4
intuitive, 4
IQs, 3, 4
life skills, 3
managerial competencies, 3
multiple, 4–7
practical, 4
social, 3–5
soft, 7–9
successful, 4
technical skills, 3
Intelligence quotient (IQ)
concept, 5
description, 4
notion, 5
tests, 4, 6

Intelligence Reframed: Multiple Intelligence
            for the 21st Century, 6
Intelligent tutoring systems (ITSs), 37, 60
Internet, 26, 27, 30, 52
Interpersonal
    abilities, 24
    areas, 2
    capabilities, 2
    communication, 20, 36
    dimensions, 3
    dynamics, 31
    intelligences, 4, 6, 7
    interactions, 14
    qualities, 15
    relations, 17
    relationships, 24
    situations, 5
    skills, 1, 3, 9, 11, 13–16, 22
    soft aptitudes, 8
Intrapersonal
    areas, 2
    capabilities, 12, 15
    communication, 20
    intelligences, 4, 6, 7
    skills, 14, 24
Intuitive intelligence, 4, 8

L
Laissez-faire leader, 125
Leadership, 25, 26, 34
    achievement, 16
    and customer service, 11
    effective, 16
    and management, 5
    negotiation, 48
    performance, 4, 18
    positions, 15
    skills, 1, 16
Learners, Eutopia
    debriefing tools, 71
    OSAs, 69
    participation, session, 70
    physical and emotional features, 69
    questionnaire, 69
Learning goals, 27, 36
Learn to Lead (L2L)
    computational and rule-based RPG,
        137–140
    description, 123, 126–130
    evaluation layer, 133–137
    leadership, 124–126
    mechanism, 130–132
    soft skill, 123–126

Level of autonomy, 49
Linguistic intelligence, 6
Logical-mathematical intelligence, 6

M
Management skills, 17
Managerial competence, 1
Massive multiplayer online role-playing
            games (MMORPGs), 27, 63
Metaphor, 35
    cultural products, 43
    EduTechRPGs, 52
    role-playing games, 52
Methodology, 39, 76
    Eutopia (*see* Eutopia)
    psychodramatic, 22
    psycho-pedagogical, 38
    role-play, 27, 30
    soft skills training (*see* Technologically
                Enhanced Educational Role-Playing
                Game (EduTechRPGs))
    training, 22
Micro-worlds, 37
Mirror technique, 21
Mise en Scène, 43–44
Moreno's role theory, 22
Motivations, 6, 7, 14–16, 25
    educational outcomes, 40
    entertainment games, 49
Multiplayer online role-play games
            (MORPGs), 28
Multiplayers, 63–65
    Eduteams, 34
    EMORPG, 30
    Eutopia
        adoption, role-play methodology, 63
        3D graphics, 64
        electronic role-playing games, 64
        game design, 64
        learning strategies, 63
        MMORPGs, 64
        MUVEs, 64
        psychodrama, 65
        skills, 64
        social, psychological and corporeal
                identity, 64
        spatial and psychological immersion, 64
    Infiniteams, 34
    interactions, 22
    MMORPG, 27
    MORPGs, 28
    ORIENT, 33
    platforms, 33

Multiple intelligence (MI)
    ambiguous and subjective concept, 7
    area of, 4
    and communication, 2
    concept, 7
    definition, 6
    *Frames of the Mind: The Theory
        of Multiple Intelligences* 1983, 6
    hard Ss, 6
    individual possessing, 4
    *Intelligence Reframed: Multiple
        Intelligence for the 21st Century*, 6
    interpersonal, 6, 7
    intrapersonal, 6, 7
    introspective and self-reflective capacities,
        7
    IQ concept, 5
    notion IQ, 5
    period of time, 5
    psychological evidence, 6
    soft Ss, 5
    traditional IQ tests, 6
    training and education, 7
Multi-user virtual environments (MUVEs), 63
Musical intelligence, 6

N
Narrative
    EMORPG, 31
    psychological models, 103
    structure and Mise en Scène, 43–44
Negotiation and soft skills, 2, 16, 25, 34, 36,
        37, 77–79
    and effective communication, 44
    Eutopia
        behaviour, 79
        communication, 79
        definition, 78–79
        objective processes, 79
        outcomes/feedback, 79
        SISINE and SINAPSI, 77–79

O
Obliging, 92
On-stage agents (OSAs), 54–55, 69, 118
Open-source platforms, 29
Open Wonderland, 30

P
PACCIT programme, 34
People skills, 1, 9

Performance
    appraisal processes, 26
    assessment, 45
    attributes, 10
    critical differentiator, 2
    director invites, 21
    effectiveness, 5
    effective/superior, 2
    employee, 2
    and intervene, 21
    job, 1, 5, 15, 22
    leadership, 4, 18
    new skill area, 17
    and potential appraisal systems, 14, 18
    run real-time visual, 30
    social performance skills, 5
    successful, 2
    team, 34
    user's, 37
Performance assessment
    educational games, 45
    game designers, 45
    level completion, 45
    mainstream video games, 45
    in psychological settings, 45
    scoring system, 45
    tutorials, 45
    video games, 45
Phenomenon of role distance, 21
Planning
    abilities, 26
    skills, 16
Platform BiLAT, 37
Practical intelligence, 4, 7, 8, 12, 16
    definition, 7
    professional intuition/business instinct, 8
Pre-validation testing data, 100–102
Proactive, Eutopia
    COPI scenario, 83
    critical thinking, 83
    fostering teachers' and trainers' creativity,
        82
    implementation, 82
    learning contest, 82
    learning objectives, 83
    LLP KA3 project, 82
    outcomes/feedback, 83–84
    role-play scenarios, 82
    soft skills, 82–83
    trainers, 82
    training, 83
Problem solving, 2, 8, 14, 15, 25, 33, 34, 37
Proficiencies, 2
Psychodrama, 19, 20, 22–25, 27, 50

Psychological and pedagogical modelling
    ABM, 53–54
    BSA, 54–55
    characteristics, 50
    computer simulations, 55–57
    digital EduRPG, 52
    drama based situations, 50
    drama-based games, 52
    DREAD-ED, 52
    EduTechRPGs, 55–57
    ENACT, 51–53
    Eutopia, 52, 53
    game domain, 50
    game plot, 52
    identification, 51
    Internet and communication technologies,
        52
    Learn to Lead, 53
    metaphor, 52
    multiplayer game, 51
    OSA, 54–55
    personal skills, 51
    psychodrama, 50
    role-playing games, 52
    SimTech EduTechRPGs, 53
    teaching and learning, 51
    type of interactions, 52
    and user-centred perspective, 50
    virtual labs, 55–57
Psycho-pedagogical dimensions, 50–61
Public relations, 111

R
Rahim model, 98
Risk communication, 106
Role-play, 26–27
    applications, 24
    characteristics, 21
    classical Moreno psychodrama, 23
    conditional knowledge, 21
    debriefing process, 25
    description, 19
    different settings and contexts, 19
    digital environments (*see* Digital
        environments, role-play)
    dramatisation, 19
    dynamic relationships, 20
    educational and training settings, 24
    educational purposes, 24
    experiential learning, 19
    group member (auxiliary), 20
    interactive training methods, 22
    learning purposes, 23

    mirror technique, 21
    Moreno developed and formalised, 20
    Moreno's role theory, 22
    multiplayers and single-player
        applications, 22
    nurtures, 19
    organisational contexts, 26
    phenomenon of role distance, 21
    postgame session, 25
    potential and performance appraisal
        processes, 26
    psychodramatic method, 19, 20, 22, 23, 25
    psychological state, 20
    role-play director, 21
    role-reversal participants, 20
    rules/guidelines, 22
    selection purposes, 26
    self-awareness, 20, 21
    share similar principles and dynamics, 20
    simulations, 19, 23–25
    skill of empathy, 20
    and sociodramatic enactments, 24
    sociodramatic technique, 19, 20, 22, 23, 25
    socio-emotional networks, 20
    sociometry, 20
    theatre of spontaneity, 20
    therapeutic potential, dramatic
        improvisation activity, 20
    thinking and interacting, 20
    training purposes, 24
    type of knowledge, 21
Role-playing games (RPG), 27–38
Role-reversal participants, 20

S
Scenarios
    backgrounds, 34
    defines, 21
    E-adventure, 32
    for learning, 28
    online learning, 30
    realistic learning, 30
    role-playing, 22, 31
    simulation, 31
S-Cube
    assessment, soft skills capabilities, 85
    blended methodological approach, 85
    design and development, 84
    enterprises, 84
    Eutopia platform, 84
    Future Positive, 85
    group-based and online software tests, 85
    inspiration, 85

intrapersonal and interpersonal, 86
  leadership style and values, 85
  online training service, 84
  outcomes/feedback, 86
  project partners, 84
  self-awareness, 85
  soft skills, 85
  TNA research, 84
  training process, 85
Secondhealth, 28
Second Life, 28, 29
Self-awareness, 20, 21, 23, 25, 31
  EI, 5
  intrapersonal intelligence, 7
  intuitions recognising, 8
  research, 4
  social skills, 17
  soft skills, 15
Self-discovery, 24
Self-reflection, 7, 21, 25
Serious games, 27
SimTech EduTechRPGs, 53
Simulations
  avatar-based gatekeeper training, 31
  commercial-off-the-shelf role-play
    simulations, 27
  effectiveness, 26
  game for learning purposes, 27
  implementations of role play, 19
  integration, 32
  large-scale, 29
  learning, 20
  motivation and interest and promote, 25
  recognises, 25
  role-play activities, 24
  scenario, 31
  simulation-based training systems, 26
  structuration, 23
  theoretical area, 25
Simulation Technology (SimTech), 37, 50,
    52–57, 59
Single-player, 22, 32, 33, 55
Skinner's theories, 60
Social competence, 1
Social intelligence, 1
  components, 5
  concept, 3, 4
  definition, 5
  description, 3, 4
  notion, single concept, 4
Social self-efficacy, 1
Social skills, 1
Sociodrama, 19, 20, 22–25, 27
Socio-emotional networks, 20

Soft intelligences
  business and management contexts, 8
  definition, 7–9
  purposive/successful adaptation, 7
  self-awareness, 8
  soft aptitudes, 8
  tacit knowledge, 8
Soft skills, 3–9
  abilities/talents, 14
  attributes/level of commitment, 15
  behaviours, 2, 18
  challenges, 9
  character, 13
  characteristics of management skills, 17
  classifications, 10
  communication and interpersonal skills, 14
  competency, 2, 9, 14
  component of educational reform, 13
  components, 13, 17, 18
  core management skills, 17
  deal-breakers, 13
  definitions, 2, 10–12
  description, 9
  development, 26, 30
  domain attributes, 15
  EduTechRPG, 37
  face-to-face settings, 18
  feedback, 5, 17, 18
  goal-directed behaviours, 14
  and hard, 10, 15, 18
  healthcare state, 13
  important to students, 1
  intelligence (*see* Intelligence)
  international relationship studies, 13
  interpersonal capabilities, 2, 15, 16
  intrapersonal skills, 24
  IT professional roles, 16
  leadership skills, 16
  learning-by-doing environments, 18
  learnt and developed, 18
  management skills, 17
  managerial factors, 16
  micro-social skills, 16
  molecular and macro levels, 13
  natural extensions, 36
  non-technical skill, 15
  non-technical traits and behaviours, 16
  people skills, 1
  personal and social skill, 15
  personal qualities, 15
  personality traits, 15
  personality-based characteristics, 9
  potential development and job suitability,
    14

Soft skills (*cont.*)
    productivity and innovation in workplace, 14
    project management research, 16
    promoting personal and collective growth, 1
    reciprocal relationship with hard skills, 1
    service and information industries, 13
    and social, 15
    software project management, 14
    training, 22, 30, 31
    trans-situational, non-technical skills, 15
    transversal competence, 10
Soft skills training and development, 30
Storyboard, 31
Stress
    and anxiety, 26
    management, 14
    resistance to, 26
Successful intelligence, 4

T
Tacit knowledge, 8
Teaching
    children, 24
    history, 32
    of language, 29
    method in curriculum, 24
    skills, 29
Team communication, 122
TeamSim, 57
Teamwork style, 122
Technology, 27, 39, 50–61
    EduTechRPGs (*see* Technologically
        Enhanced Educational Role-Playing
        Game (EduTechRPGs))
    and psycho-pedagogical dimensions (*see*
        Psycho-pedagogical dimensions)
    role-play (*see* Role-play)
    and work organisation, 13
Technologically Enhanced Educational
        Role-Playing Game
        (EduTechRPGs), 37, 38, 63, 103
    ABM, 53–54
    application domain, 42
    assessment design and techniques, 57–61
    BSA, 54–55
    categorisation, 39
    challenging process, 61
    characteristics, 39
    computer simulations and virtual labs, 56, 57
    designing and implementing, 39
    educational games, 49
    educational objectives, 43
    ERP game fundamental structure and
        functional elements, 42

European projects, 39
Eutopia, 61
evaluation layer, 43, 44
feedback, debriefing and backstage Agents,
    60, 61
formal categorisation, 39
functional elements, 42
fundamental structure, 42
game design principles, 49–50
gaming experience and education, 40–41
information and communication, 39
narrative structure and Mise en Scène,
    43–44
OSA, 54–55
performance assessment, 45
psychological and pedagogical modelling,
    51–57
soft-skill training, 42
teaching and learning, 48
technical implementation, 42
trainer/tutor, 46–47
The *Rahim Organizational Conflict
        Inventory-II* (ROCI-II), 93, 97
Theoretical model of soft skills, 9
Trainers/tutor, 46, 47
    EduTechRPGs
        artificial intelligence, 47
        debriefing, 46
        editing scripts, 66
        experience, 46
        face-to-face training settings, 46
        feedbacks, 46
        learner's profile, 47
        learning analytic techniques, 47
        learning process, 46
        learning scenario-environment, 46
        profiling, 47
        technology-enhanced role-play games,
            46
    Eutopia
        back-stage agents (BSAs), 66
        debriefing tools, 69
        editing scripts, 66–67
        function, 65
        learning objectives, 65
        online multiplayer games, 65
        participation, session, 67–69
        start role-playing sessions, 67
Training, 69
    in adults, 4
    and development courses, 15
    and development initiatives, 14
    and education, 7
    and educational programmes, 2
    and experience, 10

employability programmes, 14
entrepreneurship, Eutopia, 84–86
and learning, 9
session, 38, 67–69
soft skills training programmes, 18
trainers (*see* Trainers/tutor, Eutopia)
workplace state, 13
Transformational leaders, 125
Transformational leadership models, 124
Tutoring system, 99
guidance, 37
intelligent, 37
online group chat-based role-play
game, 33
online group/individual chats/meetings, 38
trainers and psychologists, 30

U
Unassigned personnel member (UPM), 113
Unigame, 30, 33

Unigame Social Skills and Knowledge
Training web platform, 33

V
Videogames, 33
Virtual environments, 52
avatars, 30
digital representations, 30
learning-oriented 3D, 29
multiplayers or single player, 31
ORIENT, 33
role-play methodology implementation, 30
SciLands, 28
training negotiation skills, 37
Virtual labs, 55–57
Virtual Learning Environments (VLE), 32
VirtualPREX, 29
Visual-spatial intelligence, 6
Vocal tone, 94
VoIP solutions, 116

CPI Antony Rowe
Chippenham, UK
2017-01-26 10:06